T.L.S.

ESSAYS AND REVIEWS FROM
The Times Literary Supplement · *1970*

9

T.L.S.

ESSAYS AND REVIEWS FROM
The Times Literary Supplement · 1970

9

London
OXFORD UNIVERSITY PRESS
NEW YORK TORONTO
1971

Oxford University Press, Ely House, London W.1

GLASGOW NEW YORK TORONTO MELBOURNE WELLINGTON
CAPE TOWN SALISBURY IBADAN NAIROBI DAR ES SALAAM LUSAKA
ADDIS ABABA BOMBAY CALCUTTA MADRAS KARACHI LAHORE DACCA
KUALA LUMPUR SINGAPORE HONG KONG TOKYO

ISBN 0 19 211547 2

Printed in Great Britain by
Alden & Mowbray Ltd
at the Alden Press, Oxford

CONTENTS

Contents

NOTE

TLS 9 is an anthology of review-essays originally printed in the *Times Literary Supplement* during 1970. The paper extends its coverage of the world's new books every year, and in 1970 made a particular effort to widen and deepen the attention it pays to scientific and technological books, represented here by pieces on Scientific Biography, the Soviet geneticist Lysenko, and Hovercraft. Other subjects discussed in these pages include Literature, Music, Politics, Linguistics, Education, Anthropology, War, History, Philosophy, and the New English Bible. There is also a full selection of reviews of the year's more significant novels and new volumes of poetry.

I

THE YEAR'S ANNIVERSARIES

(a) DICKENS

THE CENTENARY OF Dickens's death is certainly producing more, and more competent, tributary writing than did the centenary of his birth. From 1912 little survives that is worth turning to: an essay by Alice Meynell, a collection of E. P. Whipple's prefaces, the important series of Dickens's letters to W. H. Wills, Edwin Pugh's study (still the most comprehensive) of the 'originals' of the characters, Shaw's preface to *Hard Times*. Various prominent writers answered a questionnaire in the *Bookman*'s special Dickens number: Hardy (very taciturn), Shaw, Chesterton, and a long tail of the now-forgotten. Many of the more likely established writers seem to have made no pronouncements (James, Kipling, Wells, Bennett), nor did the up-and-coming youngsters (Forster, Lawrence). The universities were silent, except for a thesis from Halle.

Silence need not mean lack of interest or respect, of course. Around 1912 Henry James was writing of Dickens, in his autobiography published the next year:

He did too much for us surely ever to leave us free—free of judgment, free of reaction, even should we care to be, which heaven forbid: he laid his hand on us in a way to undermine as in no other case the power of detached appraisement. . . . Criticism, roundabout him, is somehow futile and tasteless.

(a) ANGUS WILSON: *The World of Charles Dickens*. 302 pp. Secker and Warburg. £4.

Dickens and Fame, 1870–1970: Essays on the Author's Reputation. Centenary Number of *The Dickensian*, May 1970. Vol. 66. No. 361. 200 pp. Dickens Fellowship. 75p.

'Dickens', *Europe*, December 1969. 16.50fr.

MICHAEL SLATER (Editor): *Dickens 1970: Centenary Essays*. 241 pp. Chapman and Hall with the Dickens Fellowship. £2.25.

A. E. DYSON: *The Inimitable Dickens*. A Reading of The Novels. 303 pp. Macmillan. £3.50.

(b) *Ludwig van Beethoven: Autograph Miscellany from circa 1786 to 1799*. (Edited by Joseph Kerman.) Volume I: Facsimile. 39 pp. plus facsimile. Volume II: Transcription. 296 pp. The Trustees of the British Museum. £25 the set.

A pity, nevertheless, that John Morley had not pressed James harder, thirty years earlier, when for this reason he declined to undertake the 'English Men of Letters' volume on Dickens: a pity too, as Professor Fielding remarks in the *Dickensian* Centenary Number, that the Dickens Fellowship did not elect James to a Vice-Presidency, where-by the course of Dickens criticism might well have changed much sooner—for James's tangle of feelings about Dickens included an unsophisticated enjoyment of the common reader's participation in the Dickens world, instanced by his exploring Rochester to see the place where David Copperfield slept. 1970 finds a more substantial contingent of novelists, as well as academics and others, enrolled for the celebrations—and fittingly, for, as Dr. Michael Slater writes, introducing his collection to which several prominent novelists contribute, Dickens might well be called 'the novelist's novelist', did not this make him sound too rarefied. As he reminds us, such diverse writers as Tolstoy and Kafka, Wells and Dostoevsky, Proust and Priestley, have spoken reverentially of Dickens and often have shown signs of his influence.

Anyone asked to name a contemporary English novelist showing some kinship to Dickens would soon suggest Mr. Angus Wilson. Surveying Dickens's fortunes in the 1960s, Professor George Ford describes Mr. Wilson as the chief torch-bearer among the novelists who have given any attention to him; over the past twenty years, he has written several much-admired essays on him and he has reported that he re-reads the whole canon of the novels every two years. To the writing of his substantial new study, *The World of Charles Dickens*, Mr. Wilson brings further qualifications than this enthusiasm and long immersion: a novelist's fellow-feeling for Dickens's craftsmanship and for the emotional pressures behind its development, a novelist's understanding too of the personalities of Dickens and his circle, and long practice as a critic in good touch with scholarship, apparent in his study of Zola and many subsequent essays and books, and kept in trim by his work as a university teacher (for he has of course been Professor Wilson for some years past). Few men in Britain are better equipped to write a study of Dickens, or more certain to have written one some day; and his expected book fulfils one's expectations. This is the finest study of Dickens by a novelist since Gissing's, and one of the subtlest and strongest interpretations of his life, mind and art.

The title so inevitably plays around with the words used by very disparate predecessors in this field—Humphry House's *The Dickens World*, J. Hillis Miller's *Charles Dickens: the World of his Novels*, J. B. Priestley's *Charles Dickens and his World*—that Professor Wilson's agenda should be quoted:

> Such a life, with the contradictions and strangenesses it inevitably involved, makes Dickens a very interesting man. . . . What matters about his public and private life is the way in which they fed his great novels. . . . It is as a guide to exploring this Dickens imaginative system. . . that this account of his life has been written.

A brilliant example of this opens his book: an analysis of Dickens's reminiscences of his childhood toys, showing how closely they are linked to some of the adult obsessions of his books—unsurprising, since (as he says) toys are the first food upon which our fancy is nourished, but no previous commentator had spotted the suggestiveness of this little-known essay, 'A Christmas Tree'.

A more central and important example of Professor Wilson's methods and merits is his exploration of what he argues are Dickens's two greatest defects. The first, the biographical origins of which are very familiar, is his obsession with childhood; among other arguments this is well suggested through a comparison with Dostoevsky's world, ultimately more universal and mature (though Dostoevsky is not always thus introduced, as he often has been, as a stick with which to beat Dickens). This obsession, however, is also acknowledged as a source of the peculiar splendour of the Dickens world ('for the general reader who is touched by his works Dickens is above all funny; but, next to that, he is compassionate. And the general reader is surely by and large right'). Professor Wilson can see no compensation for what he regards as the second great defect of the Dickens world, 'the absence of any real sympathy with, or understanding for women'. He traces this to Dickens's resentment against his mother for her attitude during the blacking-warehouse episode, and later he argues that this blockage of sympathy was reinforced and extended by all the main women in his life (Maria Beadnell and all three Hogarth sisters) until at last, from Ellen Ternan, 'Dickens acquired late in his career some sense of what it was like to be a woman'.

All this is well-argued and critically relevant. What is missing, regrettably, is an adequate discussion of how Dickens's personal and artistic shortcomings over women were related to early Victorian assumptions social and literary. Professor Wilson says surprisingly little about Dickens's English literary contemporaries, though he has some sound remarks on the theatre, asks some penetrating questions about the relationship between Dickens and the Romantic movement, and throws out some tantalizing asides which it would be good to see him substantiate, such as that Dickens was influenced by Tennyson.

Several new emphases emerge. There is a notable discussion of *Sketches by Boz*, about how and when its crudities were outgrown, and where they persisted. The account of Dickens's development is fresh and suggestive. 'From my own experience', Professor Wilson remarks, when discussing the *Daily News* débâcle, 'I should suggest that the very realization of the hopeless step he had taken probably stimulated his imagination to work again.' This is the only time that Professor Wilson becomes explicitly Mr. Wilson the novelist, but the experience and insights of a novelist are often implicit, and are helpful (for Mr. Wilson does not confuse Dickens with himself, as some other commentators, with less excuse, have done). A crucial re-interpretation of Dickens's early development appears in the discussion of *Barnaby Rudge*, here argued to be both a much finer novel and a more considerable step forward in Dickens's artistic mastery of his fictional world than has been recognized.

Professor Wilson has enough sense and penetration not to need to be over-ingenious. 'Truth, Sir', said Dr. Johnson of some intellectual opponents, 'is a cow that will yield such people no more milk, and so they are gone to milk the bull.' Recent Dickens studies have seen some determined bull-milking, particularly in the attempt to establish improbable relevances and to explain away weaknesses. No such desperate expedients appear here: Professor Wilson is sharp on what he judges to be lapses or relatively superficial effects, and these include such popular and admired episodes as Dotheboys Hall, the American scenes in *Martin Chuzzlewit*, and much of *David Copperfield* ('this most inner of Dickens's novels is the most shallow, the most smoothly running, the most complacent—indeed in the pejorative sense of that word, the most Victorian')—judgments well argued and worth considering. Altogether, a capital book, to use a Dickensian adjective, and splendidly illustrated by nearly 200 items, including forty pages of colour plates, depicting not only Dickens, his works and his circle, but also many areas of Victorian life and sentiment. Professor Wilson is acquainted with the relevant scholarship, and unobtrusively aware of the current critical debate about Dickens.

Occasionally there are signs of haste in the composition or proof-reading: five errors, for instance, in the brief account of the public readings (but this is untypical).

'The pages of the *Dickensian* over its long years of publication are an extraordinary mine of the unexpected and the relevant', Professor Wilson notes in his acknowledgements. Under its new editor, Dr. Michael Slater, the *Dickensian* continues its usefulness, with a further shift from the amateur to the academic. The annual surveys of current work on Dickens are one admirable new feature; so is the much-improved index. The reviewing section is as good as it could be, with such contributors as Kathleen Tillotson, Barbara Hardy, Steven Marcus, W. W. Robson, Raymond Williams and Richard D. Altick, besides the regulars whom Dr. Slater assembles for his notable Centenary Number.

This issue is devoted to the course of Dickens's reputation since 1870, the period being farmed out in (mostly) twenty-year lots to Professor K. J. Fielding, Sylvère Monod, Philip Collins, George Ford, and the editor himself. These scholars display the degree of competence one would expect, and a decent liveliness too. Themselves drawing liberally on the back volumes of the *Dickensian*, they discuss not only the development of scholarship and criticism but also manifestations of Dickens's popularity among more common readers and his persistence as part of the national consciousness. This book-length survey thus usefully supplements, though it rarely contradicts, Professor Ford's notable study *Dickens and his Readers*. The issue also contains a prologue on Dickens's final months by Miss Margaret Lane, a postscript on Dickens films by Miss Dilys Powell, and a full report on Centenary events. There are three dozen illustrations, ranging from Dickens in 1870 to Dr. F. R. Leavis.

Of the many other promised Centenary Numbers, the French collection in *Europe* deserves commendation. Besides containing useful essays by two leading *anglicistes*—Professor Monod on the modernity of Dickens's art and Professor Henri Fluchère on *Great Expectations*—the issue assembled twenty pieces by various hands, some inevitably much more adept than others. Of special interest to the Anglo-Saxon reader are the account of Dickens on French television, the list and discussion of Dickens films, and the essays on his fortunes in Italy, Hungary and Bulgaria.

Dr. Slater, besides editing his regular *Dickensian* number, has assembled a second and more varied team to write, for Dickens's old publishers, a set of centenary essays: three academics (Professor Barbara Hardy, Dr. John Holloway, Dr. Slater), three novelists (Miss Margaret Lane, Miss Pamela Hansford Johnson, and Lord Snow), three who are both (Professors Walter Allen and Angus Wilson, and Mr. Raymond Williams). The essays are grouped under three heads: the Artist, the Critic of Society, and the Fellow-man. Professor Allen finds new things to say about Dickens's comedy, and Professor Wilson about his presentation of childhood. Dr. Slater, who in a recent *Dickensian* contributed an unusually suggestive essay on the Christmas Books, here writes learnedly about the background and genesis of *The Chimes*.

It was a happy notion to persuade Lord Snow to write about Dickens and the civil service. The satire on the Circumlocution Office is, he argues, inaccurate and unhistorical, but

under it there is a cry against all administrative systems anywhere. It isn't useful. One doesn't make a more tolerable world like that. But we all at times feel it. When everything else is disposed of, that is Dickens's strength.

Mr. Raymond Williams's essay on Dickens and social ideas makes useful discriminations about how ideas operate in fiction, and on how Dickens relates to the Radical tradition, but it ends just when one was expecting a fuller application of this prolegomenon to the details of the novels. Mr. Williams—who must surely write a book on Dickens some day—needed more than essay length to work out these possibilities, and some substantial argument would be necessary before the sceptical would be convinced that Lady Dedlock's name deserves to be added to those of Micawber, Pecksniff, Sarah Gamp and Skimpole as examples of a kind of characterization typical of Dickens's genius, 'a unique and memorable and individual reality which yet has a lasting force as a general meaning or emphasis in life'.

If Mr. Williams seems to lack elbow-room, Mr. Dyson is sometimes more relaxed and expansive than he need be. Offering chapters on all the novels from *The Old Curiosity Shop* onwards, he is at his best when he does not feel impelled to re-tell all the circumstances of a novel's composition and say something about most aspects of its artistry. Sensible and scholarly though he is, and in happy sympathy with his author, there is not always enough pressure of new perception behind his discussions, and sometimes he worries an idea to death (the names of David Copperfield, for instance). He is happier when he selects a limited objective (as in his very brief item on *Little Dorrit*, mainly devoted to an analysis of the brilliant opening chapter), or when he teases out the roots of a personal response, such as why *Our Mutual Friend* is his favourite Dickens novel, though he would not claim it is the best. He makes out a good case for seeing it unfashionably, as a very funny, as well as sinister, novel, 'a real recovery of Dickens's great comic form' and has much that is fresh to say about it, including some nice asides, such as that Silas Wegg must be among the ancestors of Davies in *The Caretaker*.

Mr. Dyson usefully challenges some current accounts of the novels: the excessively censorious stance, for instance, that Pip has elicited from many recent commentators. What kind of boy, he sensibly asks, 'could be expected to respond impeccably to Mrs. Joe, Pumblechook and Wopsle, let alone Magwitch, Miss Havisham, Estella, and Pip's curious fate'? Or his explosion over Mr. Edmund Wilson's association of John Jasper with his creator: 'There is no major and seminal piece of literary criticism known to me . . . where a more damnable piece of nonsense can be found.' As independent, but much less convincing, are his contentions that Esther Summerson is 'extremely intelligent' and 'perhaps Dickens's greatest study of virtue'. A useful and agreeable book, then, but patchy and too long.

A long review of discussion of England's greatest humorist (besides what else he is), and not a glint of that famous humour. What could be more appropriate in the *TLS*, than to end by quoting the passage from *Dombey and Son*, which the book review section of the *Dickensian* now happily carries as its epigraph?

There was something very awful in this manner of reading. It was such a determined, unimpassioned, inflexible, coldblooded way of going to work. . . . And when the Doctor smiled suspiciously at his author, or knit his brows, or shook his head and made wry faces at him, as much as to say, 'Don't tell me, Sir, I know better', it was terrific.

Mr. Williams's phrase about 'a unique and memorable and individual reality' would not be inappropriate here.

(b) BEETHOVEN

THESE TWO splendidly-prepared volumes may well go down to posterity as the finest tribute of the Beethoven bicentenary year. The

subsidiary title 'The Kafka Sketchbook', however, needs both explanation and qualification. Although the Miscellany contains a large
number of sketches, it is not a record of continuous work like some
of the later sketchbooks, but a random collection of sheets dating
from Beethoven's early period, apparently assembled and preserved
by the composer, and later bound together. Despite his untidiness in
mundane affairs, Beethoven kept his sketches with care, and often
drew inspiration for a work from a jotting made years before: an
example is the main Allegro of the last piano sonata, Op. 111, which
derived from a rejected sketch for the slow movement of a violin and
piano sonata, Op. 30 No. 1, made twenty years earlier.

The present *Miscellany* was bought by the publishing firm of
Artaria at the auction after Beethoven's death in 1827, and subsequently by the composer Johann Nepomuk Kafka, who sold it to the
British Museum in 1875. It also included some much later sketches
for *The Ruins of Athens* and *King Stephen*, dating from 1811, which
have not been reproduced in the present volumes. Thus the unifying
factor in the collection is the period, extending from Beethoven's last
years in Bonn up to the turn of the century. The sheets include some
fragments and fair copies, admittedly of less important works, as
well as sketches for familiar masterpieces, such as the first two piano
concertos. These, the sketches, are not only valuable to the musi-
cologist and the performer but fascinating to the general music-lover.

'A source of wonder even in the composer's lifetime', writes the
editor, Joseph Kerman, 'Beethoven's sketches have in later years
been much discussed.' They have been much discussed, certainly, and
quoted at second and third-hand; yet the basic material has never
been readily available. In 1961 the Beethovenhaus in Bonn published
a transcription of sketches for the Pastoral Symphony and the Op.
70 trios, taken from the British Museum's originals; and in 1962 the
so-called 'Wielhorsky' sketchbook of 1802-03 appeared in Russia.
But the main source has long been in the pioneer works of Gustav
Nottebohm, and even these have been hard enough to acquire in
recent years. Nor, to the writer's knowledge, have they ever been
translated into English.

Professor Kerman, in his preface, rightly praises Nottebohm for
his sharp sense of the relevant, in spite of his 'parsimony over exact
manuscript references'. Nottebohm's essays, which explored a large
number of the sketches, had in their nature taken a bird's-eye view.
It is the sources themselves that the musician now wants to see, even

though editorial guidance may be needed to explain their relevance, and to decipher, or conjecture about, their rougher details.

Some of Beethoven's fair copies were hardly models of legibility, let alone the jottings he made for his own eyes alone. The ideal solution, in publication, is to provide a facsimile of the original with a separate transcription into music-type as a kind of cross-reference or 'key'. This was done with the 'Wielhorsky' sketchbook, plus a third volume devoted to commentary.

Professor Kerman has favoured a less literal, but in the long run more helpful method of transcription. His second volume falls into two parts: first, a rearrangement of the material in order of works, where these are identifiable; and secondly, a supplement containing the remaining fragments, quotations of other composers' music, &c. Part two is arranged in the page-order of the facsimile, and there are meticulous cross-references to and from the material in the first part. In the editor's own words:

The transcription presented here is not of the so-called 'diplomatic' type, which follows the original notation as faithfully as possible, adding nothing, correcting nothing, and reproducing the distribution and spacing of the music page by page and line by line. An attempt has been made to achieve a greater degree of intelligibility in the end result.

Would the ultra-purist wish, in fact, for an empty stave, an overlap, a thickening of ink, or even a blot, to be indicated in the transcription? The answer is that the original is also there to see; and Professor Kerman's thoroughness—to be expected by readers of his recent book on the Beethoven quartets—sees to it that all editorial marks in the transcription are clearly bracketed off.

His method has the advantage of grouping all the sketches for a particular work under one heading. He is fairly confident about labelling the stages of sketching—preliminary, early, later, &c.—but he is generous with question-marks too. Each volume has its preface. In addition there are indexes and inventories, and an exhaustive investigation of the different types of paper, ruling-inks, and watermarks scattered throughout the *Miscellany*. These are not always a guide to the chronology, since Beethoven was apt to use up old manuscript paper at a later date. The transcription volume has its own appendix of notes, all bearing marks of formidable scholarship. For example:

Sketched on a bifolium (ff. 58–9) which also contains a notation for WoO

B

71, composed between Sept. 1796 and Apr. 1797. It also has a sk for the trio of the minuet of the Sonata in D, Op. 10 No. 3, in the key of A flat but evidently notated in three flats; the piece may well have been first conceived for Op. 7.

There are basically two types of autograph: actual sketches, for the most part on a single stave; and written-out compositions, beyond the sketching stage, whether complete, fragmentary, or ultimately rejected. Professor Kerman reserves the term 'autograph' for the latter group, and explains the prevalence of fragments and minor works by pointing out that Beethoven, even at a much later date, would have been likely to dispose of fair copies to publishers. Nevertheless, the *Miscellany* enriches the scanty collection of early Beethoven originals, even though the most substantial offerings are the minuet from the Wind Sextet, Op. 71, the Duo 'with two obbligato eyeglasses', part of a Sonatina for mandoline and piano, and some unused variation-material for the Andante of the Op. 18 No. 5 Quartet. Several pages in full score preserve part only of a movement for flute, bassoon, piano (or harpsichord?) and orchestra, presumably a very early work indeed. There are other curiosities for the Beethovenite to relish: a fugue for Albrechtsberger, with whom Beethoven studied counterpoint in Vienna, and (much earlier) a page of alternative harmonizations for the *Lamentations of Jeremiah*, with which he is said to have 'thrown' the singers in his apprentice days at Bonn.

However interesting all this may be, it is in the sketches for important works that the real value lies. As Professor Kerman says, referring to the sketches in general, they 'constitute a source for study of great potential that has remained largely untapped'. The process of trial and error, the many rejections and rewritings, the growth of great music from humble beginnings, constitute a lesson in composition and a unique example of human endeavour.

Beethoven's first concern, it seems, was to capture some basic idea in no matter how primitive a form. From there he could set to work, and the act of setting pen to paper was in itself a vital stage. A large number of the pre-1800 works are represented in the *Miscellany*, including fourteen of the first nineteen opus numbers. Professor Kerman's remark, 'all but five works', is misleading, since many of the numbers cover groups of works. The Op. 18 quartets, for example, are missing except for No. 5, and apart from the rejected variations, only its finale is attended to in detail. Other existing sketches lie elsewhere—understandably 'since the *Miscellany* is not a true sketch-book but a collection of loose sheets'.

Those who know Nottebohm will recognize many of his finds—he obviously had access to the collection through Artaria or Kafka—such as the andante version of the prestissimo finale of the C minor Piano Trio. But if the tempo of an idea eluded the composer in the initial stages, so did its rhythmic form. The finale of the B flat Concerto, Op. 19, is a famous example. Its syncopations seem to be born out of the need for rhythmic variety, but Kerman tactfully disagrees with Nottebohm over the order of events: the most advanced sketches rejected the syncopation, and then it was apparently readopted having meanwhile 'caused Beethoven several changes of mind'. The E flat slow movement started life in D major, but this was not un-usual in intermovement relationships: there was a semitonal shift in the C minor Violin and Piano Sonata and in the 'Emperor' Concerto.

Most interesting, too, are the cadenza sketches for the first move-ment, some of which anticipate the athletic fugato Beethoven wrote (or rewrote?) years later for this earliest concerto. The C major Concerto, Op. 15, also appears in some detail with the familiar largo theme yet again in the wrong key—D flat—but with hardly a breath of the finale. Some fragments of the third C minor Concerto, not performed until 1803, are embryonic but recognizable: the timpani-part in the first movement, the striding opening of the cadenza, and the up-beat (only) of the rondo.

The first two concertos are particularly significant since they were the most important of Beethoven's orchestral works to date. Yet more than one symphony was sketched, and a C major one seems to foreshadow the eventual First Symphony (1800), even if only as 'a repository of unfulfilled ideas'. Nottebohm only touched on it briefly, and it is good to find it running to nine whole pages of transcription. In all these cases it is easy nowadays to be wise after the event and to see Beethoven's abortive attempts at a slow introduc-tion reaching fulfilment in the symphony we know, or to discover the seeds of the Fifth Symphony's Scherzo in a still earlier C minor symphony sketched in Bonn. This is, at least partly, implied by Kerman's word 'potential'. The sketches afford a unique entrance into the depths and developments of a great mind.

The question may be asked: what does one *learn* from the sketches, which were purely private documents not intended for public peru-sal? One learns, for a start, not to take masterstrokes for granted.

One learns that in spite of his fame as an extemporizer Beethoven left little to chance or to memory when it came to serious composition: everything must be written down, rewritten, and rewritten again. As he said himself:

I carry my ideas with me for a long time, rejecting and rewriting until I am satisfied. Since I am conscious of what I want, I never lose sight of the fundamental idea. It rises higher and higher until I see the image of it, rounded and complete, standing there before my mental vision.

The labours in producing the present volumes can hardly be over-praised, and likewise the initiative and cooperation that led to the project. Mr. T. C. Skeat, the Keeper of Manuscripts at the British Museum, offers his thanks to the Royal Musical Association for the initial idea, and Joseph Kerman includes in a wide range of acknow-ledgements the assistance of several graduate students at the University of California, Berkeley, where he is professor. The large oblong format was dictated by the folios themselves, and the transcription volume is to match; the Oxford University Press undertook the printing, and Messrs. Halstan the music-setting, on paper specially manufactured by Messrs. Frank Grunfeld.

On the strength of the maxim that if a job is worth doing it is worth doing well, the result is worthy; and if the expense places it beyond reach of many Beethoven-lovers, it is to be hoped that libraries everywhere will make it available for reference. What is now needed is for *all* the extant Beethoven sketches to be made accessible, and somehow integrated: those for the later and greater· works, like the Eroica and the Ninth, are a goldmine for study. Professor Ker-man, thorough as ever, gives references in his notes to 'other sources' in connexion with the works included; and to his editorship one must return with gratitude.

Apart from the need for scholarship and understanding there re-mains the problem of Beethoven's handwriting, summed up best per-haps by the composer himself in a letter to his friend Zmeskall:

Dear good Z. Don't be annoyed if I ask you to write the enclosed *Adresse* on the enclosed letter; the person whom the letter is for is always complain-ing that no letters come from me; yesterday I took a letter to the post, where they asked me where the letter was supposed to go?—so I see that my handwriting is perhaps misunderstood as often as I am myself. . . .

Beethoven's writing deteriorated in later years and Kerman modestly claims that 'reading the miscellany is a relatively feasible matter'. There is a vast difference, even in the early period, between the fair copy of the Trinklied (1790?) and the earliest of the sketches. 'Since I am conscious of what I want . . .' said Beethoven. He had, in addition, the composer's prerogative of reading between his own lines.

2

GENERALS IN COMMAND

(a) EISENHOWER IN WARTIME

EVERYONE KNOWS that General Eisenhower was a good man, but not everyone is sure that he was a good general. British military opinion, with significant exceptions like Tedder, was inclined on the whole to doubt it. He was acknowledged to be a superlative manager of men and an excellent chairman of committees. But both his combat experience and his strategic competence were seriously questioned. His own humility contributed to the somewhat negative assessment. One of the reasons why he was later acceptable as the President of a great democracy was precisely that he was so unlike the conventional stereotype of a general. As President, he behaved rather like a constitutional monarch, which is not the role of a Commander-in-Chief. Yet one of his greatest successes was to extricate his country from the Korean War, which perhaps only a trusted soldier could have done. He was in fact unquestionably a soldier through and through.

Whether he was a great captain is more difficult to judge. Among his contemporaries he lacked the tactical genius of Montgomery and the aggressive drive of MacArthur or Patton. At the present distance of time he does not seem to bear comparison with other leaders of

(a) *The Papers of Dwight David Eisenhower: The War Years.* (Edited by Alfred D. Chandler Jr.) Volumes 1–4: 2,696 pp. Volume 5: 414 pp. Johns Hopkins Press (I.B.E.G.). £35.65 the set.

(b) CHARLES DE GAULLE: *Mémoires d'espoir. Le Renouveau, 1958–1962.* 314 pp. Paris: Plon. 27.50fr. *Discours et Messages.* Volume I: Pendant la guerre, 1940–1946. 677 pp. Volume II: Dans l'attente, 1946–1958. 662 pp. Volume III: Avec le renouveau, 1958–1962. 443 pp. Volume IV: Pour l'effort, 1962–1965. 457 pp. Volume V: Vers le terme, 1966–1969. 418 pp. Paris: Plon. 35.70fr. each.

PIERRE VIANSSON-PONTÉ: *Histoire de la république gaullienne.* Volume I: La fin d'une époque. 578 pp. Paris: Fayard. 30fr.

YVES COURRIÈRE: *L'Heure des colonels.* 630 pp. Paris: Fayard. 32fr.

JACQUES DEBÛ-BRIDEL: *De Gaulle contestataire.* 254 pp. Paris: Plon. 18fr.

JOHN NEWHOUSE: *De Gaulle and the Anglo-Saxons.* 374 pp. André Deutsch. £2.50.

PHILIPPE ALEXANDRE: *Le Duel: De Gaulle-Pompidou.* 420 pp. Paris: Grasset. 28fr.

great coalitions like Wellington or Foch, though his war was as great and his victory as decisive as theirs. There is never likely to be such a command held again over vast allied armies in the field, so comparison will have to make do with the evidence already available. It cannot be said that General Eisenhower's papers, now published on a massive scale and superlatively edited, make any substantial difference to the basis of comparison. They add to the detail in a number of places, but historians have already had access to them before now, so that the general picture is not altered. Looked at as a whole, however, even if they do not make him a better or worse general than before, they do emphatically confirm his professionalism and his complete command of the forces under him. Whatever he may have been as President, he was a Commander-in-Chief and not an easy-going co-ordinator in the field.

The professionalism shows itself on every one of more than 2,500 pages: in the detailed grasp of logistics, in the thorough attention to training, in the confident handling of tactical problems and strategic disputes, in the insistence on discipline, in the tone of address to both subordinates and superiors. Whether the ultimate decisions were right or wrong, there is no doubt who took them. He insisted from the first on a single chain of command, not co-ordination by committees; and in at least one instance, over the control of the air forces in the assault on Europe, he explicitly threatened to 'request relief from this Command' unless he had his own way. It is only necessary to study a few of his extremely detailed directives to be left in no doubt of his mastery. It was recognized too, by his most unruly and brilliant subordinates. Even Montgomery wrote to him in the end: 'You will hear no more on the subject of command from me.' Coming from such an authority, and signed 'your very devoted and loyal subordinate', such a tribute is conclusive.

Eisenhower's professional skill and success as a commander tended to be obscured by his genius for promoting allied unity. In this respect propaganda did him a disservice during the war and another one after it. During the war the extreme difficulty of achieving allied cooperation was obscured in the interests of morale. The British, American, French and other forces were represented in public as cooperating in perfect accord when in fact many of their generals were squabbling like actresses and the rank and file regarded each other with amused contempt. In the circumstances Eisenhower's achievement was far more remarkable than was recognized at the time. His papers clearly chart the progression from a situation in which the confrontation was between British and American doctrines and personalities as such to one in which the confrontation was on the issues, and the divisions were no longer on nationalist lines. In this respect Tedder and Bradley were his most significant allies, Patton and Montgomery his most damaging opponents. But because wartime propaganda successfully concealed the problems which he faced and overcame, postwar reassessments, particularly in Britain, did him another injustice. Eisenhower's disagreements with Montgomery, like Roosevelt's disagreements with Churchill, became identified with basic differences between the United States and Britain. It was overlooked that there was virtually no controversy in which Eisenhower lacked British supporters, as well as American opponents.

In the light of early postwar reinterpretations, it is intriguing to look again at some of the famous matters of contention: the policy towards the French in North Africa, the decision to land in southern France instead of across the Adriatic into the Balkans, the rival merits of a broad front and a narrow thrust into Germany. The Eisenhower papers are revealing and cogent on all these arguments: not that they contain new revelations, but precisely because they confirm the true basis of the solutions adopted, which was a strictly military necessity that no political calculations could override without disaster. They also confirm that there was no diametrical confrontation on national lines within the alliance. Least of all was there an absolute Anglo-American dichotomy over the greatest of all the strategic questions, which was the priority of the European and Pacific theatres. It is interesting to see how firmly Eisenhower was committed to the European strategy long before his own destiny was revealed and at a time when he was chiefly concerned in planning for the Pacific theatre.

So far from being deeply troubled by Anglo-American differences, Eisenhower had greater difficulty in reconciling the views of his own compatriots. There were not only dissidents among his own generals, of whom Patton was no more than the most notorious prima donna; there were also serious interservice problems of cooperation. An American Admiral or Air Force General was more likely to dispute Eisenhower's judgment on professional grounds than a British General was on national grounds. Unavoidably Eisenhower had to resolve some of the resultant problems by accommodation rather than command. In other words, against his wishes and better judgment, in some respects he had to behave as if he were the chairman of a committee of colleagues rather than a commander with a staff of subordinates. The difference is crucial to the distinction between military and political or civilian activity, and had never before been confronted in so intense a form. That Eisenhower succeeded in resolving it is a fact of history, proved by his final victories. Obviously it was not done, as his milder critics have suggested, by a mere combination of kindness and simplicity. Both the subtlety and the firmness of his character, as well as his professional ability, are unmistakably revealed in his papers.

Although indispensable to historians, the papers are too voluminous and miscellaneous to command much of a general readership. Even the admirable editorial notes, which are often more interesting than the papers themselves, cannot knit them together into a continuously readable whole. This is a pity, because much of the mosaic from which Eisenhower's contribution to history is built up would be of great interest in its own right. There is personal as well as professional and historical material here. Eisenhower's letters to his friends and his family, to contemporaries who had been passed over for promotion, to war correspondents and school-children and bereaved relatives of men killed under his command, all add revealing details to the total portrait. So do the innumerable trivialities with which a supreme commander was daily beset: visiting Senators, entertainers, film producers, cranks and the rest. His remarks on the problems of enlisted women or of Negro troops are themselves contributions to social history, if only the social history of a bygone age. Perhaps one sentence of his own best sums up the basis of his success: 'I instinctively dislike ever to uphold the conservative as opposed to the bold'. It was a true judgment, though not the most generally accepted one. The value of these volumes is that they will help to put that part of the record straight.

(*b*) DE GAULLE AND ALGERIA

THE DEATH OF General de Gaulle has been very much à la de Gaulle. He always liked departures which were sudden and unexpected. The brusque resignation of January, 1946, supposedly impressed the communist leader Thorez, who remarked that it was not without grandeur. The laconic communiqué of April, 1969, and the long silence which followed, made a distinguished ending to the last confused and inglorious months of Gaullist power. Both were the subject of interest and speculation. Even as late as 1969 and 1970 people wondered whether de Gaulle was not reserving himself for some ultimate gesture which might devastate those who had succeeded him. The unexpectedly early, but carefully planned, appearance last month of the first volume of the new series of memoirs, caused many to remember the publication of the first volume of de Gaulle's war memoirs in 1955.

This was an important element in the revival of the General's reputation. It was only then that many realized, or remembered, that de Gaulle was something out of the ordinary. He was not just the leader of an unsuccessful and in some respects shabby political movement which had added to the discordance of the Fourth Republic (the Rassemblement du Peuple Français or R.P.F.). He was also a perceptive observer, a lucid analyst, an exalted visionary, whose colossal egoism was submerged within a magnificent literary gift. Critics claimed to see the influence of Montesquieu, Hegel, Tocqueville. Stylists compared him to Valéry, Proust, Saint-Exupéry. The names of Chateaubriand, Barrès, Péguy, were invoked. The memoirs were accompanied by the publication of documents which historians found very useful to have. But they were not the sort of memoirs which historians like to use. There were few revelations, explanations, indiscretions. These war memoirs were essentially a statement of belief and philosophy, a deliberate fusion of national and personal history, an essay in politics. With their publication, Gaullism became more explicit. And nobody can doubt that it was the General's intention, with the publication of a further three volumes, along with five volumes of *Discours et Messages*, to construct a formidable political monument for himself. The fact that, on the day of his sudden death, he was still working on the second volume means that the first volume of the new series, *Le Renouveau*, will arouse particular interest.

This volume begins with a rapid survey of the decline, depicted as inevitable for institutional reasons, of the Fourth Republic. It includes a brief reference to the R.P.F. and to its defeat, and a passing reference to Nato (by virtue of which, said de Gaulle, an American generalissimo, established near to Versailles, exercised the military authority of the New World over the Old). And then we are in May, 1958. The General is at pains to establish that while he was in no way surprised by what happened in Algiers on May 13 and by its effects in France, he was not in any way involved in these events. He tells us that he had had no contact with Jacques Soustelle either during the period when he was Governor-General of Algeria, or afterwards. As for those Gaullists who, in Algeria itself, were working for the General's return to power, they were acting independently and without consulting him ('en dehors de mon aval').

All the same, the General explains that once the crisis was there, he knew that he would have to act. He foresaw airborne troops arriving in Paris and the establishment of a military government analogous to that of Algiers; a movement of strikes and of resistance to this government; the eventual development of civil war and of foreign intervention in France. In these circumstances he felt obliged to emerge from his retirement; he was conscious of his position within France, 'je me sens donc l'instrument désigné'. 1958 was 1940 all over again, except that whereas in 1940 he had been almost unknown, in 1958 he was 'notoire', and that in 1958 it was necessary to calculate how he could effect a fundamental change in French development and not appear simply as a temporary moderating influence on a grave crisis.

So de Gaulle describes how, after General Salan in Algiers had launched the cry of 'Vive de Gaulle' (which he claims was May 14 whereas most people date it on May 15), he published a seven-line communiqué in which he pointed out the degradation of the state and stated his readiness to assume power. At his press conference on May 19 he again announced that he was at the disposition of the country. As he describes it, from his very first communiqué, everyone understood that his return to the direction of affairs was inevitable. All that was needed was to determine the details of how this could be done. In spite of the objections of André Le Troquer and in spite of 'quelques interventions malveillantes' from within parliament (and he specifically mentions M. Mendès-France) his investiture, on the conditions which he had imposed, was assured. On May 30, before going before the Assembly, the General was at Colombey: 'Sur ma maison je regarde alors tomber le dernier soir d'une longue solitude. Quelle est donc cette force des choses qui m'oblige à m'en aller?'

It is natural that we should pause and reflect on this account. It is, of course, obvious that the General did not seek to write the history of the 'revolution of 1958'. As he says elsewhere, 'pour traiter le sujet, je m'efforcerai sans cesse, conformément à ma nature, de le ramener à l'essentiel'. Naturally, therefore, if we turn to the admirably clear and excellently written first volume of *Histoire de la république gaullienne*, which covers the period from 1958 to 1962, or if we turn to the more dramatic events in Algeria described by Yves Courrière, *L'Heure des colonels*, we will find many details which are not present in de Gaulle. It is said, for example, that on May 15, Jacques Foccard, who was working closely with de Gaulle and who could hardly have been acting without his approval, inquired whether the generals in Algiers were in de Gaulle's favour. It was as a result of this direct and vital inquiry that Salan felt obliged to take the plunge and proclaim himself for de Gaulle.

It has been said too that with regard to the proposed plans for landing parachutists in Paris ('Opération Résurrection') de Gaulle played a game of brinkmanship, both holding off and encouraging the parachutists as a means of bullying the politicians into accepting him. And, without necessarily giving any credence to all these innumerable and uncontrollable stories which surround this period of plots and conspiracies, any analysis has to note the importance of the very uncertainty which surrounded de Gaulle's ideas on Algeria. In the *Discours et Messages* the last published statement to be made before the crisis of May, 1958, is dated September 12, 1957. General de Gaulle made it known that when he should think it necessary to explain his views, notably on the subject of Algeria, then he would do so. And it was not only such a heavy uncertainty which was cultivated; there was also a deliberate ambiguity. M. Viansson-Ponté gives many examples of different men with different ideas, each of whom had reason to believe that the General was with them. It is hardly surprising that when de Gaulle describes his entry into the Palais Bourbon, on June 1, 1958, he notes that he was surrounded by an intense curiosity.

Perhaps de Gaulle is right when he speaks of his return to power in 1958 as being the result of a 'sursaut national'. But it was also the result of a remarkable piece of political calculation. It is not surprising that when de Gaulle goes on to describe the success with which his referendum and the ensuing elections were greeted, he does not mention the considerable pressure exercised by his administration (which is described by M. Viansson-Ponté). It is clear that de Gaulle was a republican who believed in the voice of the people, but he also believed that the voice, and its representatives, should be manipulated.

There are occasions when de Gaulle deals with events and people with brutal realism. He never believed that the men of Algiers would pursue their revolutionary action; he knew that they would be only too glad to find someone who would relieve them of responsibility. As M. Soustelle has said, the General always had a tendency to believe that men were never really courageous or devoted to a cause. Equally he never thought that the government of the Fourth Republic was capable of acting energetically. Having come unescorted from Colombey for his press conference on May 19, he describes how he saw the Minister of the Interior, Jules Moch, inspecting his armoured cars on the banks of the Seine. It was this 'spectacle dérisoire', he says, which persuaded him to adopt 'le ton du maître de l'heure'. There is not much of 'l'appel venu du fond de l'histoire' here. As he supposedly told the left-wing Gaullist, Debû-Bridel, the Fifth Republic had emerged from *le 13 mai* as the Third Republic had emerged from the defeat of Sedan.

A great deal of attention will be attached to the General's claim, made in *Le Renouveau*, that when he assumed power in 1958, he knew what he wanted to do, had to do, in Algeria. He says that although he had no pre-established plan, yet 'les grandes lignes' of his policy were already decided in his mind. There was no question of assimilation. This was a policy which might have been possible a hundred years earlier or at various other times, but in 1958 integration was nothing but 'une formule astucieuse et vide'. It was equally impossible to maintain the status quo and condemn France, politically, financially and militarily, to a sterile conflict from which she had little to gain. Thus, according to de Gaulle's own account, there remained only the one possible solution, that Algeria should have the right to determine its own future. And to show that this was a reasoning which he had held for some time, he quotes his press conference of 1955, when he stated the necessity of substituting 'association' for 'domination'.

Thus his strategy was fixed. But in terms of tactics he was obliged to proceed by stages, progressively, cautiously, delicately, as he thought he could obtain the necessary movement of consent. 'Si de but en blanc', he writes,

j'affichais mes intentions, nul doute que, sur l'océan des ignorances alarmées, des étonnements scandalisés, des malveillances coalisées, se fût levée dans tous les milieux une vague de stupeurs et de fureurs qui eût fait chavirer le navire. Sans jamais changer de cap il me faudrait donc manœuvrer.

And of his speech in the Forum of Algiers, which caused such emotion, the speech beginning with the unforgettable words, 'Je vous ai
compris', he writes that he had used 'les mots apparemment spon-
tanés dans la forme, mais au fond bien calculés, dont je veux que la
foule s'enthousiasme sans qu'ils m'emportent plus loin que je n'ai
résolu d'aller'.

Not everyone will find it possible to believe that de Gaulle had so
early made up his mind in favour of an 'Algérie algérienne' or that he
had understood that 'association' could mean independence. Writing
with the advantage of hindsight he seems to forget a policy which
was experimental and devious, at times unsuccessful and often out-
paced by events and which, in any case, allowed the war to continue
or four years. It is interesting to see that M. Viansson-Ponté places
the emphasis on the means rather than on the ends. Just as de Gaulle
was determined to be institutionally secure in France so that the
politicians could not get rid of him once the Algerian war was over,
so he was determined that the Algerian affair should be dealt with by
a strong French state. He was not prepared to accept that the
authority of the French state should be challenged. He was concerned with the appearance as much as with the reality. And there is
much in *Le Renouveau* which accords with this.

After his attempt in June, 1958, to persuade Abderrahmane Farès
(whom he knew to be in correspondence with Ferhat Abbas) to enter
his government, an attempt which was unsuccessful ('mais une bonne
action est-elle jamais perdue?'), he arranged for an important military offensive to take place the following spring. It was unthinkable
that there should have been any military action in which France
might have been defeated. Then, having visited General Challes and
inspected the site of his operations, he was convinced that the re-
bellion would continue to grow. Thus he moved forward step by
step, endeavouring to understand what was happening and rarely
dominating events. It seems preferable to believe in this realistic
approach rather than to accept the General's own suggestion that
from the beginning he had foreseen the outcome, or to accept M.
Debû-Bridel's statement—in his *De Gaulle contestataire*—that de
Gaulle was knowingly carrying out the process of decolonization
which M. Mendès-France had begun but which he had not had the
courage to conclude.

All this is presented in the style which is characteristic of the
General. He continually refers to himself in the third person; the

cadences of his prose remain vigorous; repetition gives a certain drama to the most ordinary descriptions ('C'est ainsi que . . . c'est ainsi que . . .'); lists of names and details of journeys give an epic quality to every Presidential tour; the choice of words is always careful and the occasional archaic elegance helps to confer distinction; the text is filled with quotations from the General's own speeches and observations. And yet, it must be said, that the literary quality of *Le Renouveau* is disappointing. It could be that since 1955 we have grown too accustomed to de Gaulle's style to be as impressed as we were with the first page of the first volume of the war memoirs. Yet the striking phrase is harder to find; the verve is less compelling; the sharpness less evident. It is typical perhaps that only when de Gaulle is being nostalgic does his prose now leave its matter-of-factness and reach for some literary grandeur. Thus, writing of the economic changes, we find this passage about the necessary decline of the peasantry:

Comment, étant qui je suis, ne serais-je pas ému et soucieux en voyant s'estomper cette société campagnarde, installée depuis toujours dans ses constantes occupations et encadrée par ses traditions; ce pays des villages immuables, des églises anciennes, des familles solides, de l'éternel retour des labours, des semailles et des moissons; cette contrée des légendes, chansons et danses ancestrales, des patois, costumes et marchés locaux; cette France millénaire, que sa nature, son activité, son génie, avaient faite essentiellement rurale? Comment méconnaître que si, dans notre existence de peuple, la cité—et d'abord, la capitale—ne cessa jamais d'être le siège et le décor de l'appareil officiel, le foyer des arts et des sciences, le rendez-vous principal du commerce, la meilleure place pour les ateliers, c'est la campagne qui demeurait la source de la vie, la mère de la population, la base des institutions, le recours de la patrie. . . . Comment ne pas comprendre que les paysans français ont d'instinct le sentiment d'être, en somme, la France elle-même et que la colossale mutation qui diminue leur volume social et leur rôle économique suscite inévitablement leur inquiétude et leur mélancolie?

The portraits of men are neat and clear. Thus of General Salan, de Gaulle writes,

Son personnage, capable, habile, et, par certains côtés, séduisant, comporte quelquechose d'ondoyant et d'énigmatique qui me semble assez mal cadrer avec ce qu'une grande et droite responsabilité exige de certitude et de rectitude.

Of Gaston Monnerville, 'Il est exclusif dans la conception qu'il s'est faite, en d'autres temps, du régime républicain'. There are interesting inclusions of detail, as when, recounting the end of the unsuccessful rising in Algeria in 1961, we are told that the parachutists withdrew, singing Edith Piaf's song, 'Je ne regrette rien'. There are some rare moments of sarcasm, and many old enemies are not forgotten, so that as he entered the Palais Bourbon de Gaulle recalls his last visit there in 1946, when he administered to Édouard Herriot 'la réponse assez rude et ironique qu'il méritait'.

Some even older issues are paraded, such as the French resentment over their failure to receive reparations from Germany for the First World War, and the surprising suggestion that it was the Anglo-Saxons who, in 1918, insisted on the armistice, thus depriving the French army of its victory (did de Gaulle not know the most famous letter that Clemenceau ever sent to Poincaré?). But among many fine, interesting and surprising things, it is a pity to find so much complacency. We accept that General de Gaulle should attribute to himself the supreme rôle ('Quelle que puisse être l'interprétation que l'on veuille donner à tel ou tel article, c'est vers de Gaulle en tout cas que se tournent les Français. C'est de lui qu'ils attendent la solution de leurs problèmes. C'est à lui que va leur confiance ou que s'adressent leurs reproches'). It is natural that he should comment how, in spite of his age, he had nevertheless journeyed more frequently to and in Algeria than had any of his predecessors. But it is a pity that de Gaulle should find it necessary to pass on to his readers the compliments of those who took part in the abortive summit conference of 1960 or that he should quote an extract from François Mauriac's *Bloc-Notes* in praise of himself.

Two questions are of particular interest in *Le Renouveau*. They are de Gaulle's relations with Britain and America, and the references which he makes to the events of 1968 and to his successor, M. Pompidou. On both these subjects books have been published in which the authors claim to have had access to inside information. John Newhouse is an American whose account of de Gaulle's attempts to destroy the Anglo-American 'hegemony' in Europe, *De Gaulle and the Anglo-Saxons*, is an interesting commentary on American thinking. Having listened at many keyholes, he goes on to reveal the well-known secret of de Gaulle's memorandum of September, 1958 (which he dates the 17th, although de Gaulle dates it the 14th). This memorandum proposed that there should be a reorganization of Nato which should extend the organization beyond the bounds of the North Atlantic and place it under the control of three powers,

America, Britain and France. Mr. Newhouse suggests that to call this proposal a fraud would be overstating the case, 'but not by much'. The fact that de Gaulle readily admits that he did not expect his proposal to be accepted will doubtless seem confirmation to him of the trickery which he had expected. But de Gaulle's own explanation is simple enough. There was no deep-seated plot against the Anglo-Saxons. He was not seeking to remove France from the Atlantic Alliance, but from the integration which this involved. He sought to maintain the alliance ('à titre d'ultime précaution') and at the same time to come to agreements with the states of eastern Europe, with Russia and with China.

From M. Alexandre's *Le Duel* we learn of the relationship between de Gaulle and Pompidou. It has already been widely remarked that de Gaulle has little to say about his successor whom he had, in many ways, created. One incident on which M. Alexandre dwells is that of the mutinous General Jouhaud. De Gaulle was determined that he should be executed and in his memoirs comments drily on the 'astuce juridique' by which Pompidou ('devenu Premier Ministre') saved him. But M. Alexandre dwells longer on this affair which, he says, was a great shock for Pompidou, since it showed him that de Gaulle was in no way prepared to give him any special consideration. As for the events of 1968, in passing reference to them de Gaulle speaks of 'l'alliance des chimères, des chantages, et des lâchetés'. We learn from M. Alexandre that he placed Pompidou in the category of 'lâcheté' after he had consented to reopen the Sorbonne.

It is striking to reflect that after all that de Gaulle has written and all that he has said, we still have to turn to the gossip-columnist sort of writer such as M. Alexandre. For de Gaulle we will have to have the 'petite histoire' as well as the serious study. De Gaulle, as we have always known, was both simple and complex. As we read the first volume of the set of memoirs which he did not live to complete, and as we reflect on his work and character, we realize that he was even more simple and more complex than he had appeared.

C

3

HEMINGWAY'S LAST NOVEL

THE DELAY IN publishing the material Hemingway left in manuscript at his death has been long and hard to explain on any except perhaps commercial grounds. We have had an extraordinarily fine collection of memoirs, *A Moveable Feast*, and that is all. Two recent studies—*The Hemingway Manuscripts: an Inventory* by Philip Young and Charles W. Mann, and Carlos Baker's *Ernest Hemingway: a Life Story*—have given tantalizing glimpses of the range and variety of what remains in the hands of Hemingway's widow and of Scribner's, his canny and close-mouthed publishers. With the appearance of *Islands in the Stream* the process of discovery begins.

It is the book which has usually been referred to recently as Hemingway's sea novel. Between 1947 and 1951, apart from the time he took to write *Across the River and into the Trees*, it was known that he was working in Cuba on a sequence of four narratives set on the islands and waters of the Gulf Stream. For purposes of composition, he regarded them as four separate novels, but he spoke of 'welding' them ultimately into a single work. One of the sections, the third in order of composition, which carried the working title of *The Sea in Being*, was detached from the rest in 1951, and published separately as *The Old Man and the Sea*. The other three sections form the present novel. The first two were originally called *The Sea When Young* and *The Sea When Absent*, while Hemingway does not seem to have fixed on a title for the third. By 1951, he was beginning to refer to the first as *The Island and the Stream*, and it is from this presumably that Mrs. Hemingway or the publishers devised the present title for the whole work—without any indication, it should be observed, that the title is not Hemingway's. The three parts are now called *Bimini*, *Cuba*, and *At Sea*.

The central character of all three, Thomas Hudson, resembles Hemingway himself very closely, not only in temperament and outlook but in biographical detail. At the point in time reached by the novel,

---

ERNEST HEMINGWAY: *Islands in the Stream*. 398 pp. Collins. £2.

1943, he has been through the same number of marriages, had the same number of sons, and, with minor shifts in location, lived in the same places as his creator. He is an artist (a token change from writing to painting has been made); he takes the same lively pleasure (both gourmand and connoisseur) in eating, drinking, and lovemaking; and he enjoys the same outdoor sports. The novel is more directly autobiographical than anything Hemingway had written since his earliest work, the Nick Adams stories. If *In Our Time* is largely the portrait of the artist as a young man, *Islands in the Stream* is the portrait of the artist as a dying man.

In *Bimini*, the first section, Thomas Hudson is living on the West Indian island of that name in the mid-1930s. He has divorced two wives (he reflects that he should have left neither of them), and he sees his sons only for holidays. There have been inner, psychological lesions, too; like the old waiter in *A Clean Well-Lighted Place*, he has lost youth and confidence and now lacks everything but work:

> He had been able to replace almost everything except the children with work and the steady normal working life he had built on the island. He believed he had made something there that would last and that would hold him. Now when he was lonesome for Paris he would remember Paris instead of going there. He did the same thing with all of Europe and much of Asia and of Africa.

This discipline against loneliness and emptiness is helped out by another, more genial discipline of good food, 'drinks to look forward to', deep sea fishing, swimming, and a certain amount of carefully regulated social and sexual life. Very little actually happens in this section: Thomas Hudson is visited by his sons, and they talk and go fishing; there is a particularly vicious waterfront fight; and an improbably beautiful and malleable girl of the sleeping-bag variety arrives, and goes away again with Thomas Hudson's closest friend in tow. Even the news that the two younger boys and their mother, his second wife, have been killed in a car crash, does not seem to function in the novel as action. Hemingway is trying to establish the atmosphere of a particular way of life and the things which threaten it.

As fictional autobiography, *Bimini* reflects to some extent Hemingway's Key West period—the waterfront brawlers are clearly based on the wealthy riff-raff he associated with in the 1930s—but principally it reflects the psychological pressures of the late 1940s, when he was trying to put his life together again after the disruptions of the war—

physical injury, too much drinking, and something like a five-year absence from his desk.

Cuba and *At Sea* are much more closely linked to each other than to *Bimini*, and they belong to the curious period of Hemingway's phoney war, when he fitted out his cabin-cruiser with grenades and machine-guns, and set out to hunt for German U-boats in the Caribbean. He meant his boat to masquerade as a fishing vessel, so that he could approach unsuspecting submarines when they surfaced, and, at the last moment, raise the Stars and Stripes (if not the Jolly Roger) and throw grenades and home-made bombs down the enemy's companion-ways. In fact in two years he saw only one craft which, after ignoring his approach for some time, sailed over the horizon with insulting indifference.

There is no such debunking flippancy in his treatment of Thomas Hudson's service at sea, but none the less these parts of the novel have their own peculiar kind of honesty. In *Cuba*, we see Thomas Hudson ashore, communing with his cats, getting drunk at the Floridita in the company of a whore called Honest Lil, and enjoying a surprise visit from his first wife. *At Sea* describes how he tracks down the crew of a German submarine destroyed by air attack, through the keys and shallows off the Cuban coast. The Germans are found and wiped out, but at the end of the novel Thomas Hudson himself is wounded and dying, like Harry Morgan, Robert Jordan, and the narrator of *The Snows of Kilimanjaro*. The whole action is over-shadowed by the death of his one surviving son Tom, who has been shot down while serving with the R.A.F.

In many obvious ways *Islands in the Stream* is not a good novel—*Cuba*, indeed, is the very worst piece of writing, we have seen by Hemingway so far. It is colourless and boring, completely unfunny in the places where the author tries for comedy, and permeated with a particularly unattractive kind of tough self-pity. *Bimini*, which he left unfinished when he abandoned the sea novel in 1951, is formless—the boys' visit, which could have given it shape, ends abruptly—and leaves many loose ends. However, it does contain occasional flashes of good writing, and one or two passages of painful self-analysis, which prevent its being wholly unrewarding.

At Sea is much the best section—Hemingway, in a moment of enthusiasm recorded by Carlos Baker, said it was 'impregnable to criticism'. It is not that, but it is an efficient and at times beautifully written narrative of violent action. Its distinctive quality can be isolated by recalling General Lanham's praise of Hemingway's unrivalled eye for terrain, in the military sense.

The drama of the sea chase is a drama of terrain, of where to fight or where to hide up, of where to lie in ambush or where to look for trouble, above all, of where to expect death. The element of suspense can be traced back to the same source. We are made to participate in the alternations of intensity and calm with which Thomas Hudson reacts to his environment—the play of his nerves and senses in response to winds and tides: keys, banks, reefs, and channels; vegetation, the behaviour of birds, and the movements of fish. In spite of these qualities, *At Sea* does not equal Hemingway's finest episodes of violent action, the retreat from Caporetto, the destruction of El Sordo's band, and *The Undefeated*, largely because Thomas Hudson's irregulars, an inadequately characterized band of bar-flies, cut-throats, and psychopaths, do not offer the kind of interest as human beings which would complement the dramatic use of terrain.

* * *

It is easy to make damaging criticisms of *Islands in the Stream*, yet it is, with all its weaknesses, the most interesting Hemingway novel to appear since *For Whom the Bell Tolls*. It is free of the grotesque self-parody of *Across the River*, and of the rather wooden heroics of *The Old Man and the Sea*. From 1930 onwards, Hemingway, both as man and artist, had tended to hide behind the familiar mask which, for the ignorant and the prejudiced, *is* Hemingway. The features of the mask reflect the masterful and supremely competent man of action, the boastful genius, and the sophisticated wealthy citizen of the world who knows better than anyone else where and how to take his pleasures. Unlike the *personae* of Yeats and Pound, which enabled them to explore themselves on a larger stage, Hemingway's mask is one behind which the artist's true personality is in danger of disappearing altogether.

Islands in the Stream drops the mask entirely. There is something desperately wrong with Thomas Hudson which neither he nor his creator can define or cure. There is a fundamental nameless horror and emptiness at the heart of his life. As a condition, it is the same as the *nada* of the old waiter in *A Clean Well-Lighted Place*: as a feeling it is like Jake Barnes's mood after the débâcle of the fiesta, or Frederick Henry's after the death of Catherine. At Bimini, Thomas Hudson has constructed defences against it—the routine of work, a range of modest comforts and pleasures, and the resources of memory. With the death of his sons, the equilibrium is shattered. Hemingway had feared for his own sons' lives in circumstances almost identical to those in the novel: his eldest son was reported missing for several weeks during the war, and the two younger boys were involved in a serious, though not fatal, car-crash while he was actually working on the novel. In Cuba, Thomas Hudson finds that the 'anaesthetics' and 'palliatives' no longer work. On the sea chase, he scarcely eats or sleeps, and he only once has a drink. Even memory fails him: the drink he takes on the night before the final gunbattle 'unlocks' his memory, he is betrayed into happy recollections of his eldest son and of his first wife, only to be brought back to the facts of death and loss.

All experiences and all memories lead back to the central horror, directly or indirectly, and so, when not actually planning the chase, he tries to stop his mind working altogether:

He felt clean from his scalp to his feet from the soaping in the rain that had beaten down on the stern and he thought, I will just lie here and feel clean. He knew there was no use thinking of the girl who had been Tom's mother nor all the things they had done and the places they had been nor how they had broken up. There was no use thinking about Tom. He had stopped that as soon as he had heard.

There was no use thinking about the others. He had lost them, too, and there was no use thinking about them. He had traded in remorse for another horse that he was riding now. So lie here now and feel clean from the soap and the rain and do a good job of nonthinking.

But no one can ever do a good job of nonthinking; either one is betrayed through memory and dreams, or people and circumstances impinge. There is no release even through violent action. In *Bimini*, Thomas Hudson is a brooding spectator, not a participant, at the waterfront fight, and on the occasions when his son David confronts a shark in the water, and tries to land a giant marlin he has hooked. His pursuit of the Germans is a failure: he takes his ship straight into an ambush, and in the fight kills all the German sailors instead of taking the prisoners he was instructed to get.

He faces death at the end of the novel with a sense of relief ('All your life is just pointed towards it'). 'Death', he reflects, 'is really final.' Perhaps the job of nonthinking can be done at last.

The upshot is that *Islands in the Stream* is the most bleak and desolating of all Hemingway's published works. In spite of many local weaknesses this consistent and unsparingly honest self-scrutiny gives it a certain limited distinction. But honesty is not enough to make a great novel. In *The Sun Also Rises* and *A Farewell to Arms*, Hemingway was able to give the emptiness and the horror the imaginative resonance of a metaphysical condition. By relating this vision to the First World War he made it part of the history of the age, and by drawing from it a psychology of the life of sensation he gave it a universal human application. In the later novel it has shrunk to the dimensions of the private nightmare of one man's despair.

It is impossible not to revert, in conclusion, to the curious circumstances surrounding the publication—and the non-publication—of Hemingway's manuscripts. But for the breakdown of a commercial deal with *Cosmopolitan* magazine, *At Sea* would have been published in 1951 or 1952 and the delay in bringing it out is absolutely unpardonable when one knows that the author himself considered it a finished work.

This is not the only cause for anxiety. Certain statements made by Mrs. Hemingway imply that we may often be reading an unreliable text. In a press conference given at the New York publisher's offices earlier this year, she said that she had been editing the novel for months, and the blurb for the American (though not the English) edition quotes her as saying that she and Charles Scribner, Jr.

worked together preparing this book for publication from Ernest's original manuscript. Beyond the routine chores of correcting spelling and punctuation, we made some cuts in the manuscript, I feeling that Ernest would surely have made them himself. The book is all Ernest's. We have added nothing to it.

This disturbingly suggests a policy of streamlining and packaging rather than a true respect for Hemingway's work. A definitive scholarly text is not necessarily called for yet, and in an unfinished manuscript there are no doubt fragmentary or incoherent passages which could justifiably be dropped from a reader's edition. It would be easy to indicate where such omissions occur, without impeding the flow of the writing, and this should have been done. Any other kind of cutting is quite inadmissible. As it is, we do not know how much has been left out, nor what editorial criteria were used. (*A Moveable Feast* received similar treatment.)

Both Mrs. Hemingway and the publishers say that there are more posthumous works to come—according to the *New York Times* report of the press conference, an unfinished record of the Heming-ways' safari in the early 1950s is most likely to come next. It is to be hoped that all such books will be published without further delay, and that they will be edited in a more satisfactory manner than *Islands in the Stream* has been.

4

FICTION OF 1970

(a) LAWRENCE DURRELL
Nunquam

Nunquam is the second part of what Lawrence Durrell describes as a double-decker novel. At the end of *Tunc*, the first part, it is left as an open question whether Felix Charlock will be successful in trying to free himself from the golden tryanny of what is referred to in both books as 'the firm'. Felix is an inventor; his creations are used by the firm for its own purposes, but he is spectacularly rewarded for them. In marrying Benedicta, he has married into the firm, although he has not been successful in actually meeting Julian, its Western head. *Nunquam* now reveals that Felix's bid for freedom has come to nothing, and it is one of several disappointments provided by the new novel that both the narrative and the abstract implications of Felix's attempt to escape should be so weakly resolved. For 'the firm' stands for the culture in which the novels' characters exist, and both books are much concerned with the question of whether it is possible to reconcile the freedom of the individual with that association with others which being part of a culture makes inevitable. Durrell's conclusion appears to be that in the end one cannot evade one's culture, and—as a conclusion—this is acceptable if hardly startling. What is less satisfying is the fact that neither novel investigates very fully or plausibly what a sustained attempt to be free would be like to experience.

At the beginning of *Nunquam*, Felix comes to in the Paulhaus, the

(*a*) LAWRENCE DURRELL: *Nunquam*. 283 pp. Faber and Faber. £1.50.
(*b*) EDNA O'BRIEN: *A Pagan Place*. 223 pp. Weidenfeld and Nicolson. £1.25.
(*c*) SAUL BELLOW: *Mr. Sammler's Planet*. 313 pp. Weidenfeld and Nicolson. £1.75.
(*d*) ALAN SILLITOE: *A Start in Life*. 352 pp. W. H. Allen. £1.80.
(*e*) SHIVA NAIPAUL: *Fireflies*. 415 pp. André Deutsch. £2.10.
(*f*) MICHEL TOURNIER: *Le Roi des Aulnes*. 392 pp. Paris: Gallimard. 25fr.

firm's Swiss clinic: he has had a nasty blow on the head, and has lost several months. However, he picks up fairly rapidly, much encouraged by a better understanding with his wife: Benedicta seems to have achieved a new degree of freedom from Julian (now revealed as her brother), and the confidence of their relationship remains steady throughout the novel. Felix at last encounters Julian, and it is characteristic of the more gratuitous side of Durrell's manner that this portentous meeting should occur in a mountain hut above the snow-line. Just before Julian appears Felix and his wife watch an avalanche: in Durrell nature can always be relied on to have a sense of occasion. Julian induces Felix to cooperate in the making of a working model of Iolanthe, the dead Greek film star and Felix's mistress before her days of fame. Julian argues that 'the only road to freedom . . . lies through an aesthetic . . .', and that Iolanthe is particularly suitable for an experiment since she was an image of beauty that was universally available and idolized. The main narrative drift of the novel subsequently concerns the perfecting of the new Iolanthe, and can doubtless be read as an allegory of the artist's situation, as well as a satire on technology. The doll is stored with as much data about the real Iolanthe as can be gathered and recalled—here Felix's work (in *Tunc*) on 'Abel', his memory-bank, comes in useful. Other scientists endow her with nylon flesh, motor responses, and—as the reader of Durrell would expect—sexual appurtenances. A certain jaunty callousness towards the physically grotesque and bizarre is a familiar note in Durrell's writing.

When Iolanthe's current is switched on (from her point of view, she is simply reviving after an operation), her plausibility is total, and has the most striking effects on old friends and former lovers. As she 'convalesces' she wants more freedom of action, and eventually takes matters into her own hands by escaping from the vigilance of the firm. But she is fatally handicapped by the fact that her vital functions—eating, excreting, copulating—can only be simulated. In Julian's view, therefore, she cannot really relate to our culture because she has not the use of those organs upon which it ultimately rests (Freud is more than once appealed to, even though his simplifying disciples are rebuked). Perhaps as a consequence of this incapacity Iolanthe's attempt to escape the firm again ends in death—she comes to a spectacular end in another Paulhaus—not the one in which the novel opens, but St. Paul's Cathedral.

Other characters in *Tunc* are revived in *Nunquam*, if not by such extreme means. As predicted in the review of *Tunc* in these columns, Caradoc, the famous architect, proves not to have perished in the South Seas: he is discovered in a Geneva tea-room. His bid for freedom from the firm was 'the best, the most fruitful thing I had ever done. At the same time . . . it wasn't necessary at all—it could have been done another way'. Caradoc, like Felix, is content to be reassimilated into the firm, because it provides a meaningful context for his work. Other reintroduced characters include Jocas, the Eastern head of the firm, who is seen preparing for his demise with much serenity (there is a good deal of discussion about death in the book). But the return of old friends does not always seem very relevant: they tend to have the air of actors who appear in Act I but who have to hang about in costume until the final curtain call. The main character that is in a sense new is Julian. As a personality he does not have a great deal to offer and such factors as his emasculation and his addiction to gambling are not easy to relate to the novel's general argument.

The natural tendency of Lawrence Durrell's narrative style is to proliferate rather than to progress. His forte has always been the more of less sensational episode, but there are fewer of these in *Nunquam* than in *Tunc*. In *Clea* the return to the old ground of the previous novels in the Alexandria Quartet seemed to involve a considerable loss of narrative momentum, as well as a certain speciousness of effect and even a tendency to ad lib. The transition from *Tunc* to *Nunquam* gives a similar if not greater sense of deceleration. Part of the reason for this may lie in the fact that the questions rehearsed in *Nunquam* have already been adequately posed in *Tunc*. Since the choice between working within the firm and trying to free oneself from it turns out to be more theoretical than realizable, the characters who concern themselves with this question find that they are, narratively speaking, in a cul-de-sac. Even the destruction of the firm's records, which Felix plans when he succeeds Julian as its head, is just a way of posing the problem once again. Theoretically the absence of any written contractual obligation might tempt people to take advantage of a new freedom, but it is also open to them to funk it, and the evidence of both books suggests that they will. The choice between now and never is in fact less open than it looks.

But then Durrell's interest in and use of ideas has always been more opportunist than rigorous. He enjoys the kick that can be got out of certain notions more than the disciplined conclusions that can be reached through them. The ideas that lay behind the Quartet had at least the merit of leading us back to the permanently interesting imponderables of personality and point-of-view. The more abstract concerns of the new diptych not only mean that Durrell's usual command of the sensually realized scene is mostly conspicuous by its attenuation: they are not even very coherently or persuasively worked out in their own terms.

(b) EDNA O'BRIEN

A Pagan Place

NOBODY COULD ACCUSE Miss O'Brien of being an unambitious writer. She tries—even labours—to achieve all virtues at once, to be simultaneously shrewd and innocent, lyrical and earthy, funny and sad. Occasionally she brings it off—in *The Love Object*, say, or in some passages from *Girl with Green Eyes*. But all too often she falls to one of her two besetting sins: a calculated, knowing naivety, or a stylistic prettiness which Miss Brigid Brophy aptly called 'Syngesong'. Her bitter-sweet is usually too sweet by half; her 'fresh' or 'unencumbered' vision the deliberate cuteness of a child. There is something very Irish about this; or rather, something 'very Irish', a self-admiring performance by a corrupted peasantry who half believe the gentry's myths about their charming fecklessness.

At her best, Miss O'Brien can ballast this fault by the sheer roughness of her material: the clap in *August is a Wicked Month*, the drunken invasion of Gaillard's house in *Girl with Green Eyes*. Provincial Ireland is not Turgenev's Russia, nor was meant to be, although there is a great temptation for Irish writers to believe that they are carrying on the nineteenth-century Russian task of beautifying rural boredom. 'A society of *poor* gentlemen upon whose hands time lies heavy is absolutely necessary [for the creation of literature]' wrote Yeats's brother. But it tends to produce more watercolours than masterpieces, more Trollopes than George Eliots. Miss O'Brien understands the nastiness, the meanness, the destructive limitations of her country. The title of her newest book suggests that this time she will give it to us straight, unsweetened by girlish high spirits. So does the Brechtian epigraph: 'I carry a brick on my shoulder in order that the world may know what my house was like.' She has revisited scenes of her childhood, claims the dust-jacket, 'rejecting both sentimentality and neurosis'. It is an excellent intention. Unfortunately, it is not carried out.

Synge-song is the first culprit. To write an entire book in the second person might pass as a brave experiment, but the result is a disastrous extension of self-regard. Combined with staccato sentences (a child's vision is weak on punctuation), it is as soothing as a dripping tap:

You were given an oyster as a great treat. It would not go down. It was too big for your swallow. It was both cumbersome and slippery. It was a delicacy. Your father said that was the last time they would bring you anywhere. Your mother said to leave you alone.

This bears the same relation to the brisk narrative of *The Country Girls* as the self-parody of *Across the River and into the Trees* does to the best of *Up in Michigan*. The comparison is not fortuitous. Hemingway is the prime example of a writer whose lucid style began as a vehicle for observation and ended as a gigantic obstruction to it. The clear pane of glass became a baroque mirror, in which the author gazed lovingly at his own all-too-imitable way with words. There is some properly unsentimental material in *A Pagan Place*: not only the life-denying puritanism of an Irish village, nor the (less than unexpected) struggle between a patient, put-upon mother and an unreliable, drinking, indebted father; but also the agricultural dirt, the poor food, the malice, the stony fields, the island graveyard, the flashy scraps of festivity. Seen through a clear pane of glass, all this might genuinely move the reader. But seen through the eyes, heard in the lisping tones of this budding sister to Nick Adams, it is both sentimental and neurotic.

A number of borrowed plumes are sported. Mrs. Muriel Spark's marvellous adolescent mixture of the bawdy and the pedantic lends a few sentences. 'He rampaged at night to look at celestial bodies.' 'The curlew was a grallatorial bird, indigenous to sedge and damp places, more partial to wading than flying.' In *The Prime of Miss Jean Brodie* such stiffness had its place: the style which the Edinburgh schoolmistress imposed on her pupils was the subject of the book. Here, it is merely one more trick a girl can play, one more bid for sympathy—along with her pretty sister's bastard, her sexual gropings with a tormented priest—from the narrator. She leaves home, finally, for a convent in Belgium:

I will go now, was what you said, hoping that she would emerge from the house and say goodbye and have done with you, but since no such thing

happened you went anyhow and the last thing you heard was a howl start-
ing up, more ravenous than a dog's, more piercing than a person's, a howl
that would go on for as long as her life did, and his, and yours.

Indeed, indeed, the poor girl never had a chance. Better dismantle
such places altogether than 'define and celebrate' them (the dust-
jacket again) with this blurred keening.

  There is no growth here, not even in the girl's understanding of
what stops her growing. No house was ever built from such bricks.
The compulsive raconteur does not ultimately care for the heroes of
his stories (though he remembers a mass of detail): he wishes you to
be interested in his interest, to admire his fund of anecdote, to see
him—of all things—as a man fascinated by others. Miss O'Brien's
narrative voice drowns her story; by a perverse and unfruitful
miracle, she has snatched sentimentality out of the jaws of truthful-
ness. Out of the strong comes that old enfeebling sweetness, as
intrusively mannered as the old 'Irish charm' which this book should
have laid in the grave. It's a sad waste of talent.

(c) SAUL BELLOW

Mr. Sammler's Planet

IN *Mr. Sammler's Planet*, Saul Bellow has produced another of what
one might call his 'little books', a group which includes *Dangling
Man*, *The Victim* and *Seize the Day*, as against those self-consciously
'big books', *Herzog*, *The Adventures of Augie March* and *Henderson
the Rain King*. The distinction need not belittle the little side. Perhaps
it would be fairer to speak of *piano* and *forte* sections of his work, and
to confess a strong preference for the first. With a writer as intelligent
as Mr. Bellow, some sense of strain is inevitable. One might at least
be spared the anxiety of a Mailerish burst for the world record. Any
good writer must push his own talents rather than rest on them. It's
hardly surprising that Bellow, so assured in the lake of the *conte
morale*, should want to go big-game fishing in the picaresque. But it
doesn't suit him. Even in the *piano* section, some of the incidents
grunt and labour. Like the outbreaks of violence in *Room with a
View* or *Where Angels Fear to Tread* (another instance of a gentle
writer trying to beef up his own civility), such gestures as Allbee's

attempted suicide in *The Victim* arrive loaded with authorial intention. Most critics praised the traffic accident and its aftermath in
Herzog, perhaps because it was so unembarrassingly near-fetched:
something which might have happened to anyone, even Mr. Bellow
himself. *Mr. Sammler's Planet* is, for the most part, blessedly
plain.

Sammler is an old Polish Jew living with his widowed niece on the
Upper West Side of New York. He has been through a great deal,
both above and below the line of his present circumstances. In the
1930s he lived in Woburn Square as the London correspondent of
several Eastern European papers, a tenant of Oxonian certitude and
an acquaintance of the Bloomsbury great. From this height, he fell to
incredible depths, being caught on a visit to Poland by the Second
World War. He escaped a mass shooting, struggling out of a ditch
over his wife's corpse, hiding his daughter in a convent, fighting the
Germans with Polish partisans, then hiding again from antisemitic
Poles. Rescued from a refugee camp by another nephew of sorts (the
family relationships need a minute or two to grasp), Sammler now
lives with understandable caution. He reads very little: Meister
Eckhart and the Bible, while officially preparing a memoir of H. G.
Wells. His beneficent nephew Elya Gruner, a rich New York doctor,
provides him with enough money to live.

It is a harbour, perhaps, but not a haven. At the beginning of the
book, Gruner is in hospital after a carotid haemorrhage. Sammler
himself is obsessed with a private problem: a black pickpocket whom
he has seen operating on buses round Columbus Circle. Should he tell
the police? Has the pickpocket seen that Sammler has seen him, and
if so is he in danger? On top of this everyone comes to him for
advice. Gruner's daughter Angela has her sexual hang-ups: to Sammler's mind, problems of too much appetite. Gruner's son Wallace
rehearses the well-documented difficulties of a rich boy struggling to
carve out his own career. Margotte, the niece with whom he lives,
fusses herself into a desert of lonely routine. His daughter Shula, one
of those unattached, thirtyish females without whom no American
ménage seems complete, drifts around New York's campuses in a
chaos of wigs and shopping-bags. (She had a husband, a lunatic
sculptor, now in Israel.) And all these individual destinies unfold
against the background of a moonshot, a major human endeavour
nicely calculated to bring out Mr. Bellow's grandest vein of existential
speculation: the human escape from Mr. Sammler's planet.

Indeed, the whole book is a well-worked machine, with Feydeau-esque calibration of plot. Sammler's daughter nuttily steals a manu-script from an Indian professor, his only copy of an essay on moon-travel from Wells to the present. Angela asks Sammler to intercede for her, since her father has heard ugly rumours of a spot of snatch-swapping in Mexico. Wallace wants some money (from abortions? from dressing wounded Mafiamen?) allegedly stowed away in Gruner's house. The black pickpocket is finally cornered by Samm-ler's son-in-law and a young professor. Confusion mounts dizzily. In the middle of it all, Sammler preserves an old-fashioned commodity which only he seems to cherish: self-respect. It is Angela's job, not his, to beg her father's forgiveness, although her cold rage at the sugges-tion spells good-bye to Sammler's allowance. It is not right of his daughter to steal a manuscript. 'It was not stealing', she says. His reply is unashamedly a paternal rebuke. 'Other people may make new rules as they go along, but I will not, and you will not put me in that position.' When the stolen hoard turns up—another chancy lurch into the incidental—Sammler is equally uncompromising. He is a model of old-fashioned rectitude.

When he gives a lecture at Columbia, a heckler yells: 'Why do you listen to this effete old shit? What has he got to tell you? His balls are dry. He's dead. He can't come.' Sammler retires, not at all surprised that his reminiscences of Bloomsbury should bore the kids, but astonished at such crudity. Like Professor Hodgart, he finds himself in the land of the Yahoos. He is very much a stranger to the age of Aquarius.

There is a strong note of elderly counter-protest running through this book: 'My Lords, My Lords, what are we coming to?' It is not merely earthbound age against space-age youth: indeed, as Mr. Bellow is quick to point out, the youth Mr. Sammler is up against are the very opposite of the smooth technicians putting those bleeping capsules into orbit. They long to be 'whole' and self-sufficient, whereas all human achievements depend on specialization.

An oligarchy of technicians, engineers, the men who ran the grand machines, infinitely more sophisticated than this automobile, would come to govern vast slums filled with bohemian adolescents narcotized, be-flowered, and 'whole'.

If Mr. Bellow had campus fans, he is prepared to shed them now. Through his aged mouthpiece, he dins in the two lessons which young American radicals neglect: that the past is a valuable heritage, and that things can go terribly wrong. The horses of instruction, in Mr. Bellow's world are wiser than the tigers of wrath. There is nothing fortuitous in Sammler's history. Both the calm of a civilization—Oxford, Bloomsbury, the British Museum—and the fury of a civilization destroyed—Auschwitz and the Warsaw Ghetto—are facts which the Weathermen ignore. If today's young radicals are the prophets of a new reformation, preaching the sovereignty of an individual conscience, *Mr. Sammler's Planet* is the first work of a modern Counter-Reformation, preaching the value of a purified tradition, the necessity of rules, the weakness of the unaided self. 'Greatness without models?' muses Sammler. 'Inconceivable.' Not for nothing is he a 'Sammler', a collector, an assembler in search of order. A picture of the author on the dust-jacket shows him, crouching and hatted, behind a landscape painting in an old frame. Is he defending 'culture', or sheltering behind it? Either figure will do.

Wherever Mr. Sammler looks, he finds Self rampant. The pickpocket follows him home, corners him in a lobby—and then, instead of beating Sammler up, exposes a magnificent set of genitals. 'He took out the instrument of the Will.' (It is unlikely that the Elizabethan pun escaped Bellow's erudite notice, but he typically leaves it to the reader to pick up the reference.) Angela is the same, unable to believe that opening her legs where she fancies is—what's the word? —wrong, just as she is unable to see that turning up at her father's death-bed in a micro-skirt is offensive. Sammler's daughter Shula is the same, desperate to find in her father a divine spark which justifies her theft. 'For the creative there are no crimes. And aren't you a creative person?' She is much too stupid to see the point of Sammler's work. The only book by Wells which she has even attempted is *God the Invisible King*, which Sammler himself put down after a few chapters because he could foresee the rest of the argument. But some undisciplined assertion is essential to her; as it is to her husband, whose heavy medallions in a sack are finally used to smash the black pickpocket over the head: art as a cosh, the final act of the theatre of cruelty.

To these confused appetites, Sammler offers only traditional piety. But he has earned the right to it: perhaps too easily, since Mr. Bellow loads the biographical dice in his favour. Shula has suffered too; but when she pleads with her father in Polish, invoking her own

D

grief as an alibi, he orders her not to. There is no simple self-fulfilment for him, no easy options as there are for his young lecturer friend Feffer, a bearded blusterer looking like François Premier, the all-time teacher on the students' wavelength. When Sammler is being heckled, Feffer is in a phone booth wheeling and dealing. Like Wallace, he admits no obligations. He is a sharp cookie, sharp enough for casuistry even about elementary politeness. Sammler will not have it. Over Gruner's death bed, he prays:

At his best this man was much kinder than at my very best I have ever been or could ever be. He was aware that he must meet and he did meet—through all the confusion and degraded clowning of this life through which we are speeding—he did meet the terms of his contract. The terms which, in his inmost heart, each man knows. As I know mine. As all know. For that is the truth of it—that we all know, God, that we know, that we know, we know, we know.

A name not mentioned in Sammler's Bloomsbury days, but clearly present in this speech, is G. E. Moore. Through Moore, we come to Forster, whose humanism might equally well get a raspberry on campus these days. At his splendid best, Mr. Bellow is a mixture of Forster and Camus. The extraordinary music of his style enables him to confront basic problems with unfashionable directness. Here, as in *The Victim* and *Seize the Day*, the moral lessons of a death are rubbed in with Victorian intensity. When Sammler and Wallace are discussing a murderer's ability to kill, Sammler tells the episode from *War and Peace* where General Davout spares Pierre Bezukhov's life because they have exchanged 'a human look'. The conversation continues:

'Oh, that's marvellous! What do you think?'
'I sympathize with the desire for such a belief.'
'You only sympathize.'
'No, I sympathize deeply. I sympathize sadly. When men of genius think about humankind, they are almost forced to believe in this form of psychic unity. I wish it were so.'
'Because they refuse to think themselves entirely exceptional. I see that. But you don't think this exchange of looks will work? Doesn't it happen?'
'Oh, it probably happens from time to time, Pierre Bezukhov was altogether lucky. Of course he was a person in a book. And of course life is a kind of luck, for the individual. Very booklike. . . .'

Very like a book by Mr. Bellow, at any rate. All his strengths and weaknesses are in that passage: the ability to make philosophy sing, but also (Camus again) the temptation to make a sing-song into philosophy; the consistent flicker of intellect, with only a rare gleam of character. All Mr. Bellow's characters speak with the same lyrical-metaphysical voice, piling up the short speculative sentences each with its grand simple word. The fact that Mr. Bellow is much cleverer than Camus does not save him from bathos. Sometimes it makes it worse, and one wonders if all that stylistic carapace does not conceal a latter-day Aldous Huxley, an essayist whose novels *manqués* happen to come in the form of moral rather than social comedy.

Sammler quotes Sydney Smith: 'Short views, for God's sake, short views.' But when the sympathetic Dr. Lal, author of the purloined manuscript, engages him on his own level of conversation, short is hardly the word that springs to mind. A touch of obligatory comedy interrupts them: Wallace, hunting for his father's secret savings, has burst a water-pipe. Characteristically, it is the high-minded Dr. Lal who finds the main stopcock. Someone once asked Malraux why all his characters were intellectuals. 'Je n'écris pas pour m'embêter', he replied. Mr. Bellow casts his net wider, but does not set his sights any lower. Intelligence is intelligence, right is right; self-development is a fairly low moral priority. Like Mazzini answering Paine, Mr. Bellow is much concerned with man's duties. He is—so far as Sammler speaks for him—the last of the Kantians, with some stern words for a generation who resent all external imperatives. For that, one can forgive much verbal and intellectual self-indulgence. Mr. Bellow's planet has a thin atmosphere, like mountain air; but the views are magnificent, and even ennobling. Some people even feel nearer to God up there, or at least to Meister Eckhart. Almost all will feel better for the climb.

(d) ALAN SILLITOE

A Start in Life

IN THE STORIES in *The Loneliness of the Long-distance Runner* (1959) and *The Ragman's Daughter* (1963) and in *Saturday Night and Sunday Morning*, which also began as sketches of life in Nottingham, Alan Sillitoe was able to recreate, in its own idiom, a whole vein of experience which had usually got into literature only as material for comic character stuff in the way of Alfred Doolittle in *Pygmalion* or for

militant reportage in the way of Orwell's *Wigan Pier*. The life concerned is one of hard grafting, in all senses of that word—of living
in old rows of industrial housing, working in down-town factories,
getting outlet and satisfaction through semi-licit or illicit pleasures,
from screwing the overlooker's wife to shooting foxes on a Sunday.

The idiom matters as much as the experience. Its hard snap and
unpredictable humour still crop up in his novel of 1965, *The Death
of William Posters*, whose title (not really made good in the book) is
based on the splendid joke that 'Bill posters will be prosecuted'
means the authorities have it in for a scapegoat called Posters. In this
new novel that sort of voice can be still heard in snatches, like 'Her
middle name was Audrey, which she favoured most, Tawdry Audrey
from Tibshelf, who got off the bus one Saturday night in Worksop
market place'.

This ability to root his art in the life of the poorly-off has made
Sillitoe our outstanding portrayer of what Arthur Miller has called
(in his classic introduction to his *Collected Plays*) 'that sub-culture
where the sinews of the economy are rooted, that darkest Africa of
our society from whose interior only the sketchiest messages ever
reach our literature or our stage'. It is presumably what Raymond
Williams means when he speaks (in *The English Novel*) about finding
in Sillitoe and David Storey late 'followers' of Lawrence, a 'narrow-
er, more jagged edge' of evoked communal experience. Sillitoe
himself, in a recent *Guardian* interview and in his introduction to the
'Heritage of Literature' edition of *Saturday Night*, has repudiated the
label of 'working-class writer'. But the label is surely invidious only
when it implies that the artist is dealing with a rather limited area
that is somehow less human than other ways of life. What matters is
that since, in *William Posters*, Sillitoe took to presenting the London
middle-class scene, his touch has become fatally uncertain; whole
tracts of his novels have been sketchy or forced; and he has resorted
to literary modes which he cannot master.

A Start in Life is (yet again) about a man who breaks out of the
hard-grafting life of the unskilled worker in the Midlands. The first
seventy pages are (yet again) in the vein of the brutally breezy life-
story told by the rogue male himself. But Sillitoe clearly signals his
desire to break away from 'regional' naturalism in the devices he
resorts to. Narrative is interrupted for minor characters to tell their
life-stories, in the manner of a Fielding novel: names are ludicrously
fitting—Claudine Forks the husband-hungry Nottingham girl,

Claud Moggerhanger the London racketeer, Bridgitte Appledore the rosy *au pair* girl from Holland, and Kundt the womanizing journalist from Sedenborg in Sweden. . . . This kind of thing, along with the deliberately unlikely meetings and re-encounters and getaways, prompts the publishers to credit Sillitoe with 'reviving the picaresque'. He also 'revives' Ian Fleming by bringing in a master criminal, who organizes big-time gold smuggling from inside an iron lung.

The result is inchoate. A thriller must be tightly plotted or it is nothing. A typical turning-point in *A Start in Life* is when the hero, quite implausibly, confides certain crucial details to a girl-friend. This might suit the deliberately cavalier linkings of picaresque, but here it jars horribly with a wholly different vein—the quite deep and subtle probings of psychological contrariness which Sillitoe is able to give the narrator when he is introspecting:

If I had taken the pains to see, which wouldn't have been all that far beyond me, to the deepest recesses behind his eyes in which that picture lurked in black and grey and red, of his wife's head tilted in the mud and staring at some innocent barge going by in the moonlight, I might have saved her, and him. But I didn't because somehow my feet were no longer plugged into the earth, and my aerial was withered in its contact with heaven. It seemed I had been living underwater not to have known the truth of what was so obvious . . . I saw everything clear and sharp with the bare eye, but a lazy idleness inside kept a permanent clothbound foot on the deeper perceptions that blinded me from action.

His best work of some years ago and the force which he still fitfully commands continue to give Sillitoe a claim on our attention. But there is a chance that his talent may fray itself out for good unless he now makes himself become less headlong in his output, perhaps by holding back from easy identification with the rogue male and by weighing up more thoughtfully what it is that he has against our present way of life.

(*e*) SHIVA NAIPAUL

Fireflies

DICKENS'S LARGE NOVELS are based on networks of families, their members sending out threads in many directions, so that the complex web seems, finally, to present a comprehensive account of a whole society of eccentric persons caught in different areas, different classes, but interrelated. In England and the United States, there are only a few good novelists (Angus Wilson is one) who still want to do this sort of work. But in parts of the Commonwealth, particularly West Africa and the West Indies, the Dickensian network comes naturally. Writing for the whole English-speaking world, about little-known minorities, Commonwealth writers need plenty of space, so that local and peculiar relationships and institutions can be explained, in the novelist's way, through hints and particularities, not lectures and generalizations. In this fine first novel there is a chapter about a Christmas dinner in Trinidad which could surely stand on its own as a witty, allusive short story—for a sophisticated Trinidad reader. But most of us will need to know the family history of the characters before we can understand what is happening. The 170 preceding pages are all necessary to its interpretation.

The host is Ram Lutchman, a clerk and a former bus-driver, of Indian stock. His wife comes from a grander family, the Khojas, powerful in the island and determined in the maintenance of Hindu religion and ceremonies. She is known as Baby to her family. Baby and Ram have two young sons. Ram has invited two guests to dinner, Doreen James (a headmistress's daughter) and Mr. Wilkinson (a fellow-clerk). This last, 'Wilkie', is to Ram rather as Gowing is to Pooter: he is always talking of his mysterious social circle, 'the boys', and selling Ram things like camera equipment, with which Ram has Pooterish failures. It is only at the Christmas dinner that we are told about Wilkie's racial stock:

> Mr. Lutchman had never realized quite how black Wilkie was, a blackness that the eau de cologne, in a curious sort of way, served to emphasize. . . . Mr. Lutchman felt a definite satisfaction at having lured Wilkie away from his natural surroundings and suspected that he had him at a disadvantage.

Miss James, we gather, is white-skinned. Brought up by a rather 'progressive' mother, she went to college in the United States, had been several times engaged to marry, thinks herself an anthropologist, likely to write a good book about East Indian families in Trinidad. She approached Ram because she thought he might introduce her to his wife's family, the important Khojas: in the event, Ram and Doreen have had an affair. They have motored together in her car, and bathed on beaches (like American tourists, in a manner which made Ram uneasy), and visited poor rural Indians (so that Doreen was made uneasy by Ram's more matey than anthropological behaviour, his rum-drinking with illiterates). Ram's wife seems remarkably tolerant of the presence of her husband's ex-mistress—in spite of the fact that Doreen seems to have arranged the American-style yule-log and Christmas tree, in spite of the cutlery, which no one else needs for the eating of chicken, but which all must try to use for Doreen's benefit.

The person who irritates Baby is the cocksure Wilkie, who supposes himself superior to her husband. She is blatantly aggressive toward Wilkie, though normally she is the most submissive of women. A foreigner might suppose that Baby, coming from the grand Khoja family, would be a proud, dominating wife—a woman like Mrs. Sparsit in *Hard Times*, boasting of her connexion with the Powlers. But we have been shown the nature of her upbringing: she is, as a Khoja, a valuable prize, a useful property in an arranged marriage, but she has no Khoja distinction in her own right. Obedience and loyalty are required of her. The difference between Baby and the other women of her family is that she has become fond of her husband. Baby is, in both senses, the heroine of this long, intricate novel. She is rightly treated with tenderness by the author, despite her many faults. The first sentence ('For Baby, the marriage was a bad one . . .') shows her briefly before marriage: in the last, she is alone, a widow, with her two once-promising sons gone, in their different ways, to the bad.

The character most harshly treated is Mr. Khoja, the head of the important family. He seems a rather kind, generous person (for a rich man): his piety and regard for tradition, his ecumenism, his Rousseauesque educational theories and his populist political ambitions are all attractive to the reader—who may wonder why the author has so clearly got it in for him. Only gradually do we recognize the elements of Pecksniff and Chadband in him. At one of his ceremonies, a girl is singing a *bhajan*. The scene is agreeable: we are attracted as by Godbole's song in *A Passage to India*. The author continues:

There was another typical sound. A child was being beaten, and its piping wail blended with that of the singer's. It was like a duet, so well did the two voices complement each other. . . . No Khoja function was considered complete without a beating.

Shiva Naipaul's handling of this kind of spare, chilly English is all the more effective in contrast with the spirited vernacular of his dialogue.

We may recall a typical sentence from a story by his brother, V. S. Naipaul: 'It have nothing in the whole world so funny as to see a man you know flat out on his arse and catching good hell.' This is only one of many resemblances: the old Indian lady, secretly tempted by Roman Catholicism, is bound to recall V. S. Naipaul's story, 'My Aunt Gold Teeth'. It looks, too, as if Shiva Naipaul might agree with his brother's criticism: 'I knew Trinidad to be unimportant, uncreative, cynical. . . . Power was recognized, but dignity was allowed to no one.' It seems to be thought tasteless or invidious to compare these two brothers; but they are both very good in the same way (unlike the Waughs, for instance) and their novels have more in common with each other than they have with any other novels—from Trinidad (Selvon, Mittelholzer) or anywhere else.

(f) MICHEL TOURNIER

Le Roi des Aulnes

IN HIS ONLY PREVIOUS NOVEL, *Vendredi ou les Limbes du Pacifique*, Michel Tournier revamped the story of Robinson Crusoe: the cast-away forced to renegotiate his place in the natural world. Crusoe the plucky Anglo-Saxon handyman was shelved and substituted by an altogether more theoretical model of explorer, who was obviously a graduate of the Sorbonne and seemed to have been shipwrecked not in the South Seas but on some atoll in the collective unconscious, down where the myths begin. *Le Roi des Aulnes* is a bigger, odder and more enthralling book still. This time, the events which M. Tournier has appropriated and raised to the power of myth are real instead of fictive ones.

The jacket-note on his book is helpful: it explains that the 'deep' intention of *Le Roi des Aulnes* has been to 'déduire la "drôle de guerre", l'hitlérisme, les camps de concentration et le déferlement de l'armée rouge selon une voie purement symbolique et sans recourir aux vieux ressorts de l'histoire et de la psychologie'. This super-human prospectus, for the rectification of a human chaos, may seem implausible or even offensive, ranking as an infidelity to the real sufferings of the Nazis' victims. But all history, however mundane its principles, is figurative in relation to lived experience, so M. Tournier's ambition is unusual only in degree. Anyway, his exercise in meta-history is enormously clever and *Le Roi des Aulnes* a lusty *jeu d'esprit*, generated by the impact of a high and often jocular intelligence on intractable historical events.

The novel has five sections, two long ones mirroring each other at the start and finish, and three briefer chapters of transition. The opening section is a splendidly sustained piece of grotesquerie. It is the journal, kept with the left hand because the right has been damaged by a starting-handle, of Abel Tiffauges, a Parisian *garagiste* whose brain is much too sharp and profound to be kept still when putting Mobilgas into Citroens. His name alone is a gauge that he is meant for something higher, or at least more complex: he is Abel because he belongs, like Hitler's chief butts, the Jews and the gypsies, to the family of the rootless; and Tiffauges, after Bluebeard's castle, because he is, or so a behaviourist would assume, an ogre, with an appetite for young broiler-house flesh.

Tiffauges writes up his diary with some regularity from the beginning of 1938 until the outbreak of war in 1939. It is a rollicking document, in which he plies between the rather colourless present and his very *mouvementé* schooldays. As recreated by the vindictive Tiffauges, St. Christopher's—the name is of great importance—becomes the almost definitive parody of a walled-in, monosex community, and its former pupil's rationale of its odd procedures is both incisive and diverting. But St. Christopher's is also the more momentous scene of Tiffauges's initiation into his privileged role in *Le Roi des Aulnes* as the hero who pierces the opacity of the visible world and decodes its sybilline transmissions. His tutor in this is Nestor, masterful but misshapen son of the school concierge, who has grasped that all sensibilia can be marshalled into parables if only we pay adequate attention to them. Under Nestor's robust tuition, Tiffauges turns into a sort of demented yet heroic structuralist and ultimately brings off some sensational *coups* in his feud with the superficial disorder all around him: above all in his integration into one biological system of the pointage of a stag's head with the size of its testicles.

He also finds out at school that he has a special relationship with the course of history. When he finally runs away he is saved from any punishment by a fire that burns St. Christopher's down, killing at the same time Nestor, whose function has thus been usurped by events. Later, it is the outbreak of war that saves Tiffauges having to face

trial for rape. Such top-level meddling in his private affairs makes him
both a hero and a villain, since the contract between him and history
is reversible: is it the war that gets him out of prison or is it the rape
that has brought about the war? *Le Roi des Aulnes* lobs a good
many sarcastic grenades of this sort into the dug-outs of the causalists.

So instead of going into gaol Tiffauges goes into the army, and his
early war service is phoney even by the standards of the time. He is
attached to a carrier-pigeon unit in Alsace, in which the regulars are
warped and fixated men as memorable as those in Evelyn Waugh's
army. But Tiffauges himself is more interested in the birds, sinless
creatures who can stand in for a time as his paragons of an abused
innocence.

From the Franco-German borderlands, Tiffauges's next step, as
France crumbles, is into Germany, the country of 'pure essences' as
he sees it. He fetches up in the most essential part of Germany of all,
East Prussia, where he is employed as a 'trusty', as an assistant game-
keeper on the estate maintained for the pleasure of the Grand
Veneur himself, Hermann Göring. Innocence here is embodied in the
stags, pursued viciously but sometimes comically by Göring and his
toadies.

But the fun dies out altogether in *Le Roi des Aulnes* when Tiffauges makes his final move: to Kaltenborn, one of the special
schools established by the Nazis to bend the more promising local
twigs. This last section of the novel is a grisly transformation of the
first, as well as a commentary on it, with the two schools as exemp-
lars of different grades of perversion. M. Tournier supports his
description of Kaltenborn from the relevant source material, and
gives references.

By the time Tiffauges gets there, Kaltenborn is over the top,
because the stocks of desirable recruits are falling off. The crazed
eugenicists are still in harness, however, and the hunt goes on for
Aryan males whose skulls match up to the shape and dimensions laid
down for admission to the élite. Tiffauges's job is to travel the
vicinity as a salesman for the school, and con the parents into donat-
ing their beautiful boys to the Fatherland. He, and Kaltenborn, are
finally trapped in the collapse of the Reich before the Russian troops
from the East.

The conclusion of *Le Roi des Aulnes* is visionary and grotesque but
the book as a whole is a journey from a contrived surrealism to, as it
were, the real thing. The novel is so charged with symbols that it is

hard to tell whether it is intended to have one meaning or many, or just how menacing an ogre Tiffauges is. For all his connivance in Nazi bestiality, he is no simple monster. On the contrary, he is a man with a keen and lasting sense of innocence, a primal state which he is fond of distinguishing from its corrupt simulacrum, purity. What is innocent is good, what is pure is merely the false ideal of an impure society.

Tiffauges also has a Manichean obsession with what he calls 'malign inversions', spiritual turning-points at which the white is dyed black with diabolical suddenness; the specific 'malign inversion' for a Christian being that perpetrated on Christ himself, first the cross-bearer and then borne by the cross. Tiffauges himself, the anarchist and solitary, dies equivocally, marching into a bog bearing on his shoulders a Jewish child rescued from the rubble of Kaltenborn. His death identifies him with the King of the Elves in the poem by Goethe from which M. Tournier has taken the title of his novel.

Throughout *Le Roi des Aulnes*, Tiffauges's most persistent and elegant exercises in the symbolization of reality are concerned with the 'phoric', or the act of carrying. The carriers may be mildly absurd, like the pigeons, or deadly serious, like the figures of Christ and St. Christopher, the Christ-bearer. What M. Tournier is investigating, therefore, is presumably the metaphorical portage of one generation of human beings by the previous one, and the dreadful perversion of innocence which takes place in education. Tiffauges's death, as the saviour turned executioner, is thus itself a 'malign inversion' which not only completes the parable of a rich and complex book but may also resolve, for the novelist, a personal search for what he explicitly invokes as 'the quintessence of the German soul'.

5

SCIENTISTS AS INDIVIDUALS

(a) THE As AND Bs

In 1840 William Whewell wrote: 'We need very much a name to describe a cultivator of science in general. I should incline to call him a *Scientist*.' He was looking for an inclusive term that would cover the workers in any and all branches of the subject. The astronomer, the chemist and the anatomist, for example, had already made their appearance; and scientists of course flourished before a generic name had been found for them.

A recent authority tells us that full-time teaching and research posts in chemistry existed in the eighteenth century, though, until the latter part of that century, 'it would be a serious anachronism to think of almost any figure as purely and simply a chemist'. Tycho Brahe, in the latter half of the sixteenth century, can clearly be described as an astronomer—one of the particular sort that specializes in the work of actual observation. A little later Francis Bacon wrote that 'natural philosophy, even among those who have attended to it, has scarcely ever possessed, especially in these later times, a disengaged and whole man (unless it were some monk studying in his cell, or some gentleman at his countryhouse)'.

At this period, however, things had not quite specialized out, and he was thinking not just of the sciences as we understand them, but of natural philosophy in its aspect as 'the mother of the sciences'. The laboratory and the observatory were older than Bacon and by this time a high degree of specialization had been achieved here and there. But, in general, the figure of the scientist as we conceive him was beginning in his day to crystallize—something of a synthesis perhaps between the older natural philosopher and the artisan or technician—

(*a*) Charles Coulston Gillispie (Editor): *Dictionary of Scientific Biography*. Volume I: Pierre Abailard—L. S. Berg. 624 pp. Volume II: Hans Berger—Christoph Buys Ballot. 628 pp. McGraw-Hill. £16.80 each.

(*b*) Zhores A. Medvedev: *The Rise and Fall of T. D. Lysenko*. Translated by I. M. Lerner. 284 pp. Columbia University Press. £4.50.

with possibly also a suggestion of the artist of Renaissance Italy, the artist at least in one or two of his aspects.

In its crudest state, the history of science was something like a succession of biographies—a record of discoveries accompanied by miscellaneous notes about the men who made them—the intention apparently being to commemorate the achievement and identify the person rather than to elucidate the course of development. The object was to find the man who had put the 'right' idea into currency —the idea of the circulation of the blood, for example—for such a man could be recognized as one of us, and everything around him could be ignored as merely bad science. A policy of this kind, which means picking out from Galileo just the things that we recognize today, has the effect of reducing the history of science to dullness. The movement of the earth, the circulation of the blood, the right formula for the acceleration of falling bodies—these are things that every schoolboy knows, things that have become second nature for modern man. What emerges from this type of history, therefore, is not any impression of the genius of a Copernicus or a Harvey or a Galileo, but a conviction that everybody else in those days must have been more than ordinarily stupid.

The progress and enrichment of the history of science has de- pended in the first place upon a radical departure from the notion of it as merely a succession of biographies. In *The Advancement of Learning*, Francis Bacon, having recognized this point, provided cer- tain guidelines, and perhaps only in the twentieth century has his programme been fully carried out—extended indeed in some ways further than he had conceived to be possible. His plan involved tracing out the continuities and the lines of development, reading the actual texts and studying the whole miscellany of factors that en- couraged or discouraged progress, or otherwise affected the course of things. He drew attention to the problem of the transmission of knowledge, and the migrations of knowledge, and to the importance of the institutional background. It was in connexion with all this that he wrote: 'I wish events to be coupled with their causes.'

The history of science failed for a long time to measure up to this pattern. Its progress was slow and peculiar, partly because the scientists, though highly conscious of their own techniques and their methodical handling of evidence, seem to have thought that historical- mindedness and the criticism of sources was merely a matter of ordinary common sense. A further obstruction was caused by the fact

that the histories of the separate sciences could so easily be regarded
and treated as mere technical adjuncts to those sciences themselves.
For this reason much of the advance in the subject in the nineteenth
century was due to the great generalizers, the men who came closer to
history because they envisaged the development of a single all-
embracing science. Much was owed indeed to the philosophers of
science, who were conscious of this unity in the subject and who inquired into the implications of the thinking of ancient scientists. At a
later stage, however, they were to become something of a menace. In
re-thinking for a Galileo, they might be inclined to depreciate the
humbler task of discovering by historical evidence what Galileo
actually thought.

In spite of all this, the dynamic moment came in the closing decades of the nineteenth century and the opening decades of the
twentieth century, when there occurred an intensification of research,
together with a certain revivification of the biographical method.
Among men still fervently faithful to the ideal of a single history
embracing the whole of science, the work became much more detailed, and masses of source material—the writings, the working-
papers and the correspondence of scientists—were published, or
more closely examined. Attention came to be turned to the great
number of forgotten scientists—those who had made small contributions or whose hypotheses had proved to be misfires—those who had
been outshone by Galileo or who had been engaged in controversy
with him. Long-buried texts were now re-read and, at this point in
the development, historical-mindedness itself could get a better hold
on the subject matter, for things began to fall properly into place.

It became possible to discern the multitude of smaller links in the
chain, to see more of the antecedents of the great discoveries, and to
bring analysis to bear on lines of continuous development. Also—
as quite a momentous matter—one gained a better impression of the
intellectual hurdles which the scientific thinker at a particular period
had to surmount. Now one could trace a closer history of such a thing
as the idea of the *impetus*, and learn more accurately where a Leo-
nardo da Vinci or a Galileo had been original. One could dream of
following, through little discoveries here and there, through debate
at different levels, and even by way of hypotheses that led to dead
ends, the story of the advance to the Newtonian idea of gravitation.
The work of Antonio Favaro, and still more that of Paul Tannery—
the inspirer of George Sarton and Aldo Mieli—and that of Pierre

Duheim set many things in motion. In the last generation Sarton's *Introduction to the History of Science* and Lynn Thorndike's *History of Magic and Experimental Science*, sum up this stage of the story.

There have now appeared in the United States—blessed by enormous scholarly patronage—the first two volumes of a large-scale *Dictionary of Scientific Biography.* This is edited by Charles Coulston Gillispie, who has won a leading place among historians of science in the United States; it has secured the collaboration of an impressive collection of international scholars. The magnitude of the enterprise might be sufficient in itself to prompt a new effort at stock-taking; but the work, in the generosity of its conception, in its many moments of interest, and, sometimes in its actual distinction, might well serve to enhance the importance and prestige of the history of science itself. In any case it assembles so much of recent knowledge, and brings so many corrections of view that are still current—it even involves a flexibility of treatment, and carries at times an unexpectedness and originality, which are so unlike the usual encyclopedia article—that it is bound to stand as an indispensable work of reference and a particular treasure for people who love to browse in this field.

We might have wondered in advance whether there was likely to be sufficient urbanity in the conception of it—sufficient inclination to see that modern science emerged out of what was essentially a humanistic culture. On this topic George Sarton, at the previous stage in the development, had had high ideals. He was prepared to push his notion of the history of science to the point at which it covered almost all positive knowledge and envisaged the whole advance of methodical thinking as such. He was ready to say that the theologians had been scientists, and to recognize a stage at which theology was the queen of the sciences—even to suggest that 'the notion of monotheism may be considered a scientific hypothesis'. The first volume of his *Introduction* (published in 1927, and carrying the interesting sub-title: 'From Homer to Omar Khayyam') therefore included the prophet Amos almost at its beginning; and when he produced the first volume of an actual history of science towards the end of his life, he wore his heart on his sleeve, bringing Greek tragedy and the Book of Job into the picture. In some respects, however, his ingrained habits of mind conflicted with his charming disposition; and, when it came to the point, he would be tempted just to quote from the theologian or the historian the evidence that they supplied about the state of contemporary science. St. Augustine, he says, 'taught that the fetus is besouled during the second month and besexed during the fourth, and that premeditated abortion is equivalent to homicide'. He notes also that this writer's *Confessions* contain something of modern psychology.

The new *Dictionary* sets out to deal more specifically with the natural sciences but it is prepared to cast a wide net in its search for their origins, and in some respects it gets a better hold on the very things that Sarton had had in mind. A considerable article by Ernan McMullin takes the line that the importance of St. Augustine

was often overlooked by early historians because it lay at a deeper level of thought than they were wont to regard as relevant. Yet it was at this deeper level that really crucial changes were occurring over the next millennium, so that by the seventeenth century the West was prepared in both attitude and motivation for a great new effort of understanding.

Augustine, extending the achievement of the ancient Greek philosophers, is treated as 'marking the second crucial stage in the development of the peculiar matrix of thought and value within which natural science as we know it emerged in the West'. His theory of knowledge and his attitude to what we should call natural science are examined, and they are balanced against the implications of his literalist interpretation of scripture; though we are shown the difficulties that are involved in his view—a view which Galileo tried to use against the Pope—that an interpretation of the scriptures would have to be reconsidered where it contradicted something that had actually been scientifically established. At the level at which this article is treating its subject matter, it might have been relevant and profitable to consider also what Augustine did with the Christian interpretation of history.

Sarton was most anxious to make it clear that both the Arabian and the Christian medieval worlds were worthy of careful historical interpretation and had a place in the development of science. His capacious mind conceived of scholasticism on a generous scale— existing as a synthesis of religion, science and philosophy not only in the Christian and Arabic realms but (earliest of all) amongst the Buddhists, then amongst the Jews, and finally in China. Sarton attained his views on the Middle Ages only after a struggle within himself, however, and his thought continued to retain signs of the struggle. Scholasticism to him was in fact an obstruction to progress and science in the Middle Ages really sprang from sources outside its sphere. Concerning St. Thomas Aquinas, he wrote: 'Though interested in science, he utterly failed to understand its true spirit and methods, and no scientific contribution can be credited to him.'

In the *Dictionary*, however, William A. Wallace, a Dominican—though, oddly enough, he thinks it 'unfortunate' that Aquinas should have believed in 'the existence of spheres that transport the heavenly bodies'—sees the same man as using 'what was then a rigorous scientific method, learned from investigating the world of nature, for probing the mysteries of revelation'. Aquinas, moreover, turned in his later life 'from his unfinished *Summa theologiae* to comment on all the physical works of Aristotle', and, 'for a man not usually recognized as a scientist, he made notable contributions to medieval science'.

It becomes a main object of Wallace's article to specify the marginal points at which Aquinas has something relevant to say, points which touch 'the medieval counterparts of physics, astronomy, chemistry and life sciences'. It is interesting to learn that 'at least once, commenting on Ptolemy's cumbersome theory of eccentrics and epicycles [Aquinas] voices the expectation that the theory will one day be superseded by a simpler explanation'.

The ancient Greeks present fewer problems than the Middle Ages and the first letter of the alphabet offers an opening for handsome accounts of Aristotle, Archimedes and Apollonius of Perga. For technical reasons, India and China are left for illustrative treatment in future supplements, so that essentially this is a biographical dictionary of western science—the science which now can claim universality. The earliest stages even of this, the developments in Mesopotamia and Egypt, are also necessarily relegated to supplements; but, even for western purposes, it was important to have the Arabs, and these—al-Battānī and al-Bīrūnī, for example—prove to be interesting on the scale which this work permits.

It is too soon to say whether the *Dictionary* will do as much justice to what might be called the 'technological' as to the humanistic antecedents of progress in the natural sciences. The question is clearly momentous; for a point that worried Francis Bacon was the fact that inventions and medical cures had often come first (possibly by fluke) and the scientific theory had been drawn out of them retrospectively. Here is a whole aspect of the story that was too long neglected, and, though we have histories of technology, the interaction with doctrine is a more difficult matter, perhaps not amenable to biographical treatment.

E

In the present volume an expert on Agricola gives a useful biography while another expert tells us only that Biringuccio represents
'the strain of practical chemistry that had to develop and to mingle
with philosophy before it could become science'. The imposing article
on Tycho Brahe has special interest because of the full account it
gives of this man's instruments. Adequate attention is paid to the
important question of the transmission of scientific knowledge; and
this is illustrated by a considerable study of Boethius, a special
section in the account of Aristotle, and the interesting note on
Nallino's translation of al-Battānī's *Zij*—a translation published in
1899 and itself described as 'one of the masterpieces of the history
of science'.

It is particularly true in the most important cases that the amount
of purely biographical narrative has been curtailed as far as is reasonable. In general, contributors appear to have been instructed to deal
essentially with a man's thought, his points of originality, his antecedents and his influence. Certain of the accounts of minor people
may read like encyclopedia articles, but at times we are given something more like an essay, as in Mary Hesse's interpretative piece on
Francis Bacon. The result of a plan so highminded is that there is
much to interest the humanist, though in many articles there comes
a point at which the mathematics or the natural science will defeat the
lay reader.

It is clear that when the history of science has moved from a crude
biographical form to historical understanding (through analysis and
synthesis), it can return at the finish to biography, loading into this
the result of all the processing, so that there emerges a picture of
greater depth. In the case of many of the minor figures in the present
volumes this is bound to be lacking, but, where the smaller men are
concerned, what the historian often wants is just the material for
identification and a rough delineation of the personality.

There is much history-mindedness in the *Dictionary*, as in the
account of Jean Buridan or in the article in which Frances A. Yates,
abridging her own previous works, produces a Giordano Bruno
thoroughly relegated to his proper context and seen as 'a Hermetic
magician of a most extreme type'. The sketch of Aristarchus of
Samos gives much of what the historian looks for, since it is almost
an essay on heliocentrism in ancient Greece, tracing its beginnings,
discussing the reasons for its rise, inquiring why it provoked so little
interest and showing how it went underground. There is a fine crop

of significant seventeenth-century studies. Great care has often been taken with the bibliographies at the end of the articles, and these are intended for serious students.

Apart from the fact that an encyclopedia of the minor figures of science is a valuable auxiliary, we need the vision of history in its concreteness, so that biography is a value in itself; and if the volumes could have contained a considerable selection of actual portraits, even these might have had their interest. It is useful in any case to have an account of Neils Bohr by one who knew him and worked with him, and to catch glimpses of the personality of al-Battānī.

Perhaps the neatest piece of pen-portraiture in the two volumes is the account of Airy, the nineteenth-century astronomer. Olin J. Egger tells us of

the habit he adopted, as an undergraduate, of always keeping by him a quire of large-sized scribbling paper, sewn together, upon which everything was entered: translations into Latin and out of Greek, several lines of which he attempted every day, no matter how pressing other business might be; mathematical problems; and nearly every thought he had, complete with date. The sheets, even after the more important items were transferred to exercise books or diaries, were kept, together with nearly every communication received and a copy of those sent throughout his life, and are still extant. He seems not to have destroyed a document of any kind whatever: stubs of old checkbooks, notes for tradesmen, circulars, bills, and correspondence of all sorts were carefully preserved in chronological order from the time that he went to Cambridge. . . . He wrote his autobiography up to date as soon as he had taken his degree, and made his first will as soon as he had any money to leave. . . . No independent thought could be tolerated . . . he rapidly became the type of the modern government scientist.

There is a sense in which it is both true and relevant to say that history is the essence of innumerable biographies. Those who overlook the point will fail to have a sufficiently flexible view of the time-process or an adequate regard for the number and variety of the possible alternative futures that confront the human race. Those who keep their eyes on merely sectional processes, in limited realms that have been abstracted from the rest of history, will see a simplicity of pattern which they too readily transfer to their picture of overall change. They too easily forget the role of contingency and of human wills in the history of mankind, and the smallness of the pivot on which great things may turn. For this reason, when the experts and the technicians have contributed all they can, we still need the statesman to survey the whole complicated scene and to make a judgment about the policy that is practicable at a given moment. And, similarly, the economist and the rest of the social scientists may do wonders to enrich historical understanding, but we still need the historian in the traditional sense of the term, not merely because he answers the human need for either narrative or commemoration, but because only by watching men as individuals, and surveying the complexities, and heaping all the concreteness back into the picture—and only by seeing the motions and interactions of everything as a story—can justice be done to something that lies in the very nature of human events.

(b) THE RASPUTIN OF GENETICS

THIS BOOK has a curious history, as befits its curious subject. The author is a patriotic Soviet citizen who doesn't doubt the basic beliefs of Marxism-Leninism, but he is a bitter opponent of the once all-powerful agro-biologist T. D. Lysenko. An established scientist of the middle rank, with 100 publications to his name including a massive monograph on protein biosynthesis, translated into English in 1966, he is (let us hope that he still is!) Director of the Molecular Radiology Laboratory at the Institute of Medical Radiology in Obninsk, near Moscow.

The present book was written between 1961 and 1967 in three separate parts, being somewhat disjointed as a result, and it was submitted for publication in the Soviet Union but rejected. However, a typescript was already being circulated privately and a microfilm of this came into the possession of Professor Michael Lerner, an eminent American geneticist who already had some slight acquaintance with its author, and who had been in correspondence with the Soviet Academy of Sciences about producing an authorized translation, with no success. So in the end he decided to go ahead anyway: as the introduction puts it, 'For obvious reasons the author did not see the translated, abridged and edited manuscript. It is to be hoped that he may one day see a copy of this book.'

The story is one of the murkiest in the history of science. From about 1935 onwards, Academician N. I. Vavilov, a geneticist and plant breeder of international renown who was the founder and first President of the Lenin All-Union Academy of Agricultural Sciences (L.A.A.A.S.) and Director of the All-Union Institute of Plant Breeding (A.I.P.B.), came under increasingly severe attack from a rival agronomist, T. D. Lysenko. Lysenko was a follower of I. V. Michurin, who had been a highly successful practical horticulturist in his time, and who neither knew nor cared anything of modern 'Mendelian-Morganist' genetics, which he had vigorously criticized in the ten years before his death at the age of eighty in 1935. In this campaign Lysenko was ably assisted by I. I. Prezent, a Marxist theoretician without biological pretensions, and the sinister V. R. Vil'yams (his father had been a Mr. Williams who went to Russia to help run the railways) who was a soil expert of the 'muck and mysticism' school.

With the support of Stalin himself, Lysenko supplanted Vavilov as President of the L.A.A.A.S., and in 1938 he intruded an N.K.V.D. agent, one Shundenko, into the A.I.P.B. as Vavilov's deputy who, assisted by G. N. Shlykov, a member of the scientific staff, was busily doing his best to make the Director's position impossible. But Vavilov managed to hang on until August 6, 1940, when finally he was arrested while on a botanical trip to the Western Ukraine (in the then newly occupied Soviet zone of Poland), possibly in the belief that he was about to flee the country.

Charged with 'sabotage in agriculture, rightist conspiracy, and spying for England' (those being the days when there were not many other countries a Soviet citizen very well could be accused of spying for), he was duly condemned to death. After many months in a windowless underground dungeon, this was commuted to ten years' imprisonment. Beria's wife had apparently been persuaded to intervene on his behalf, for by a happy chance she had been a plant physiologist and a pupil of Professor D. N. Pryanishnikov, a former colleague of Vavilov's who was most courageously doing all he could to help a friend in need. By now broken in health and spirit, Vavilov was transferred to the somewhat better conditions of the general cell block in Saratov prison, where he died of pneumonia on January 26, 1943, shortly after his election as a Foreign Member of the Royal Society in London.

All this in outline is already known well enough, but Medvedev had access to Vavilov's 'private archives', which rather surprisingly survived, and he has been able to fill in much fascinating historical detail. What is still not satisfactorily explained is why it ever happened at all. Some of the work started by Vavilov and his collaborators was perhaps open to the criticism that it promised no immediate benefit to the economy. But he also had an extensive programme, prescribed by Lenin, for developing cultivated plants and seeds, and farm animals, purchased from capitalist countries abroad. Given the admittedly backward condition of Russian agriculture at the time, this could not have failed to produce some striking short-term improvements straight away.

As for Lysenko, he seems to have been a complete charlatan, and an almost Rasputin-like personality. Yet he contrived to gain and retain the confidence of Stalin, no less; not, one might have supposed, a man excessively susceptible to charisma. There was a time when many biologists outside the Soviet Union, whatever their doubts about the theoretical explanation, felt that there must be something to the practice of 'vernalization' (the cold treatment of wheat before sowing) for which outstanding success was officially reported. But Medvedev will have none of this, pointing out that no farm manager told to try the new methods would have kept his job if he had not claimed success, fudging the figures as best he could. At any rate vernalization is now no longer used in Soviet agriculture.

After a pause for the war, Lysenko returned to the fray, and finally routed what remained of orthodox opposition at an extraordinary session of the L.A.A.A.S. in 1948, a 600-page verbatim report of which was afterwards published in English, with its never-to-be-forgotten conclusion:

Hail to the progressive Michurinian biological science! Glory to the great Stalin, the leader of the people and coryphaeus of progressive science! (*Stormy, prolonged and mounting applause and cheers. All rise.*)

With his chief opponents soon all exiled, dismissed or demoted to laboratory assistants (it is fair to say that few were imprisoned and none were executed, though there were one or two suicides), Lysenko's position for the next four years was unchallenged, and he enjoyed a popular cult second only to Stalin's. He was even immortalized in song.

It was not until the end of 1952 that doubts were again publicly expressed, by the innocuous Moscow Society of Naturalists and in the *Botanical Journal*, where Lysenko's theory of speciation by saltation came in for some criticism. This taught that one species could give rise to another in a single generation: rye into wheat, for example, or cabbages into swedes, or alder into birch. After the death of Stalin a few months later the dam burst, and soon many of Lysenko's enemies had got back into their former positions, ousting his friends in the process and with plenty of hard feelings on both sides.

Medvedev is now describing events in which he personally took part, but it is a confusing story. Basically, Lysenko continued to have political support from the Party and the public, and most of the younger biologists in posts of power had been his protégés. But with the terrible figure of Stalin no longer behind him he couldn't begin to hold his own in purely scientific dispute. There were many ups and downs, but at the end of 1955 Lysenko was removed from the Presidency of the L.A.A.A.S., and Academician A. I. Oparin, a celebrated biochemist and scarcely one of Lysenko's disciples scientifically, who had been playing a very equivocal role, was replaced as Biological Secretary to the Academy of Sciences.

After 1958 there was a decided reaction, when Khrushchev gave his support to the Michurin trend, with the disastrous consequences in agriculture which did so much to bring about his own downfall in 1964. Since then there has been some real progress in Russian biology, though there is a long way still to go. And Academician Lysenko seems to have gone into semi-retirement, full of years (he is now 72) and if not of honour at least of honours, as a Hero of Socialist Labour and the proud possessor of no fewer than nine Orders of Lenin. He is still a political power in the land, and nobody need wonder that the present book cannot yet appear in the Soviet Union.

It is, however, an historical document of the first importance, even if there remains much of this sorry tale still to be told, and thanks are due to Professor Lerner, without whose efforts it could well have been lost. We must be grateful also to the many Russian biologists who, with no help from outside in their private fight, so steadfastly withstood pressures which scientists elsewhere have not experienced for hundreds of years. It is good to know that scientific sense and intellectual integrity still flourish in the Soviet Union, and seem in the end to have prevailed.

6
COLLOQUIAL JEWISH

A LANGUAGE, according to Professor Weinreich, is a dialect that has an army and a navy. Hebrew has never been more of a language than in these last few years; Yiddish remains what it has always been—chief common tongue of the diaspora (11 million speakers before the Second World War), a vital and very human world Jewish colloquial, a great literary and rhetorical medium impatient of demagogic inflation, a mere dialect of German.

Solomon ben Isaac of Troyes, the eleventh-century Talmudist, calling it *loshen Ashkenaz*—'the German tongue' (Ashkenaz was the name medieval rabbis gave to Germany)—did not particularize enough. The Jewish emigrants from the north of France began the making of Yiddish (or Jüdisch or Jewish) along the Rhine, adding Rhenish German to their stock of exilic languages. They wrote down the new tongue of adoption in Hebrew characters—not always a satisfactory alphabet for an Indo-European language, but curiously, and ironically, fitting for German.

A Semitic alphabet is concerned chiefly with consonantal notation: consonants are the visible 'body', vowels the invisible 'soul'. Hebrew stakes out three consonantal letters—M, L and CH, for instance—and, whatever the vowels that come between, the semantic denotation of those consonants is roughly the same. Thus the M-L-CH triad must always have something to do with kingship, as the Arabic K-T-B conveys, without vocalic addition, the general notion of book-reading. German, far more than its sister English, plays vocalic variations within a consonantal frame in order to modify, in tense, mood or number, the semantic idea expressed by that frame. *Traum* is pluralized to *Träume*, but a Hebrew T-R-M will take care of both, the context clarifying the accidence, SCH-R-B will carry a fair number of the tense shades of *schreiben*. A good number of Hitler's slogans would have gone well, alphabetically speaking, into Hebrew.

Yiddish proved, in its medieval phase, a tough travelling language.

LEO ROSTEN: *The Joys of Yiddish.* 547 pp. W. H. Allen. £3.15.

When the Black Death and the Crusades drove the Rhineland Jews to South Germany, Austria, Bohemia and Northern Italy, Yiddish went too, maintaining its basic German genius but absorbing new words. These Rhinelanders became, in Poland, notable traders; their language had prestige and was soon spoken by the long-settled Jews of Poland, though it was quick, as ever, to enrich itself with the new Slavic elements it found. From the fifteenth century on Yiddish has maintained a pliability, an eagerness for loanwords, a structural 'progressiveness' (it has never cared for the huge grammatical battery of High German) that bring it closer to English than to any other cognate language. The fine literature that Yiddish has produced— from fifteenth-century Elijah Bochur to twentieth-century Isaac Bashevis Singer—attests the vitality, the unwillingness to set into 'literary' clichés, that characterizes a medium more demotic than academic.

Hebrew, of course, is the noble traditional language of all the Jews, the tongue of the scriptures, the national speech of the Jewish State, but most Jews would admit its stiffness, its odour of sanctity and, since it is the language of rabbis, Talmudic exegetists, lawyers and political leaders, its remoteness from the affairs of ordinary life. It has never been domesticated: it is not a language for women. As writers like Philip Roth never tire of telling us, the Jewish mother is almost wholly responsible for the joys and nightmares, or the stability and dynamism, of Jewish life. Yiddish is, literally, the mother-tongue of the exiled Jewish race. A boy may learn to read Hebrew in the *shul*, but at home he is weaned into Yiddish. Hebrew may be about the great ineffables, but Yiddish is about chicken soup and chopped liver. The mothers themselves regard Yiddish as the essential voice of Jewishness. The following story long went the rounds in Israel, where Yiddish was still officially disapproved recently:

On a bus in Tel Aviv, a mother was talking animatedly, in Yiddish, to her little boy—who kept answering her in Hebrew. And each time the mother said, 'No, no, talk Yiddish!'

An impatient Israeli, overhearing this, exclaimed, 'Lady, why do you insist the boy talk Yiddish instead of Hebrew?'

Replied the mother, 'I don't want him to forget he's a Jew.'

This anecdote comes from Leo Rosten's new book, a very gemüt-lich tribute to the Yiddish language. Mr. Rosten first made his name with a series of stories—themselves little more than leisurely anec-dotes on a linguistic theme—about a Central European Jew, an immigrant to New York, called Hyman Kaplan. Kaplan learns English, but he does not learn it well. He is puzzled, for instance, over the meaning of 'A big department'. His teacher explains, but the explanation does not fit any context or situation that Kaplan knows. He has heard it frequently in the street, when one man bumps into another and then says, 'A big department'. Neither Mr. Rosten nor his readers ever wanted Kaplan to learn English well. What Louis MacNeice called the drunkenness of things being various animates the linguistic life of New York, which is, predominantly, a life of which the phonemes, structures and vocabulary of Yiddish have impregnated English. A language cognate with both these—Dutch—still shows its influence, as in the peculiar diphthongization of the vowel in *work*, *learn* and *dirty*, but the true demotic English of New York is Yidglish, nor would anyone wish it to be otherwise.

Mr. Rosten is, in this book as in the Kaplan ones, less concerned with Yiddish than with Yidglish—not the malapropriation, the mad vocalic confusion (heard at Kennedy Airport: 'Where are you living?'—'I am living by the next plane'), but the semantics of the loan-words that New York speech has taken from Yiddish, the speech of Goyim and Jews alike, as well as the lexical significance of stress, intonation, word-order, and subtle modifiers like *yet* and *already*. Naturally, he is more concerned with what Yidglish means to Jews than to Gentiles, but there is a sense in which all New Yorkers—and for that matter many members of the English-speaking world—have become a sort of secular Jew. In Mordecai Richler's *Cocksure* it is a Wasp from Canada who is recognized as the archetypal Jew, even though he has never entered a synagogue and is fully prepuced. The voice of literary America is heard by many as an essentially Jewish voice—the voice of Bellow, Malamud, Gold, the two Roths. The Jew is the world's urban expert, skilled in establishing an identity in the anonymous brick jungle. He brings to the task a passionate rhetoric learned in the ghettos.

English takes well to the loving assault of Yiddish. Both languages are Germanic, but they have thrown off the shackles of traditional Teutonic grammar and they are prepared to increase their vocabularies with foreign importations. They depend a good deal on the nuance of stress and intonation. One of Rosten's stories is about a man who went to a kosher restaurant and was served by a Chinese waiter. To his surprise, the waiter spoke Yiddish perfectly, complete with the appropriate grunts and sighs. The customer asked the proprietor how this was possible and was told: 'Not so loud: he thinks we've taught him English.' In a sense they had. At least, they had taken him a good part of the way towards Yidglish, which is New York English enough.

The primary assault of Yiddish on English is not verbal; it is, to use a technicality, suprasegmental. The anecdote about the letter sent to Stalin by Trotsky encloses a fair linguistic truth. The words of the communication were: 'You were right and I was wrong. You are the true heir of Lenin. I should apologize.' Read aloud by a Jewish tailor in Red Square they remained the same words, but the meaning radically changed: 'You were right and I was *wrong*? *You* are the true heir of Lenin? *I* should apologize!' English can perform this kind of trick without help from Yiddish intonation patterns, but the Jews have brought Levantine drama to it. Stress as a weapon is a fine Yiddish art: 'I should pay him for such devoted service?' So is reversed word-order: 'Already you're discouraged?' And then there are what Rosten calls 'contempt via affirmation' ('My *son*-in-law he wants to be'), 'fearful curses sanctioned by nominal cancellation' ('A fire should burn in his heart, God forbid!') and 'sarcasm via innocuous diction' ('He only tried to shoot himself').

An article in this journal (February 3, 1966) contained the statement 'Should, shmould, shouldn't, shmouldn't'. For the shm-rhyme to find its way into a *TLS* review represents its elevation from a mere slang-device to an indispensable engine of contemptuous dismissal. Indeed, the economy is brilliant. 'Oedipus-shmoedipus—what's it matter what he's got so long as he loves his mother?' A Yale professor dismissed the theory of a colleague, saying 'I can disprove it, I've got data.' The reply was: 'Data-shmata—I *like* my theory.' It is to be noted that we have not yet, in this discussion, arrived at the absorption of Yiddish *words*. But the shm-rhyme trembles on the verge of the lexical perhaps because of verbal association. *Shmaltz* is literally chicken-fat; metaphorically it stands for sentimental mush. A *shmatte* or *shmotte* is a rag, a piece of junk, a person you can wipe your feet on, a slattern, a sycophant. A *shmeer* is a bribe. A *shmegegge* is a petty person, a person without talent, a whiner, a sycophant. A *shmuck* is a dope or a jerk or a boob. There are few consonant-groups that, in initial position, carry so powerful a hogo of the pejorative.

A large number of phrases, long absorbed into British English and accepted as mere 'Americanisms', seem to be Yiddish in origin: 'Get lost'; 'O.K. by me'; 'I need it like a hole in the head'; 'It shouldn't happen to a dog'; 'On him it looks good'; 'Excuse the expression'; 'Go hit your head against the wall'. The *tone* is Yiddish; sometimes the syntax is palpably so. The 'by me' is *bei mir*: it is an admirably brief way of saying 'as far as I'm concerned'. A locus classicus in popular art can be found in the Rodgers-Hammerstein musical *Flower Drum Song*, where a San Francisco Chinese sings 'I'm a girl, and by me that's only great'. *Yet*—cognate with *jetzt*, though with greatly expanded connotations—is a sure Yiddish signal: 'This I need yet?' In an advanced poetry circle a newcomer reads a poem in traditional rhyme and metre. After the first couple of lines the comment is: 'A sonnet yet.' *Already* is a rendering of the ubiquitous *shon*, fairly colourless in German but rich in Yiddish: 'Al*right* already.' It is a pity that Mr. Rosten gives no guidance to the use of *yet* and *already* (as they are not Yiddish words they have no place in his lexicon, but why so strict?). They are popular with British television people, pointing the strength of the American-Jewish showbiz tradition. 'I've already done that' is a straight statement. 'I've done that already' is subtly irritable.

The Yiddish lexis makes its primary impact on Anglo-American Gentile speech through the Jewish cuisine. The referents, as well as the words, are there in kosher restaurants; the first are goyishly appreciated; the second become part of the general urban vocabulary. *Nosh* has been in British English for a long time now ('nosh bar'; 'anybody fancy a bit of a nosh-up?'), and its popularity in the general, as opposed to merely Jewish, context of eating may have something to do with onomatopoeia—it suggests the munching of the gnashers. Its etymology—German *naschen*: 'to eat on the sly' (Rosten)—is alive in Yiddish usage, which has nothing to do with large sitdown fryups. A *nosh* is a snack or titbit; *to nosh* is to have a little bite of something before a main meal is ready; a *nosher* is a snacker or between-meals nibbler. In some New York delicatessens there is to be seen an open plate of titbits—salami, halvah (cake of honey and sesame seeds) and so on—with the legend 'Nem a nosh a nickel' (*nem* is ultimately German *nehmen*, to take: imperative *nimm*).

Individual Jewish dishes show their place of origin in their names. *Gefilte fish* is German stuffed fish, but its accompanying horseradish —*chrayn*—is Russian *chryen*. *Borsht* also is Russian, but New York Jews are not happy about the original transliterated spelling *borshch*, which is finding its way on to restaurant menus. *Borsht* is regarded as altogether Jewish: the Jewish summer resorts in the Catskills make up what is known, to travelling entertainers, as the Borsht Belt. *Lox*—smoked salmon—is German *Lachs*. *Latkes*—pancakes, often made with potatoes—seem to be Slavic in origin. A *bagel* comes from German *Beugel*—a round loaf—and is defined by Rosten as 'a hard doughnut-shaped roll, simmered in hot water for two minutes before baking, then glazed with egg-white'. It is so much part of the furniture of urban America that it has entered the world of Gentile metaphor. A Pentagon officer said of the bombing pattern round Haiphong: 'You might call it the bagel strategy.'

Macy's—on St. Patrick's Day, 1968—advertised, in the New York press, 'BAGELS, BEGORRAH! (green ones yet)'. Subway posters show a cop munching a matzo, Non-Jewish New York gets its Yidglish direct, along with such referents as are esculent. England is learning from the American periodicals. From, for instance, an Irish whiskey advertisement that says: 'Scotch is a fine beverage and deserves its popularity. But enough is enough already.' Or the announcement of a British cod espionage film: 'By Papa he's a spy, by Mama he's a spy, but from spies he's no spy!' But British readers of magazines like *Time* must now buy a book like Mr. Rosten's if they want to take in more than the nuances of mere syntax and word-order. A recent *Time* article spoke of the chief editor of Alfred Knopf as 'mavin Robert Gottlieb'. Not even the largest English dictionary, British or American, helps here, but Mr. Rosten does. *Mavin* rhymes with *raven* and is the Hebrew for 'understanding'. A mavin is an expert, a judge of quality, a connoisseur. A newspaper advertisement for herring titbits showed an empty jar with the legend 'The Herring Mavin Strikes Again' (thought up, says Rosten, by a real advertising mavin). Once learned, *mavin* remains, indispensable.

Indispensable, as the *-nik* suffix already is—*beatnik*, *Vietnik* (a bearded protestor for peace), *nogoodnik*, *sicknik* (lover of sick humour), *Freudnik*, *straightnik* (homosexual term for a heterosexual). As *megillah* soon will be (a prolix rigmarole, like the Book of Esther; hence 'Cut the *megillah*'). Or *mensh* ('He's a *mensh*, after all, not an animal'). Or *momzer* ('She left home and gave birth to a *momzer*'). Or *nexdooreker* and *nexdoorekeh* (male and female next-door neighbours respectively). Or *mish-mosh* (not *mish-mash*—when a Congressman used *mish-mash* on the Groucho Marx television programme *You Bet Your Life*, Groucho told him he would never get votes in the Bronx with that pronunciation). Or. . . .

Mr. Rosten's book is a big, lavish, loose, loving compendium that looks less scholarly than it is. It is not just about Yiddish but the makers and users of Yiddish. It is crammed with ritual, taboos, customs, jokes. The best tribute that a British Gentile could pay to it would be an expression of regret that he was not born a New York Jew. But British English, no longer the language of an empire and hence no longer quick to absorb exoticisms, may well find it refreshing to lay itself open to the influence of so vital, homely and ironic a lexis. Yiddish is German stripped of Aryan *Reinheit* and needless grammatical complexity and dressed in, so to speak, the reach-me-downs of the human condition. It has survived pogroms, genocide, wandering. It is pleasant to think that so many of its elements find themselves at home in the chief language of the free world. Free, yet. Free-shmee.

7

I. A. RICHARDS

CHRISTOPHER ISHERWOOD has given in *Lions and Shadows* (1938), a lively description of the first impact of I. A. Richards in Cambridge:

Here, at last, was the prophet we had been waiting for . . . he was infinitely more than a brilliant new literary critic: he was our guide, our evangelist, who revealed to us, in a succession of astounding lightning-flashes, the entire expanse of the modern World. . . . Poets, ordered Mr. Richards, were to reflect aspects of the World Picture. Poetry wasn't a holy flame, a fire-bird from the moon; it was a group of interrelated stimuli acting upon the ocular nerves, the semi-circular canals, the brain, the solar plexus, the digestive and sexual organs. It did you medically demonstrable good, like a dose of strychnine or salts. We became behaviourists, materialists, atheists. In our conversation we substituted the word 'emotive' for the word 'beautiful'; we learnt to condemn inferior work as a 'failure in communication', or more crushing still, as 'a private poem'. We talked excitedly about 'the phantom aesthetic state'.

This well suggests the dual attraction of Richards's early writings. On the one hand, he sounded austere, clinical, disinfectant, the man in a white coat. In this respect, his criticism was a counterpart to T. S. Eliot's early verse. Eliot had administered a cold douche after the over-poetical poetry of the Georgians: Richards's dry astringent style counteracted the rhapsodical excesses of critics in a late nineteenth-century tradition, such as A. C. Bradley with his 'Poetry is a spirit'. On the other hand, with all its dry scientific air, the early work of Richards made (as Mr. Isherwood testifies) a strongly 'emotive' impact. There is in it an atmosphere of buoyant optimism, a sense that age-old mysteries are being at last unravelled, the 'chaos of aesthetic theories' brought to order. It is possible that contemplating the remarkable diagram in *Principles of Literary Criticism* which is supposed to depict schematically what happens in the nervous system when the eye reads a line of Browning, some readers may have received a fleeting suggestion of the Grand Academy of Lagado. But

I. A. RICHARDS: *So Much Nearer.* Essays Toward a World English. 274 pp. New York: Harcourt, Brace and World. $7.50.

JEROME P. SCHILLER: *I. A. Richards' Theory of Literature.* 189 pp. Yale University Press. £2.70.

more must have been impressed by the Aristotelian sweep and breadth of Richards's concerns, and the promise of new and powerful intellectual disciplines.

All that was in the 1920s, before Richards made his home in the United States. Today his vogue-reputation is over. On this side of the Atlantic he has been superseded, as an influential literary critic, by his one-time admirer F. R. Leavis; on the other side, perhaps by the ebullient Canadian 'anatomist' of criticism, Northrop Frye. And his recent book of essays, *So Much Nearer*, though in its studies of 'communication' it plunges enthusiastically into the world of computers and advanced technology, is unlikely to range him, in the world of cultural fashions, beside a Marshall McLuhan or a Noam Chomsky as a 'maker of the modern mind'. This still active thinker is widely regarded, it seems, as a mere survivor from the avant-garde of the day before yesterday. Once it appeared to be Richards's strength that he could bridge the communication-gap between general readers and the technically qualified—the psychologists, the philosophers, the linguists. Today he may have lost the interest of both publics. He has fallen, as he once rose, between two stools. Many readers today will accept as their own the account of him which Jerome P. Schiller, in his excellent analytic study *I. A. Richards' Theory of Literature* ascribes to 'the average critic':

Richards may be important as one of the founders of the New Criticism. This can be due only to his conviction that poetry is important and to his technique for studying it. His theory of poetry is absurd: he claims that the only way to study poetry is through psychology; he maintains that poetry does not say anything, so it has nothing to do with our beliefs. No wonder he lost interest in poetry years ago and started worrying about Basic English and general education.

But if we go and read Richards, and if we also read this book by Mr. Schiller, and the longer book on Richards by W. H. N. Hotopf (*Language, Thought and Comprehension*, 1965) we shall soon find reasons to revise that account. One way in which it is unfair is in its ignoring of the unity of Richards's work—notwithstanding occasional shifts of nomenclature and emphasis. His concern throughout his career has been the same: a concern with understanding, and with misunderstanding. It should be remembered that his first major work was *The Meaning of Meaning* (1923), written in collaboration with C. K. Ogden, that idiosyncratic genius who translated Wittgenstein's *Tractatus* and invented Basic English.

The Meaning of Meaning deals with the influence of language on philosophical theories: it has something in common with the attempts of contemporary philosophers, under the influence of Russellian logic, to create an ideal unambiguous language. In the background are books like Bertrand Russell's *Philosophy of Logical Atomism* (1918) and Wittgenstein's *Tractatus Logico-Philosophicus* (1921). Perhaps the most memorable part of *The Meaning of Meaning* is the authors' exposure of the role of 'word-magic' in traditional modes of thought: here they enlisted the help of modern anthropology (Malinowski contributed a long appendix). Its copiousness and gusto, its exuberant if eccentric erudition, and its gay iconoclasm, make the book highly enjoyable, and help us to overlook its philosophical crudities and the improbability of its general thesis—for surely it is very doubtful whether the long history of metaphysics can be explained merely as the result of 'word-magic', or of grammatical confusions. But *The Meaning of Meaning* was less a sober treatise than a manifesto. Human thought, it proclaimed, had become diseased through the misuse of language. The cure was the cultivation of the right kind of linguistic awareness. The authors were not slow to offer their therapeutic programme. Something of the book's essential aim —and something too of its youthful confidence and over-optimism— have survived in Richards's work in all its phases.

In the books that followed, down to *The Philosophy of Rhetoric* (1936), Richards made that long detour through literary criticism during which his most popular writings were published. *Principles of Literary Criticism* (1924) made his reputation current. It is his best book, because it is more of a *book*, and less of a paste-up, than any of the others. In *Principles* Richards denied that poetry (there his main concern) belonged to a separate aesthetic realm. He defined a poem as 'a class of experiences which do not differ in any character more than a certain amount, varying for each character, from a standard experience'. And this 'standard experience' he defined as 'the relevant experience of the poet when contemplating the completed composition'. Richards does not specify in what way, or how much, experiences may permissibly differ from the standard experience. Nor does he explain the usefulness, as a standard, of an experience which presumably is inaccessible to us. But his phrasing does serve to suggest the psychological bent of his work, his determination to disentangle criticism from mystifications and metaphysics.

Richards believed that aesthetics was in principle amenable to

F

science. Yet, contrary to the average critic's belief, he did not offer to make *criticism* a science. Nor did he think aesthetics at present susceptible to laboratory methods. What he did do was to sketch a *possible* psychological analysis of the effects and value of poetry. Literary readers tended to be mystified or repelled by this analysis, with its talk of 'impulses' and 'the nervous system'. They did not recognize its purely speculative character. Nor did they give Richards due credit for the ingenuity with which he connected the technical psychology of his day (expounded in text-books like George F. Stout's) with his quasi-utilitarian theory of value, and both in turn with his aesthetic theory.

It may indeed be as a 'scientific' *jeu d'esprit* that *Principles* is most vulnerable. But its lasting interest is to be found in its aesthetic theory—or rather, in its articulation of a modern taste which the new poetry of Eliot was doing much to form: a taste which rated complex poetry above simple, encouraged intellectuality and irony, and promoted an attitude Eliot had already detected in Marvell's poetry, 'a recognition, implicit in the expression of an experience, of other experiences which are possible'. (Irony, Richards maintained, is a quality of the greatest poetry.) But besides this 'period' interest, *Principles* also demonstrates clearly the most engaging aspect of Richards's work: his lifelong enmity both to pedantry and to preciousness. The one emerges, with lasting effect, in those parts of the book which demolish the pretensions of formalists, prosodists, and a priori literary theorists of all kinds; the other is seen in those passages which insist on the continuity between the 'values' of poetry and the 'values' of general living.

One of the most controversial elements in *Principles* is the idea Richards was soon to popularize in *Science and Poetry*: that the 'Magical View' of the world, on which poetry and art had hitherto depended, cannot now be sincerely held. Richards always stressed the vital importance of sincerity, even proposing a 'ritual' for inducing it in *Practical Criticism*. 'I would meet you upon this honestly' is a note he constantly strikes. His acclaim for the Eliot of *The Waste Land* was founded on his conviction that Eliot had succeeded where Yeats or D. H. Lawrence had failed: Eliot had achieved sincerity by accepting 'the neutralization of nature' and freeing his poetry from dependence on any beliefs. This last suggestion was to bewilder many readers, including, it soon appeared, Eliot himself. The average critic takes it to mean that poetry is meaningless. But Richards did not think that. The beliefs he had in mind seem to have been religious beliefs; and Richards's concern was, rather in the spirit of the later Matthew Arnold, to retain the beneficent effect of 'literature' while dropping untenable 'dogma'.

In this spirit, employing the distinction adumbrated in *The Meaning of Meaning* between 'emotive' and 'referential' uses of language, Richards allocated poetry to the emotive use. Here again he was often misunderstood. He was thought to have pronounced—with manifest unsoundness—that certain *words* were emotive (rather than certain uses of words). And he was much criticized for his use in *Science and Poetry* of the term 'pseudo-statement' to distinguish 'emotive' utterances like 'God's in His heaven' from 'referential' ones like 'There is life on Mars'. Richards was accused of dismissing poetry as beautiful nonsense in abject deference to a shallow scientism. And the term he used is certainly unfortunate, since the prefix 'pseudo' sounds derogatory, though it is not meant to be. In fact, his concept of 'pseudo-statements' can easily be interpreted so as to satisfy the most exalted traditional claims for the poet. For when Richards says that 'a statement in poetry arouses attitudes much more wide and general in direction than the references of the statement', he could be taken as saying not that the statements of poetry, in contrast to those of science, are meaningless, but that they are more general, or even universal, in their application.

The Meaning of Meaning had been concerned with therapy of the intellect: *Principles*, and *Practical Criticism* (1929), were more concerned with therapy of the sensibility. Richards agreed with those who stress the importance of literature and its capacity to fulfil social needs (though his emphasis, as Mr. Hotopf complains, is 'individualist', and he dwells almost wholly on personal self-culture.) In *Principles* he describes art as both the product and (if properly received) the source, of a greater and more various and, above all, a more *ordered* set of experiences than can be got elsewhere. The 'release', the 'repose in the midst of stress', the 'balance and composure' we should find in art were for him given most of all by great tragedy; for it is tragedy which supremely provides a 'balance and reconciliation of opposite and discordant qualities'. Richards's interest in Coleridge which was to become a cult, is apparent here. But his usual way of speaking about art, in his early work, is like Pater's, as when he speaks of 'those hours', experienced by the artist and conveyed to the recipient, when 'habitual narrowness of interests or confused bewilderment are replaced by an intricately wrought composure'. He criticizes Pater, however, for stressing the intense 'moments' that art can give us, rather than the lasting dispositions and emotional habits which it encourages us to form.

Art, then—above all, poetry—is, according to Richards, not a luxury but a necessity, for that 'self-completion' and 'increased order' without which our mental life is shapeless and confused. To appreciate it is to defeat the fixations of habit and convention, to overcome our 'stock responses' in favour of ever finer and more discriminating ones. But when Richards carried out the well-known experiment he describes in *Practical Criticism*—of setting poems without authors' names before Cambridge students, and recording their sometimes hilarious misapprehensions—he became convinced that much more educational work was necessary before poetry could perform its function. The analytic part of this book has had a great influence, not only on the incipient 'New Criticism', as John Crowe Ransom was to call it, but on pedagogic practice in schools and colleges. That 'practical criticism' has now often become at the same time irresponsible, and a sterile routine, is acknowledged, regretfully, in *So Much Nearer*.

Richards himself went on from *Practical Criticism* to explore the theoretical implications of his growing conviction that poetry is best seen, not as 'the emotive use of language', but as language requiring multiple interpretation. In *The Philosophy of Rhetoric* he wrote some of the few valuable pages there are on metaphor—pages which should enlighten those who think of it too simply in terms of likeness between 'vehicle' and 'tenor' (to use the helpful terminology Richards introduced). In *Interpretation in Teaching* (1938) he applied the methods of *Practical Criticism* to the study of prose, criticizing elementary books on logic, rhetoric, and grammar, and finding them full of mistaken doctrines. Once again Richards showed himself the enemy of pedantry. He came forward as the advocate of 'ordinary fluid language with full settings', against those logicians and grammarians who are 'stuck fast in an injudiciously technicalized set of words'. And in *So Much Nearer* he has some spirited and amusing criticisms to make of the new pedantries and abstractionist illusions (such as 'the fluent speaker') in the linguistics of Professor Chomsky and his school.

How much has Richards achieved? If the answer is uncertain, this is because (as he good-humouredly complains) he has been found hard to interpret. And this is not entirely on account of the intrinsic difficulty of his subject-matter, or the obtuseness of his readers. Richards's procedures are frequently confusing. The most obvious obstacle is stylistic. Sentence by sentence he can write trenchantly and wittily. But all too often the reader is distracted by sudden coynesses, ambiguous obscurities, the unexplained presence of out-of-the-way quotations or enigmatic Chinese fables. Cryptic hints are dropped, tips thrown out, bright ideas gleam and vanish in opaque contexts. We feel that Richards often digresses waywardly, goes off at tangents. He seems too capricious to submit himself to any particular discipline of thought. Sometimes his exposition is roundabout to the point of perversity. Thus in *Interpretation in Teaching* he is concerned to discuss the common belief that grammar summarizes usage. But we have to pick our way through his intricate commentary on the ill-formulated opinions of immature protocolists on what an old-fashioned grammarian said in attacking the views of another author, before we can divine what Richards's own views are—if then.

It is noteworthy that Mr. Schiller, a philosopher, and Mr. Hotopf, a psychologist, constantly remark on Richards's obscurities, inconsequences, and vagueness. Richards recognizes that 'talk about poems may have all sorts of purposes behind it: social, suasive, literary, comparative, analytic, scientific'. The trouble is that he himself is apt to switch without warning from one purpose to another; whether the aesthetician's or the critic's, the psychologist's or the logician's, the linguist's or the lexicographer's. This greatly adds to the ambiguity which—with ironic appropriateness in an opponent of the One Proper Meaning superstition—is the main defect of his work. Above all, ambiguity overhangs the nature of the *claim* Richards makes for what he does. Sometimes he seems only to make a modest claim, for the value of clarity in thinking and writing. But at other times his tone suggests that his proposals are truly momentous: he promises 'a general theoretical study of language capable of opening to us new powers over our minds comparable to those which systematic physical inquiries are giving us over our environment'. Yet the use he makes in *Coleridge on Imagination* (1935)—from which this quotation comes—of Coleridge's distinction between Fancy and Imagination cannot be thought to advance that 'theoretical study'. His claims for it are unconvincing.

As a theorist, then, Richards seems to promise more than he performs. His place in the history of criticism is secure: but as a critic in his own right he is insubstantial. Apart from interesting pioneer essays on writers like Gerard Manley Hopkins or E. M. Forster, his contribution here is small. His prose writings in general, like his poetry, suggest an excess of headwork and ingenuity—though this is in itself attractive and amiable—and a deficiency of deeper human involvement. In the end the best of his writings may survive in a generous selection from those asides, those pregnant suggestions, those insights into 'words and their ways', which abound in his work. It may be that he could have achieved more if he had not insisted on always being a 'loner' and confined himself to a discipline not invented by himself. His work as a whole leaves us with a sense of squandered talents. But, as George Orwell said of H. G. Wells, what a thing it is, after all, to have any talents to squander.

8

POETRY OF 1970

(a) ROBERT CREELEY
The Charm and *A Quick Graph*

ROBERT CREELEY'S NEW COLLECTION, *The Charm*, is mainly made up of works the author failed to reprint in earlier volumes, and might properly be read not on its own but as a supplement to *Poems 1950–1965* (published in England four years ago). Yet this miscellaneous sample does suggest Creeley's appeal and his range. The blocks to one's enjoyment of the poetry are big enough; they are not immovable. In too many poems Creeley seems to defy the reader with the question, 'Who is speaking?' or 'What am I thinking about?' He has been known to ask listeners whether or not he is audible and then to tell those too far back to hear well that he would spoil the effect of the lines if he raised his voice.

The truth is that his technique limits him to a fairly small number of subjects; if one keeps those in mind, one can usually sift out the meaning. Anyhow, Creeley could only produce his bright but ambivalent illuminations behind the screen of his impudent vagueness. Often the subject is a curious detail of somebody's sexual habits. In 'Two Times' he compares the inexperienced lover's shock on being handled by a woman with the experienced lover's ease:

(a) ROBERT CREELEY: *The Charm*. Early and Uncollected Poems. 97 pp. $2.50. *A Quick Graph*. Collected Notes and Essays. 365 pp. $4. San Francisco: Four Seasons Foundation.

(b) A. D. HOPE: *New Poems 1965–1969*. 76 pp. Angus and Robertson. £1.50.

(c) IAN HAMILTON: *The Visit*. 45 pp. Faber and Faber. 75p.

(d) ROBERT LOWELL: *Notebook*. 265 pp. Faber and Faber. £2.25.

(e) JOHN CROWE RANSOM: *Selected Poems*. 159 pp. Eyre and Spottiswoode. £2. ROBERT PENN WARREN: *Incarnations: Poems 1966–1968*. 64 pp. W. H. Allen. £1.25.

(f) PETER PORTER: *The Last of England*. 67 pp. Oxford University Press. 75p.

(g) HUGO WILLIAMS: *Sugar Daddy*. 55 pp. Oxford University Press. £1.25.

It takes so long to look down,
the first time thinking it
would then and there either
shoot up or else drop off.

One hand on
the trigger one
hand on the hand.

The blurred reference of 'it' is a mark of Creeley's style. He is fond of nouns like 'thing', pronouns without clear antecedents, demonstratives that seem to point nowhere. The effect (when it succeeds) is to make the reader an accomplice of the poet's: we are presumably both on such good terms that the reference will be clear.

The complexities of the relation between men and women are a favourite subject, especially as shown in marriage. Human nature depends on loyalties that last. Yet close, deep-rooted ties snarl one another and make people frantic. Creeley plays with the oscillation between mutual need and mutual rejection, marriage as grace and marriage as yoke. Here is 'For an Anniversary':

Where you dream of water
I have held a handful of sand.

My manners are unprepossessing.
I stand here awkward, and a long time.

I am mainly an idiot.
You are almost beautiful.

We will both be miserable
but no one is damned.

The arbitrary changes in tense suggest Creeley's preoccupation with time, his insistence that whatever was meaningful in the past becomes part of the present. The variety of verb forms in the poem—not only tenses but persons, numbers, voices—suggests the variety of experiences contained by the marriage. In this effort to make syntax expressive, one meets a normal element of Creeley's style.

The act of composition itself often becomes part of the poem if not the central subject. In 'The Late Comer' Creeley rewrites the poem as he goes along, and comments at the end, '(better)'. In 'Chasing the Bird' he suggests that each time the poet tries to convey his experience of 'night', the task grows harder:

The sun sets unevenly and the people
go to bed.

The night has a thousand eyes.
The clouds are low, overhead.

Every night it is a little bit
more difficult, a little

harder, My mind
to me a mangle is.

When Creeley shifts without warning from the theme of nightfall to
the theme of writing about nightfall, he acts in character. The reader
must simply identify himself with the poet to the point of 'acting'
with him, and seeing what 'it' refers to. The passive reader will miss
out. In the expressiveness of the rhythm (if one stops for what
Creeley calls 'terminal juncture' at the end of each line), in the change
from the mildness of the first half of the poem to the harsh movement of the second, one can hear the most subtle of Creeley's
accomplishments. Fuller demonstrations of this rhythmic power
appear in 'The Rhythm' and 'The Woman' in *Poems 1950–1965*.

Finally, there is the examination of selfhood or consciousness, implicit in all Creeley's work—for the creative imagination is only a
purified form of the human sensibility—but primary in a number of
poems. The relation between perception and recognition, experience
and memory, the difference between the self as agent and the self as
witness, the 'I' who *am* and the 'I' who *is*—these themes provide
centres for Creeley's verse, essays, and fiction. On the poet's uncor-
rupted mind the world of sensible particulars imposes its fresh
objects; these the poet grasps, giving them meaning as he embeds
them in his associations; and thus he joins several different times
with the place of the immediate experience. In 'Not Again', a poem
about self-consciousness, Creeley enacts the sudden appearance of
the 'I' as witness before the 'I' as agent:

It was a breeze and a seashell
brought in Venus—
but I can be here
without going anywhere.

So goodbye
until we meet again,
and when you come, walk right in.
It's I.

The comic slyness that suffuses this poem and many more alternates or mingles itself with a despair that rises as easily. So long as a
man upholds the integrity of his soul while reaching out to those who
love and resist him (especially his wife and children), he is bound to
feel regularly defeated. Yet he must keep renewing the effort. These
conflicts find an audible outlet in deliberate and often mischievous
bathos.

Disappointment with people verges on disappointment with self—
the failure of the imagination to work well against routine monotony
and anxiety. Fears of death, of losing creative power, may be embodied in despair or transcended in the ironic pathos of a poem like
'Helas'—here are the opening lines:

> Helas! Or Christus fails.
> The day is the indefinite. The shapes of light
> have surrounded the senses,
> but will not take them to hand (as would an axe-edge
> take to its stone . . .)

Creeley's style, tentative and recapitulatory, slows down the surges
of feeling without explaining them away. It sounds like his hesitant,
low-pitched voice. The movement between poet and world becomes
the quietest possible drama but draws in every resource of language.
When his lines break off or dwindle into ellipses, they evoke the
poet's rueful admission that no words are right for some reflections,
or else his confidence that the sympathetic reader needs no further
hint. When the voices speaking in a poem change with hardly a sign,
Creeley implies that all the voices—despair, humour, confidence, and
lyric passion—emerge ultimately from the single poet who represents
the human spirit.

The prose pieces collected in *A Quick Graph* will help those who
wish to study Creeley's career as a teacher and editor. But the over-
killing assertiveness here is less charming than the hesitancy of the
verse. Now and then, as in the essay, 'I'm given to write poems', or
the review article, 'The New World', he illuminates his own poetry.
Often he celebrates men—Whitman, Pound, Williams—whose work
opened doors for him: or he recommends younger men—Charles
Olson, Robert Duncan—whom he has worked with and learned
from (or taught). But the programmes he sets up are not always
consistent with one another or his practice. He delivers his eulogies
and slogans in a humourless prose that remains ugly and obstructive.

When one is not rattled by the solecisms, one is puzzled by the exotic syntax.

(b) A. D. HOPE

New Poems 1965–1969

AGAINST MODERNISM and for classicism; against the bloodlessly refined and for the sensuously robust; backing the past against the present and both against the technological future; and yet with all this, backing the undernourished and perhaps crippled Australian culture against a European civilization run to seed: there were all these reasons, as well as the sheer quality of his poetic performance, that A. D. Hope should emerge as the most distinctive poetic voice in Australia since Slessor stopped writing. With as much going for him as Slessor ever had—imagination, authority, touch—and a greater range than Brennan, Hope is by now established as the poet who matters most in all of the largest island's short but variegated cultural history.

Yet Hope doesn't fit into that history any better than Brennan did. His alignments against, his contests with, a tradition, are all against or with a *European* tradition. The regional emphases don't really matter much. It's far more pertinent to ask why he approves of Swift's rage (and why he approves of that rage as *reasonable*) than to ask about his precise attitude to current Australian society, for although that society might be the immediate stimulus of his opposition it is a whole modern era he objects to. In making this objection he writes two main kinds of poetry, one a choleric railing against all dunces in which the powder flies off his wig, the other a bitter and desperate taking of solace either in the contemplation of past greatness (Swift, Yeats, and notably in this volume Baudelaire) or in the embrace of unnamed ladies who emerge from his heroic imagery as tending to be on the strapping side.

Both strains in his work long ago became predictable. But neither strain has ever become predictable as to the actual handling of it, and each continues to throw up a remarkable number of excellent poems. For anybody who first owned the beautiful Edwards and Shaw edition of *The Wandering Islands*, and later slipped the *Collected Poems* into the shelf beside it, and now must add this latest volume, it is the combination of bulk and solidity that impresses. There have been plenty of Australian poets who have had bulk, in the same way that a trailer-load of sponge-rubber has bulk. Similarly there have been more than a few Australian poets responsible for a handful of intense, solid performances. But Hope has managed to add density to density, and already, with a lot of writing left in him, he has established the kind of presence we associate only with truly formidable talents.

It's ironic (not in history, which allows no other process, but certainly in regard to prevailing cultural pressures) that he should have won his way through to the European poetic tradition by the sheer cogency and power of his contesting almost every one of its manifestations in the modern age, and also won his way through to a pre-eminence in Australian cultural history while never once going in search of an heroic Australian past, as James McAuley did, or getting himself identified with the soil, as Judith Wright did. It shows just how hard it is to get the individual talent taped, when the talent is there.

Hope's twelve 'Sonnets to Baudelaire' are at the physical and thematic centre of the new book. Baudelaire is addressed as an equal, which takes nerve:

> For we are fellow travellers in a land
> Where few around us know they walk in hell,
> Where what they take for the creating Word
> Is a blind wind sowing the sand with sand.
> Brother, it is our task of love to tell
> Men they are damned, and damned in being absurd.

As in his earlier alliances with Swift, Blake, and Yeats, Hope has here found a way of ducking back into the past in order to recruit reinforcements for an attack on his own present. Baudelaire's position vis-à-vis his critics becomes, by adoption (presumption?), Hope's own:

> He warms my heart, your Monsieur Monselet;
> —Such culture addicts, such genteel amateurs
> As scold us for 'abominable verse,'
> While, savage with joy, we let them have their say—
> Poor fellow, I see him scan your lines, his eyes
> Moist with fine feeling, till they meet the words
> About the hanged man's belly ripped by birds:
> 'His dangling bowels dribbled down his thighs!'

'What else could I do?' Hope has Baudelaire say: 'A poem is not a game; the image I chose/Was what my theme required.' The implication, in part justified, is that Hope himself has had to say some superficially horrible things in order to penetrate to hidden truth. But to write, as Baudelaire indeed did, 'Les intestins pesants lui coulaient sur les cuisses', is one thing: he was out to show that Cytherea was a trifle disappointing. To write, as he also wrote, 'Là, tout n'est qu'ordre et beauté/Luxe, calme et volupté', was definitely another. When Baudelaire mixed these two thematic worlds it was by force of circumstance—because the facts said so. 'Les Petites Vieilles', for example, gets its huge force because the pitiable facts batter through all such cheap defences as superiority, disdain, even art: it's a compassionate poem. But with Hope these worlds are scrambled into one from the start, and that one world is acutely, narrowly personal. He sees the skull beneath the skin right enough, but his trouble—and it's his limitation as a poet—is that he expects us to fall down in astonishment on being told that life is made up of bones, blood, gristle, guts, and unpalatable, rank juices. He can't leave it alone. He's really much more like Swift than like Baudelaire: the thing that gets him is that Celia shits. And the answer to that one is still Lawrence's: how much worse it would be if she didn't. Finally Hope overcomes his repugnance and utters 'the heart's unhesitating: Yes!' to life. But his contemptuous objection to *this* life, the one we are trying to lead now, is that we are all busy trying to deny the harsh facts. Hence the condescension of tone, and the regression in time, of almost everything he writes. The only consolations offered are fatalistic, and then you see that the fatalism is private too.

(c) IAN HAMILTON

The Visit

IAN HAMILTON'S WORK marks an epoch in recent poetry. Writers have always celebrated the agonies due to passionate love or jealousy; and English poets of this century have often pitied themselves in verse either for their inadequacy in love or for the poverty of their attachments. A newer, more private theme has been the poet's inadequacy in handling his own painfully ambivalent emotions. Mr. Hamilton follows such tendencies to an elevation on which he throws a glow of heroic virtue. In place of the struggle against sexual passion or one's own catastrophic ambivalence, he deals with the futility of tenderness, the poet's incapacity to relieve the afflictions of those he loves.

Mr. Hamilton explores the situation until it becomes not narrowly pathetic but emblematic of human fate; for he reminds us of the condition on which one receives imagination and sensitivity—that one sees beyond futility to an illuminated resignation. Without imagination there would be no grief, but without grief there would be no wisdom: some of the most important things can only be discovered through helplessness.

The characteristics of Mr. Hamilton's poetry flow from the nature of his explorations. To avoid the note of self-pity, he concentrates his work on the feelings of an observer. The poet becomes a register of the impressions that intractable suffering engraves on the most sympathetic witness. His regular mode of discourse is in the second person, addressed to the beloved. His flat, declarative sentences suggest exhaustion but make a poignant contrast to the depth of the reactions they deal with. These reactions, by their acuteness, peculiarity, and discontinuity, indicate the strain under which the poet works. Yet, by avoiding direct comment on his own case, he maintains his dignity and privacy.

To establish the fidelity of his account, Mr. Hamilton sacrifices most figures of speech; for the act of understanding should exalt the act of seeing but not distort it. The poet's metrics, his leaps from curious impression to bleak reflection, could hardly work more subtly. The reader feels moved to fill every gap with an awed sympathy. Nothing marks Mr. Hamilton's personal voice more than the muted ironies and small anticlimaxes that suggest an abysmal familiarity with disappointment. Visiting his beloved in a mental hospital, he wryly sets 'new' against 'old' and turns each enjambment in a strange, chilling direction:

> They've let me walk with you
> As far as this high wall. The placid smiles
> Of our new friends, the old incurables,
> Pursue us lovingly.

('The Visit')

To imply the flattening weight of pain upon the beloved, Mr. Hamilton practises a rigorous economy in descriptive detail. Unparticularized hands take up the expressive burden that most poets would assign to vivid features of the face. Less often the head, sometimes the hair, eyes, or lips emerge, quite without specific colour or shape, as if the poet could not bear to look closely. The typical atmosphere is hushed, windless. Apart from varieties of white, grey, and black, Mr. Hamilton hardly employs colour. Flowers and landscapes appear usually with no more qualification: what matters is not their look or smell but their participation in the suffocating moment. The reader can seldom transfer his attention from the suspended anxiety to a restorative conceit. When the poet does particularize, therefore, the epithets operate with a sudden power of mysterious evocation. Always unpredictable, but beautifully placed, his images resonate with each other in sense and sound: for example, 'I', 'eye', and 'ice' in the following lines:

> 'That's where I live.' My father's sleepless eye
> Is burning down on us. The ice
> That catches in your hair melts on my tongue.
>
> ('Home')

Because the poems are short, one attends to small, local effects. Rhythms often start with a brave regularity but collapse in despair. Lines that float slowly in an air of promise alternate with lines that come to a rueful halt:

> Ah, listen now
> Each breath more temperate, more kind
> More close to death.
>
> ('Poem')

Often a short, regular line raises expectations that a longer, irregular one defeats:

> Enough to build
> A few melancholy poems on.
>
> ('Epitaph')

Or a fine play of sound patterns gives ironic harmony to a sequence dealing with disintegration—for example, this flow of *P-B* and *F-V* around *L*, as a dying man misinterprets an omen:

> You lean forward to watch the thorns
> Pluck on your skin white pools
> That bleed as your fist tightens. 'My hand's
> In flower', you say. 'My blood excites
> This petal dross. I'll live."
>
> ('Father, dying')

(*d*) ROBERT LOWELL

Notebook

IN A 'Note to the New Edition' of *Notebook*, Robert Lowell tells us that in the six months or so between the publication of the book's American edition and the preparation of the text for English readers, he made alterations to 'about a hundred of the old poems' and added more than ninety new ones. He treated, he says, his published work (the American edition) as a manuscript. On the page facing this explanatory note, Lowell gives a list of the uglier historical landmarks of the last three years—'The Six Days War, first week in June, 1967', 'Martin Luther King's Murder, April 4, 1968', 'Robert Kennedy's Murder, June 5, 1968', 'The Russian Occupation of Czechoslovakia, August 21, 1968', and so on—and justifies the inclusion of this aide-mémoire as follows: 'Dates fade faster than we do. Many in the last two years are already gone; in a year or two the rest will slip.'

Together, these concluding notes constitute a kind of apologia for the method of the total work we have just read. They speak of haste, the haste with which awful events arrive and pass away, the haste with which the poet-diarist must register them on his pulses before it is too late, the ensuing haste of both composition and revision. And in that rush, it is implied, the artist can attend but patchily to art's rush-refusing obligations. Lowell attends a good deal less patchily than any other poet would have in the circumstances, and it is this that makes the book depressing: *Notebook* is just rich enough to keep reminding us of what is being wasted. Lowell has written carelessly in the past, he has always been prone to over-exploit his best gifts and to allow his linguistic fertility to outpace his impulse. But nowhere in his earlier work—except maybe in *The Mills of the Kavanaughs*—has he surrendered so forlornly to self-parody, the strenuous but machine-like animation of dead mannerisms, as he does throughout this volume.

In the age of the short poem, the poet seeking to be called ambitious will be tempted to package his brevities in the form of a sequence. He will then insist that the sequence is not what it seems to be—a random bundling of independent works—but is in fact a 'single poem'. John Berryman's *Dream Songs* offers a key instance of this kind of marketing, and Lowell has confessed to having got the idea for *Notebook* from that 'poem'. In the same way, just as Berryman tailors his individual songs to a strict, if strictly arbitrary, pattern, so Lowell here elects to allot each of his poems-within-the-poem a ration of but fourteen lines (rhyme and metre optional). And just as Berryman challenged us, teasingly, to contemplate the possibility of structure in what he had done, Lowell too advances his collection 'as one poem, intuitive in pattern'. That 'intuitive' is, of course, a way of warning us that, although we ought to look for patterns, we ought not to be surprised if we don't find them.

Thus structure, both overall and as it is applied to individual poems, is employed as a receptacle, a spacious bin that can take and tidy anything the poet chooses to dump in it. And although we may never grasp the total pattern, individual poems—because they are offered as part of a pattern—can be as flat, ragged and inconsequential as they happen to turn out. Arbitrarily curtailed after fourteen lines, they can simply bump to a halt—after all, they do not *finish* there. The effect of the accumulative strategy is to permit the poet to abdicate from actually completing anything, and thus from the need to ever ask himself if what he has written is in fact a poem. The internal organization, the rhythmic and imagistic shaping, the dramatic pace and timing of the single poem: these become optional objectives also.

Here and there, in *Notebook*, one can disembed poems in which Lowell has seen such objectives as essential, and some of these—see poems 3 and 4 from the 'Through the Night' section—are as beautiful, as beautifully *made*, as anything Lowell has written. But how rarely, from a close-spaced book of over 250 pages, can this be said. The vast majority of the poems are, simply, shoddy; shoddy in one or another of the many ways Lowell can now be so; in ways, that is to say, which do not necessarily eschew intelligence or cultivation or, even, the eruption intermittently of an image or a cadence or a four-line burst that only a poet of his genius could have been subject to. The real shoddiness of *Notebook* is that time and again it debases into facility the poet's most potent qualities. The tightly conversational voice is frittered into chatter, the heartfelt, in extremis, plaint sounds thin, forced and vain, the appetite for history, for heroes and detritus, becomes gluttonous and indiscriminate.

But worst of all, Lowell's powers of language have degenerated into a ready-for-anything rhetorical machine: you name it, I'll write it up with urgent vigour. Consider the three-adjective device, once

G

surprising and supple, but now trundled out mechanically: 'over-white, overobserved, ignored', 'angular, night-bluish, blear-eyed, spinsterish', 'elastic, curved and cool', 'each day more brutal, oracular, and rooted', 'poised, warm and cool'. One could list dozens; and note with each, despondently, that not one of them is *bad*. Consider too, the empty, flogged melodrama: 'Revolution/dragging her terrible pre-menstrual cramps/marches with unbra'd breasts to storm the city', 'Earth the great beast, clanks its chain of vertebrae'; the slickly colourful, but essentially unseen, descriptive thrusts: 'Your sinewy lips wide-eyed as the honey-comb/your tongue as smooth as truth': the philosophical banalities: 'the poverty all men must face the hour of death', 'laws imprison as much as they protect'; the sleek agonizing: 'the soul groans and laughs at its lack of stature'.

The temptation to shrug off such things, and to point instead to (what, admittedly, needs mentioning) the work's size, range, assimilative energy, and so on (it moves back and forth through the poet's autobiography, hymning dead friends, lost loves, and heroes ancient and modern, against a backcloth of contemporary political misfortune and the despair of an individual haunted by his own griefs and nostalgias) would be a mistake, for it seems to have been in pursuit, in expectation, of such applause that this fine poet has allowed himself to let things slip—as life slips, and with it life's applause.

(*e*) JOHN CROWE RANSOM

Selected Poems

and ROBERT PENN WARREN

Incarnations: Poems 1966–1968

THOUGH CRITICS often treat John Crowe Ransom as a Southern poet, they rarely show how remote his best work is from a defence of 'Southern' traditions. It is one thing to say, as Ransom does in 'Philomela' and 'Amphibious Crocodile', that a poet will travel farthest if he starts from home. It is quite another to say his idea of home must resemble that of his forebears. Reading Ransom's 'Old Mansion', one finds the poet's sympathy with the old ways barely surviving in its contention with hostile emotions. In this poem an historian who knows foreign castles tries to visit a Southern mansion in order to secure material for an account of the house. But the ailing old lady of the manor sends a deathlike servant to refuse him entrance; and he learns nothing. While the historian will persist in his vocation, he is sorry to lose this interesting subject and be forced to 'dip, alas, into some unseemlier world'.

Like many writers of his region and generation, Ransom endlessly criticizes the legend of the Old South but never gives up his attachment, whether despairing or smiling, to her land and people. If the Lady has nothing to tell even her own children—spoilt by cosmopolitanism for the duty she would exact—they in turn withdraw reluctantly from her impressive but ruinous past, to spend their own lives in a less seemly present. Admittance to the manor would mean death. When Ransom introduced the periodical he helped to found, and with which he fostered a remarkable literary movement, he said: '*The Fugitive* flees from nothing faster than from the high-caste Brahmins of the Old South.'

In 'Antique Harvesters' the Southerners of the legend appear as old reapers, presumably in the Lady's fields. When a raven redolent of Poe utters a deathlike croak, one of the men asks what the bird has said. 'Nothing', another replies. It is new action and new love—'the song / Of passionate birds'—that excite the young men here, and not the legendary raven. A voice that does not speak for Ransom urges the 'dainty youths' to help with the harvest and remain loyal to the 'Proud Lady'. But the poet's own judgment seems at best suspended.

The pride of the Lady blends wryly with the pride of the spinsters who live in the nearby town. Rejecting their proper suitors as too low, they wait, fearful of passion, for the aristocrat who never shows up; and after their beauty has faded, they succumb to the last bridegroom, death. 'Emily Hardcastle, Spinster', written in the meter of 'The Raven', is an elegy on such a beauty, delivered by a rejected suitor. Her sisters turned against the legend and 'married them to merchants, being unbelievers both'. Emily is true to her surname and takes her proper reward:

But right across her threshold has the Grizzled Baron come:
Let them wrap her as a princess, who would patter down a stairway
Where the foreigner may take her for his gloomy halidom.

If this is the end of the maids of honour, that of the gentlemen is no brighter. Those who dedicate themselves to the Lady become like

'Captain Carpenter'. Nobody beats the captain fairly, but everyone deprives him of an essential limb or feature; for he never meets an enemy who accepts his own high code. He fails in every station, mutilated by effeminate men and masculine women, to be robbed at last of his heart and left with only a voice. In the poet's fondness for the captain humour alternates with indignation, but envy is never expressed. The poet cannot emulate those who sacrifice action and passion to a legend of knighthood during an age unacquainted with chivalry.

Satisfaction in love or marriage is almost forbidden to the subjects of the legendary Lady, whether or not they are loyal. Those whom the myth cannot seduce are undone by the chaos of modernity, the feud between intellect and passion. When marriage does occur, it produces another form of emotional starvation. In 'Man without Sense of Direction', the traditional love-making hero shows up the modern hero manqué. The hero of the past attacked external, substantial evil, and died true to his cause. The baffled modern has no ideal to magnetize him; his enemies are within; he lives on, but with no power to love. Finally, there are the children of such marriages, found dead or encountering death in some of Ransom's best poems: 'Bells for John Whiteside's Daughter', 'Janet Waking'. Innocence is their perishable amulet, against self-consciousness and prudence. 'First Travels of Max' is the story of an heir of the legendary Lady, running off as a boy to try the dangers he will face again as a man: the burden of tradition, religious confusion, lust. He escapes them all and comes home safe because 'young knights only armed in inno-cency' are not required to join in 'unequal contests'. But one knows what will happen when he returns to the 'Fool's Forest' of adult morality.

If the great private experience of these figures is sexual, the great public event is military: at the centre of the legend remains the War between the States; the metaphors of armed attack and defence are the most common in Ransom's poetry. But except in 'Antique Har-vesters' the battles are more symbolic than historical. Ransom com-monly infuses the private realm with public meaning by a representa-tion of love through the imagery of war. A walled city is the beloved; a besieging army is the lover. Within the person the relation of feeling to intellect becomes a losing struggle of body against head. 'Judith of Bethulia' gains extraordinary power from the deployment of such symbols. Here the maiden liberates the city; the invader succumbs to the beauty; the lover both figuratively and literally loses his head; and after Judith's triumph she provokes in the young men of Bethulia the same fever and chills—or lust and despair—that killed the frustrated heroine of 'Here Lies a Lady'. In unveiling herself to Holofernes, this Judith marries and destroys him. No sexual consummation, no swing of an axe, is needed. Her beauty alone unmans the great prince, reducing his body to a carcass. For the rest of her life, she needs no suitors because by keeping his head, she enjoys the perfect husband.

The language of Ransom's people suggests the old-fashioned speech of pious Southern farmers in his boyhood; and it is not without a parodical trace of Southern oratory. The words are often Biblical in flavour or otherwise archaic; the phrasing is angular or enigmatically concise. Mixed with rarities are coarse words and slang. Often an obsolete or etymological sense is preferred to the normal meaning. Like his admired Thomas Hardy, the poet has invented an idiom that both connects him with and separates him from the situations he describes. His language implies a judgment on the people around him, a distance between present and past, speaker and story. But it also implies an ironic depreciation of the poet; for this is only *his* judgment.

The landscape of the Lady's country has inspired some of Ransom's best-known lines. But they depict a sad region, recalling the darker aspect of Hardy's Wessex: bleak weather and colourless prospects, in a season that promises little fruit. 'Autumn days in our section Are the most used-up thing on earth.' Spring and summer are lost ages or tantalizing visions. The pathetic fallacy is integral to Ransom's style. Since man is not at home in the world, nature can supply him with no sympathetic climate.

The coherence of these various elements reflects the brevity of Ransom's great period of poetic composition. Nearly all the poems he or his admirers wish to see preserved were originally published during the four years 1922–25, when *The Fugitive* was appearing; but the high spirits typical of the 'Fugitive' enterprise could not overpower Ransom's notorious severity in judging his own performances. Severity took over while the high spirits levelled off. As the poems were collected and reprinted, Mr. Ransom added few to their small number. Rather he trimmed and sifted the canon. It is now twenty-five years since his *Selected Poems* first appeared; and the present volume may be described as a third, freshly revised edition of that

book. He has tended to neglect the spring of his metre and to prefer
rationality; he has tried to clarify meaning at the expense of connota-
tion. But even Mr. Ransom is hardly the same person he was in 1922;
and many readers will think of him as one of themselves (though
primus inter pares) rather than as the rightful owner, privileged to
remodel his own creation. In 'Emily Hardcastle, Spinster', for
example, the lines quoted above have become the following:

But right across the threshold has her grizzled Baron come;
Let them robe her, Bride and
Princess, who'll go down a leafy archway
And seal her to the Stranger for his castle in the gloom.

Surely the poet will not reproach somebody who has lived so long
with the older lines that he cannot hear the new.

Although Robert Penn Warren was a pupil of Mr. Ransom's, he
has been less concerned to judge a society than to define a self. In his
new collection, *Incarnations*, as in earlier poems, his motion seems
centripetal, lingering on the private response to mutability and
anguish. Like most of his later verse these poems seldom depend on
regularity of structure. They gain what force they possess through
belonging to sequences, some narrative and some lyric. In neither
mode, unfortunately, has Warren's language, imagery, or attitude
the freshness and life that should distinguish it from the efforts of less
expert writers. But he maintains a semblance of depth and drama by
an equivalent of cinematic montage, shifting his point of view back
and forth between landscape and observer, painful incident and
pained sensorium.

(*f*) PETER PORTER

The Last of England

BY NOW the Porter territory is pretty well known: an Earls Court
bedsitter in a German or Central European tower, with some
baroque opera on the hi-fi record-player and a Perspex bust of Martial on the mantelpiece. The inhabitant is a middle-aged copywriting
hypochondriac, who shudders and winces at the modish goings-on
that assault him on all sides: from a rear window, there is a good view
of Hell—colour supplements, concrete poets, gossip columnists,
slaughterhouses. There is not much laughter but a good deal of

self-defensive smiling. The host keeps on breaking into thick German. There is a strong smell of death.

This familiar terrain is to be found again in *The Last of England*, Mr. Porter's fourth collection of poems. The fears and dislikes are given their most extensive and exuberant run so far in 'Applause for Death', a hurtling catalogue of couplets densely studded with neatly avoided libel actions. There is 'More from Martial'—more of those ribald, wittily anachronistic versions of a poet already mined in *Poems Ancient and Modern* and *A Porter Folio*. 'Real People' rings changes on an earlier sequence, 'Porter's Metamorphoses'. On a deliberately smaller scale, there are the 'Japanese Jokes', unashamedly deriving from seventeen-syllable forebears and using the form to laugh at those who find it most congenial:

> William Blake, William
> Blake, William Blake, William Blake,
> Say it and feel new!

In another manner, 'A Consumer's Report' ('The name of the product I tested is *Life*') seems to hark back to another piece of sardonic investigation, 'To Start a Controversy', in which some archaeologist of the future descanted on the meaning of two human beings preserved in the act of love.

All this, though familiar, is not wearyingly so, for Mr. Porter's inventiveness is as robust as ever. But it is good to see him trying more difficult things, and not necessarily in the direction of greater complexity. True, some of 'The Sanitized Sonnets' (described as 'a continuing sequence') are disconcertingly oblique and show a randomness which comes close to impudence, but most of them have a hard-edged conciseness and a contained brilliance which exhibit very well Mr. Porter's gift for the apophthegm. But the greatest advance is seen in such poems as 'The Sadness of the Creatures', 'At Whitechurch Canonicorum', and 'On this day I complete my fortieth year', in which, without becoming vapid or merely personal, he seems to speak most directly from his concerns. There is a wonderful weightiness and richness here:

> The weight of before
> stands here for faith; so many are born and go
> back, marvellous like painting or stones:
> I offer my un-numinous body to the saint's care
> and pray on my feet to her merciful bones
> for ease of the ulcer of feeling, the starch of despair.

The grand manner—which Mr. Porter has seemed to admire in others but distrust in himself— is proper and sounds natural here, as it does in the typically pessimistic close to 'There are too many of us':

> we world-eaters
> Are eaten in our turn and if we shout
> At the gods they send us the god of death
> Who is immortal and who cannot read.

Such eloquent sententiousness, spoken so directly, confirms the feeling that Mr. Porter is not only one of the most entertaining but also one of the most serious poets we have.

(g) HUGO WILLIAMS

Sugar Daddy

IN *Sugar Daddy* the deadly seriousness of the business at hand— mainly the loss of love, partly an alienation accepted and even wooed —is punctuated flashingly by confessions of ambition:

> Washing my hair and dreaming of fame,
> I thought you came into my room.
>
> Were you saying something?
> I was in America, attending my new play.

But this is a train of thought as valid as any of the others, and bringing it in makes the others clearer. In Hugo Williams's poetry there is usually only the one man speaking, but that one man is many-selved: despair can slip abruptly towards delight, even a delight in (and this is a rare thing in these days of high speeds) making poems. In the first part of a poem called 'Motorbike' the determinedly deadpan reportage gets engagingly sick of itself in the last line and the pose (which is to have no pose, in fact hardly even to be there) breaks down into the kind of solitary snort of laughter we emit when we catch ourselves daydreaming. In 'Motorbike' the daydream has been one that features the poet as the self-effacing master of an unswerving objectivity. Cheerfulness breaks in:

> The saddle is frozen solid.
> The chronically wet rubber sponge
> Inside the leopardskin cover
> Crunches like shingle.

> I hold my cuff
> And wipe off the surface rain,
> Lean over and flood the carburettor,
> Jump on the start again.
>
> A sneeze.
> A little plume of steam.
> The old tubes cough up a bit of phlegm
> Then fade.
>
> I have chronic catarrh, a raw ankle,
> Pinkeye, blackheads and foul hair.
> I have a humiliating sheepskin coat
> And I lust strangely after a new alternator.

None of the poem's mood is dissipated: rather, it is intensified. The set of accurate descriptions is referred back to a personality, and for once you feel that the machine is not just flying, but being flown. The characteristic poseless pose of some of Mr. Williams's contemporaries has here been transcended; made to look monolithic, cumbersome. When produced by his multiple self, even the smaller poems work:

> Voices at night in summer.
> I lie in bed
> And hear them upside down
> And think I am in France

When produced by the mono-man reporter, the smaller poems remain very small indeed:

> Broken mauve lightning.
> The rooks
> Explode upwards
> Out of the mauve bracken.

Doubtless this is accurate, but then so were comparable notes in Turner's sketchbooks. Afterwards, however, he was always careful to go home and do the painting.

Throughout *Sugar Daddy* there are small moments of information about a smashed marriage. Hamilton-style, the information is pushed at you one piece at a time, each piece with one flat edge so that finally you can assemble the perimeter of the jigsaw puzzle. With Ian Hamilton the expanse of tabletop inside this frame leads straight to the unutterable abyss. With Hugo Williams it remains a trifle wooden. He is at his best when most unguarded, consciously the poet making a poem, finishing his book with an unashamed flourish:

We move singly through streets,
The last of some sad species,
Pacing the floors of zoos.

Our luck homing forever
Backward through grasses
To the brink of another time.

9

CARING FOR CHILDREN

(a) INSTANT ADULTS

IVY PINCHBECK and Margaret Hewitt have undertaken a substantial sociological survey of *Children in English Society*, from which it appears that childhood is a modern luxury. Not until compulsory education provided a protected growing-period did it acquire 'an independent and recognizable status'. In the mid-eighteenth century, 75 per cent of the children in London were dead before they were five. It is not surprising that parents deliberately trained themselves not to place their hopes and affections in barks so frail. There was little encouragement to make plans for them before they had demonstrated that they would survive to become adults by actually doing so. There was moreover every reason to hasten the desired end. If life is to be short it is as well to enter into the fullness of it early. Now that we have made a safer world for them, they can be children more completely and for longer than ever before, a situation ironically little to their taste. In every child there is an adult trying to get out, and if in the past it was the child that was suppressed today it is the adult, condemned to the artificial and insulated world of the classroom and not very grateful for it.

At one time, the precocious maturity for which modern children yearn was forced upon them whether they would or no. They had not even, Miss Pinchbeck and Miss Hewitt say, any special dress before the end of the eighteenth century; but that is to overlook the distinctive 'motley' of the household fool, which was simply a child's long petticoats, made up in a hard-wearing, stain-resistant material, and retained in adult life by someone who was recognizably immature.

(a) IVY PINCHBECK AND MARGARET HEWITT: *Children in English Society*. Volume I: From Tudor Times to the Eighteenth Century. 346 pp. Routledge and Kegan Paul. £2.80.

LEVIN L. SCHUCKING: *The Puritan Family*. Translated by Brian Battershaw. 196 pp. Routledge and Kegan Paul. £1.75.

(b) C. LACEY: *Hightown Grammar: The School as a Social System*. 214 pp. Manchester University Press. £2.75.

The long coat of the blue-coat boy reproduces this uniform. Formal portraits are another matter. There the child is in his best. Cornelia Bunch, aged two months in 1581, is still swaddled, but her braided velvet jacket and elaborate starched cap would not disgrace a maid of honour. When her two months became seven years—if they ever did —she was legally ready for the marriage-market. She is plainly a lady of property and marriage for her would be a deal in real estate. Marriages were in fact celebrated between even younger children, a girl of two contracted to a boy of three, 'hired for an apple bie his uncle to go to the Church'.

If she escaped marriage in infancy, a possible fate but not a common one, she was likely to be sent away at an early age to be brought up in some other household and perhaps never see her home again. She might not particularly want to, since deaths in the family and remarriages quickly changed its composition. Whether they liked it or not, boys and girls were forced to be early independent. The extreme reserve of the Elizabethans, their wariness and secrecy, was something they acquired very young. The queen herself had been through this mill, introduced in girlhood to ambition and intrigue at their most ruthless, though it was never demanded of her, as it was of seventeen-year-old Jane Grey, that she practise her carefully inculcated decorum on a scaffold.

It is possible that the society that demanded such early maturity was in some ways itself immature, so that children had less to live up to. Many must have carried an unfulfilled childhood into adult life and acted it out there. It was a decorous and formal but also a violent society. Life was hard for everybody. It was peculiarly hard on the children who, when they were given an adult rating early, were obviously going to be given a low one. Their youth kept them at a perpetual disadvantage. Life in the teens was in some ways not so unlike what it is today.

Pleasures and desired responsibilities were prohibited because a child was still a child, frustrations and duties imposed for the same reason. A girl might marry at fourteen, but was not therefore judged to be emotionally mature. Daniel, writing his *Civil Wars*, fears he may be criticized for making Richard II's little queen speak so eloquently of her griefs, in a way beyond a child's capacity. But the poet appeals for justification to 'the young Ladies of England (who peradventure will thinke themselves of age sufficient, at 14 yeares, to have a feeling of their owne estates)'.

It would be wrong to suppose that in the sixteenth century child welfare was not taken seriously, if unsentimentally, to heart. Arranged marriages were to benefit the family, of which the child was a member, and to secure his future. The training given by strangers was to avoid the partiality of parent for child (still a major reason for the existence of boarding schools) and to cement valuable connexions as early as possible. It shocked foreign observers, who thought it callous and unnatural, but the children were placed with care in good households, and it has always been an open question whether parents are the best people to bring up their own offspring; Thomas More made Utopians regulate the number of children in any one family, 'of the age of fourteen years or thereabout . . . for of children under this age no number can be prescribed or appointed', by putting 'them that in fuller families be above the number into families of smaller increase'.

Tudor legislators showed to advantage when confronted by a destitute child. They acknowledged that he must be adequately equipped to take his place in an ordered society. He was to be housed, clothed, fed, educated, taught his duty to God and man and, with proper regard for his aptitudes, instructed in a trade or profession. He might be an embarrassment but he was potentially a good citizen. The diet sheets of Christ's Hospital are generous, feather beds, sheets and blankets were provided. Some waifs were said to have been so shaken by the change to good food and clean surroundings that they 'dyed downe righte'. For those who could take it, it was enviable comfort and excellent training, only too successful in making men of the boys. Half the country had children they would have been glad to install in such an institution. There were destitute children in abundance, and destitute parents if it comes to that. The tide of need always rose higher than the means to contain it, and you cannot make men on the cheap.

But not till every squalid and callous shift had been tried did the country finally face this fact. The Tudor approach was paternalistic, idealistic and authoritarian. The authors of this survey find it came nearer to realizing the aims of the welfare state than any period in between. By the late seventeenth and eighteenth century the picture had altered. The child in care was then painfully at risk. Few were willing to lay out on him anything like what he cost or to make any but the most illiberal assessment of his need. He was no longer seen in terms of what could be made of him, not even of what it would cost to make it, but simply, as long as he lived and breathed, as a charge. His latter end was nobody's concern provided he ceased to be chargeable. A destitute child was a burden on the rates. Put him to work as soon as possible, which meant at seven years old, and send him to a parish as far away as possible, where whatever became of him he would be seen and heard of no more.

John Locke was a humane and enlightened man. His *Report for the Reform of the Poor Law*, presented to the Board of Trade in 1697, bears a chilling resemblance to Swift's *Modest Proposal*. It has precisely that sensible, rational, calculating tone and the conclusions, though they fall far short of breeding the children of the poor for the tables of the rich, as in Swift's horrible fantasy, are sufficiently disquieting to modern ears. The children are to be taken from their parents and brought up in Work Houses, whereby

the mother will be eased of a great part of her trouble in looking after and providing for them at home, and so be at more liberty to work and the children will be kept in much better order, be better provided for, and from their infancy be inured to work, which is of no small consequence in making them sober and industrious all their lives after

instead of being 'maintained in idleness, so that their labour is also generally lost to the public, till they are twelve or fourteen years old'. The age at which Locke proposes to set them to lucrative work is three, for

it may reasonably be concluded that computing all the earnings of a child from three to fourteen years of age, the nourishment and teaching of such a child during the whole time would cost the parish nothing, whereas there is no child now which is maintained by the parish, but before the age of 14 costs the parish fifty or sixty pounds.

Even outside the workhouses, the working child was no rarity. Defoe reports of Yorkshire in 1724 that there was 'hardly anything above four Years old but its Handes are sufficient to itself'. Locke envisaged clean and decent residential training centres. Few such existed in fact, and it was an open question whether a child fared better in a fetid herd or boarded out for a lump sum.

So much for the Restoration and the voice of Reason. What of the Saints? Inevitably one wishes to know what contribution puritanism made to the treatment of the child. Was the change of attitude between Elizabeth's Privy Council and Locke's Board of Trade in any way attributable to the Interregnum? The Civil War could not do other than disrupt civil life and the disappearance of the Privy Council meant that there was no central authority with power to see paper-schemes properly implemented. It is only fair however to acknowledge that the puritan system itself enjoyed no long period of peaceful establishment and what we see of it after 1660 is its ruins, many of its ideals cynically prostituted to ends abhorrent to it.

The centre of puritan life was the Christian family, and this might seem to promise well for child-care. But it had faults of self-centredness and self-sufficiency. It made life particularly hard for those outside its bounds, and they were many. Sixteenth-century Norwich had noted how the poor 'when their bellies were filled . . . fell to lust and concupiscence, and most shamefullie abused their bodies, and brought forth basterdes in such quantitie that it passed belief'. By the eighteenth century the attitude to foundlings was that they ought not to exist and even to take cognisance of their existence was to encourage them unduly. Captain Coram had to fight heavy prejudice before he could found his Hospital and provide London, in 1739, with an amenity that the great continental cities took for granted. Christ's Hospital, designed for poor boys, had already been taken over by higher income groups.

Education was by no means undervalued by dissenters and, with the church schools closed to them, they began to provide their own academies, progressive because unfettered by tradition. But however important education for life and labour might be, there was a prior claim on every parent and teacher, and that was the child's soul. The sober respect for divine authority, carefully fostered under the Tudors, because upon it the whole social order was founded, gave way to an impassioned pursuit of salvation, a great drama in which the child was called upon to play his part almost as soon as he stepped on to this mortal stage. The worst misfortune that could possibly happen to him was to remain unaware that hell gaped beneath the boards. The burden of Bunyan's pilgrim could be irksome and even crippling when it was laid on young shoulders. Though casualties in this psychological war are hard to assess, Miss Pinchbeck and Miss Hewitt have the support of Professor Schücking when they assume them to have been considerable. Certainly among the adult population the suicide rate soared, and after the Restoration it dropped in a spectacular way.

The Puritan Family traces the influence of puritan patterns of conduct upon English life, using as sources the proliferating conduct books, such as *Oeconomia Christiana* by William Perkins (1590), *Of*

Domesticall Duties by William Gouge (1622), *Matrimonial Honour* by Daniel Rogers (1642) and many more. From the teachers he turns to the creative writers, Milton and Bunyan, Richardson, Defoe and the later novelists, among whom the urge to teach is still very much in evidence. They show principles put into practice. We have waited forty years for this work to be translated from the German. Nothing published in the meanwhile replaces it or even goes far towards taking up its particular challenges, though an introduction generously acknowledges that valuable work has been done in the field.

Puritanism, for Schücking, is a very English phenomenon. He surveys it with a lively interest, eyebrows sometimes raised a little or lips twitching, but basically with respect. Few people who actually consult the conduct books or who see their ideals realized among the Cromwells, the Hutchinsons, the Baxters, fail to pay them this tribute. The English puritans, determined to live in the world without being of the world, to compete for the immortal garland in the dust and heat where alone they thought it was to be won, set themselves a task truly heroic, and possible only to those capable of a most rigorous self-discipline. Thus Schücking can distinguish the puritan by his sobriety and self-control, which means that, rightly or wrongly, he overlooks the ranter and the enthusiast. He sees reason set above passion (and hence husband above wife, and parent above child). Emotion was suspect, and English life has been in some respects the poorer ever since. It has also been riddled with hypocrisy and mealy-mouthed materialism. This—at any rate among our neighbours—is notorious. More admirable consequences are less advertised.

The puritan teachers set a high value on marriage, accepted sexuality as natural and good, and at the same time could conceive of a relationship between husband and wife which transcended it. This is mirrored in Milton's divorce pamphlets, which Schücking does not invoke, and in his prelapsarian paradise, which he does. Yet Milton's Adam and Eve betray a major source of tension in the puritan family. They dramatize the subordination of the woman and the disregard of her maternal role. Milton's attitude is more subtle than Schücking's interpretation of it, but certainly Eve can never attain her full stature so long as she is childless, and Adam, if it comes to that, is hampered by the absence of his fellow men. Two people cannot represent society, even though they ask an angel to breakfast and meet the devil under an apple tree. Milton's obsessive regard for God the Father is repeated in the puritan concept of the family, where the

father is paramount. The extent of his control over his children's
marriage-choices is without parallel among Catholics, Lutherans or
Calvinists: 'Here we come upon one of the most characteristic
qualities of English civilization—namely, a tendency to cleave with
quite remarkable strictness to the principles of the very oldest ecclesiastical law, which tends to follow Roman Law.' That puritan piety
was not new-minted, but derived many of its features from the
medieval past, is one of Schücking's major contentions.

The absence of social contacts in Eden may reflect another facet of
puritan life, or at least of puritan teaching. The many handbooks
which instruct children in their duty to their parents, and parents to
their children, pay no attention to how children should behave to one
another. The brother-sister relationship, barely acknowledged, seems
to have been exploited largely for the purpose of a rivalry in righteous-
ness. One remembers how terrifying is the loneliness of the human
soul when Christian abandons his wife and family in the City of
Destruction and sets out on his perilous journey. But Bunyan makes
ample amends, especially in the too-often despised Part II of *The
Pilgrim's Progress*, where women and children, the weaklings and
cripples, the self-doubters and all the poor miseries gather under the
conduct of Mr. Great-Heart, and find the Valley of Humiliation 'as
fruitful a place as any the crow flies over'.

Having noted how delicate and true is the feeling often displayed
by puritan writers, especially with regard to the marriage relationship, Schücking finds it the more surprising that they had so little
comprehension of a child's mind. Miss Pinchbeck and Miss Hewitt
join him in calling attention to that 'ignorance of developmental
psychology, which is so striking a characteristic of the thinking of our
forebears'. One wonders whether it was ignorance so much as a dis-
parity of aims. What our forefathers elicited from their children was
something that they wanted and we do not. Moreover the children
were capable of supplying it. Much of it was harmless mimicry, as
when babes in arms were taught to lisp pious phrases like Presby-
terian parrots croaking 'Down with the Pope'. Probably children
still play at preaching sermons, if—though it seems less probable—
they still sit through them. When it comes to the moral training given
in the home, as instanced by the way Susannah Wesley brought up
her family, just at the turn of the seventeenth century, Miss Pinchbeck
and Miss Hewitt are more than respectful, both to its aims and its
efficiency:

H

The positive advantages of contemporary training, of building up character and of instilling a profound sense of social and moral obligation should not be lightly dismissed. It may well be asked whether more recent generations have yet devised as effective a system of moral training for the young.

It may also be asked what sort of world these young people made in the nineteenth century for their less fortunate or less enlightened neighbours. It was by no means uniquely their world, but their pattern of self-discipline spread far beyond the frontiers of faith. Self-discipline lays a firm platform from which the self can operate effectively. It is a beginning. What sort of self then operates and to what ends is another question. It is to be feared that the second volume of the survey may make painful reading, with the Industrial Revolution looming. But at the same time it is the volume that will discuss the cures which have been found for pressing evils. History proceeds by trial and error and error must often be gross indeed before it is recognized and corrected.

Miss Pinchbeck and Miss Hewitt have sifted a great deal of very varied material, much of it hard to assess. Their presentation of it is orderly, balanced and fair-minded. They quote a good deal, and are not immune from the difficulties of proof-reading texts from the sixteenth and seventeenth centuries. Nothing is highly coloured. Nothing needs to be. This is the story of how the children of England lived and died through three centuries, what society did about them and why. They were not little rabbits to run off into the grass and fend for themselves. They were and still are a charge upon us; only the word charge can be differently interpreted.

(b) NORTH COUNTRY SCHOLARS

HERE IS an attempt to study a school in detail as part of a wider purpose, which is to see how in practice the broader statistical analyses of the sociologists stand up to examination at very close range. Mr. Lacey is apparently by training a social anthropologist, and his work was done largely under the direction of Professor Max Gluckman and in association with Professor Peter Worsley of Manchester University. He chose the grammar school of a small county borough in Lancashire, presumably near Manchester, which under almost any reform of local government would be swallowed up by a larger authority. Lancashire has a number of small county boroughs which are education authorities in their own right, and most of them do not have a reputation for outstanding educational leadership. Some of the reasons become apparent in *Hightown Grammar*.

'Hightown' is a predominantly working-class community, and such middle-class children as there are seem to go to the direct grant schools in the neighbouring town. The school was first of all a higher level secondary school, which even in the early 1900s was remarkable for the number of its pupils of working-class origin. Since working-class origin and early leaving age tend to be closely correlated, especially in the north of England, it was inevitable that it would be some time before the school developed a strong sixth form. Indeed, one of the first lessons of the book is that the grammar school, as presented by its more staunch protagonists, is largely an invention of the 1950s. They were, of course, originally created by the 1902 Act, and they were named by H. T. (father of M.) Muggeridge, so as to give them status. Few, if any, have a tradition going back beyond the 1902 Act which would bear close historical examination.

In his study of the material surviving from the 1910s and 1920s, Mr. Lacey shows the average age of entry falling towards $11\frac{1}{2}$; thus the pattern, which now seems so common, of a transfer at the age of 11 was only firmly established in the 1930s. In those times the normal secondary school course was three years. A substantial number of boys did not complete this course and, as Mr. Lacey points out, the pattern of academic qualifications was largely irrelevant to their employment opportunities. What employers were looking for was 'a good class of boy'—probably in many senses of that phrase—with some kind of secondary education. In Mr. Lacey's terms, the school was largely a finishing school—this although four-fifths of its entry were scholarship boys, and the town was predominantly a working-class town.

In 1932 the national government reduced the number of scholarships and replaced them by a system of free places, thus anticipating the heroic response to a national economic crisis adopted by Mr. Gordon Walker thirty-five years later. By this time, however, the school had become much more closely related to examinations, school certificates, and matriculation. In the 1930s a sixth-former won a state scholarship. This was so unusual that the school was given a whole day's holiday. At the same time a higher proportion of children from parents with relatively high social backgrounds started going to the

school. Now Hightown Grammar School became more representative of the local community and also manifested some of the later
social trends which were to be regarded as characteristic of grammar
schools in the 1940s and 1950s.

Interestingly enough, at this period the working-class boys began
to do better in examinations than the lower middle-class boys. Mr.
Lacey examines a number of reasons for this, of which the most
subtle and possibly the most cogent seems to be that the lower-middle-
class boys still had access to jobs, whereas the working-class boys
faced unemployment and therefore remained at the school and
worked hard to get qualifications which would enable them to get
jobs like teaching. And the evidence for this is that after the Second
World War, when the grammar school as we now know it began to
emerge and the sixth form grew in size, the lower-middle-class boys
again began to do better in examinations than the working-class boys.
Parents were beginning to recognize that education led to good jobs,
the teachers were beginning to think that their main function was to
prepare pupils for further education and in particular the universities
and, above all, the local authority was beginning to give its support
for a big and successful grammar school, since this was a hallmark of
progressive educational policies. Thus the reform of 1944 was not
followed to any degree by an increased working-class recruitment.
Indeed, by 1957 the proportion of working-class entrants was the
same as in 1905. The change was in the rise of the school's social
status, which was reflected in an increase in the number of pupils
from the more prosperous middle-class.

Many people still find it difficult to accept the evidence of a
relationship between social class and educational performance, but
there is one astonishing table in Mr. Lacey's book which shows that
the range of percentages of children chosen for grammar school
education at the eleven-plus in six selected junior schools ran from
90 per cent at one prep school to 2 per cent at one Church of England
junior school, which reflects almost precisely the social class composition of those schools.

Interestingly enough, among those boys who pass the eleven-plus,
a proportion of able working-class boys choose the technical school
or schools with a lower social and academic status than the grammar
school, while of course a fairly high proportion of the clever middle-
class children go to direct grant schools outside the area. The author's
explanation for this is largely in terms of the attitude of the teachers in

the junior schools. These attitudes, of course, are not necessarily merely snobbish, but they may be based upon a realistic assessment of the likely progress of a child from a manual working-class home in what has undoubtedly by this time become the highly academic environment of the grammar school, progress which may be halting and difficult even for a clever boy and which may lead to an early drop-out.

This process of anticipatory socialization is a subtle one, and a valuable footnote shows exactly what Mr. Lacey is getting at:

The expectations are acquired over a long period of time. An illustration of this process concerns two cubs who were examined for their 'house orderly' badges some three months before they were due to take the eleven-plus examination, and nearly a year before they entered secondary schools. They were both middle-class boys who lived in the same district, and went to the same school. During the afternoon I observed the boys at a number of tasks, for example, cleaning windows, sewing on buttons and cooking a simple meal. One boy immediately impressed by his self-assurance, competence and politeness. The other struggled with his tasks, frequently giggled, made silly remarks and, in all, only narrowly passed this essentially practical test. In conversation afterwards, the competent boy revealed that he expected to go to B school, a high-prestige direct grant school. His sister had gone there, so had several boys from his school and he felt fairly confident he could make the grade. The other boy said he was going to go to the Technical High School. He said he liked and was good at practical things and, therefore, preferred the technical side. In fact, he had shown that he was relatively poor on the 'practical' side, but had learnt, mainly from his junior school, that this was the standard to which he could aspire.

The author is fascinating when he describes the mechanism by which successful pupils remain successful. He shows that the school takes what are—quite justifiably—regarded as the 'best pupils' from the junior schools. The boys from the successful junior schools come into the grammar school with a considerable number of friends from the same school, and they are therefore accustomed to rivalry among themselves to be best pupils, and they soon adapt wholly to the norms of the grammar school. He then, in a detailed description of the way the classes behave, shows how different pupils create expectations of what they will do and then live up to these expectations. Sometimes clever boys from poor homes are able to win the sympathy and engagement of the school, including their own fellow pupils, in order to do much better than those boys who come from advantaged homes. This is obvious, of course, to anybody who has ever been to

school, but the actual mechanism has rarely been better described
than in this book.

Mr. Lacey develops a model based upon social and academic
differentiation which develops into polarization—that is to say, there
will be some pupils who identify strongly with the school and its
values and go on to academic success, and others who consciously
reject the school. Incidentally, it emerges from remarks occasionally
occurring in the book that the school was deeply concerned about
the progress of its pupils. There were parent-teacher evenings and
many other occasions on which the teachers and the parents discussed
in great detail the progress of the children. Mr. Lacey refuses to
accept the polarization as being total. Some very 'bad' boys were
interested in their work while some boys who were very good at
their work can be very bad outside it. This somewhat obvious statement is a summary of a fairly complex piece of interpretation of the
evidence, which suggests that a very strong 'anti-group' rarely
develops in the grammar school, whereas in other schools there is
evidence of anti-groups persistently developing who oppose the whole
culture of the school.

Mr. Lacey comes to the important and alarming conclusion that, as
educational achievement becomes increasingly stratified, many working-class parents may well recognize the value of education but find
themselves without the knowledge or understanding to sustain their
children through academic courses, and will therefore seek to protect
their children against the school in some sense rather than to interpret
one to the other. In his detailed case studies Mr. Lacey shows an
astonishing amount of effort by the school to help the pupils who
need help, but quite often this attempt to give help is misinterpreted
by the parents, thus leading to academic failure.

The masters at the school were predominantly local boys, many of
whom had been to the local university, though six had been to Cambridge. There were some non-graduate members of the staff teaching
art and physical education (which perhaps is fairly characteristic of
the low status of these subjects in northern grammar schools).
Though local boys, however, the masters lived not in Hightown but
in the middle-class areas near by. The turnover of staff was fairly
high, usually in order to seek promotion. In striking contrast to
American schools (as revealed in American sociological studies cited
by the author), there was no control by the community over the staff;
the teachers were free socially to behave as they wished and were free

academically to teach as they wished. Though there was a fairly
articulated bureaucratic system within the school, the author emphasizes how unbureaucratic the system actually was, and how frequent and informal the contact was between masters and boys
throughout the school.

There was a house system which the headmaster had introduced in
order to help individual children, but this obviously was a fairly artificial system and was resented by older members of the staff who felt
that it involved extra work to little purpose and for little extra pay.
Their career pattern depended ultimately upon the academic department more than upon the house work. It is interesting to learn how
far the masters were involved in the very vigorous sporting programme for the school, which was running eight or more rugger and
soccer teams every week. Furthermore the whole spirit of the school
depended upon the enthusiasm of the staff:

The jobs available within the school were open to innovation and enlargement. A keen new member of staff might start a judo club or resuscitate a
moribund cross-country running or canoeing club. Activities of this sort
could bring an aspiring teacher into the limelight. The activity would be
mentioned by the headmaster in prayers, the member of staff praised for
his initiative, and once the activity was established it became a regular and
public part of school life. As it became established, so the name of the
master responsible became associated with it and gained acceptance.

One criticism that Mr. Lacey makes of this highly motivated school
is that the staff were expected to teach too much. They would have to
see between 120 and 180 faces in one day, and this was too many for
them to get to know all the boys intimately. On the other hand, it was
obvious that a great many of the masters got to know individual boys
extremely well, even though it was rare for a boy and a master, at
least in the junior years, to have private conversations outside the
classroom.

One important point is obscured, which is that to a considerable
extent the school is an intellectual community, indeed almost the
only intellectual community in a rather run-down place like Hightown. Many of the staff and some of the boys would come to appreciate the intellectual and cultural tradition of which the grammar
school in this town is part. Mr. Lacey obviously values this tradition,
but it is difficult to find out from this study exactly what part it plays.
In any case, Mr. Lacey's important conclusion is that there is tremen-
dous energy and drive towards academic achievement. Unfortunately

a great deal of this energy and drive goes to waste because what is only *relative* failure in the competitive process at an early stage demoralizes a number of boys. In absolute terms they are doing fairly well. Relatively, however, they are failures. They become anti-school and they leave. He argues strongly that all children respond to praise and encouragement, and that a system which gives them praise and encouragement at frequent intervals will probably bring a large number of failures forward. He also argues that even greater personal involvement by the staff on an individual basis with the lives of the boys and a systematic and trained attempt to deal with social problems would help many children.

Altogether, parents and teachers as well as people interested in the social sciences are likely to find this a fascinating, thoughtful and sympathetic study.

IO
NEW USES FOR ANTHROPOLOGY
(a) CONFRONTING THE CLASSICS

THE FIRST EDITION of Frazer's *The Golden Bough* was published in 1890. It was a work of orthodox scholarship which adopted the unusual device of using ethnographic comparison to help explain the classical legends surrounding the shrine of Diana Nemorensis near Aricia in Roman Italy. This was only the beginning of a liaison between classical scholarship and the unscholarly world of social anthropology which lasted for several decades. Much of this later development resulted from the enthusiasm of another Cambridge classicist, Jane Harrison. Inspired by functionalist arguments which appear in their final form in Durkheim's *The Elementary Forms of the Religious Life*, she carried cross-cultural analogy so far that study of the cult practices of Australian aborigines became an essential preliminary to any reading of the plays of Aeschylus.

Perhaps it is not altogether surprising that in subsequent generations the more orthodox members of the Cambridge classical faculty have found the mere mention of anthropology an embarrassment. Even so, there has been a persisting Cambridge tradition, currently reflected in the work of M. I. Finley, which holds that despite the

---

(a) G. S. KIRK: *Myth.* 299 pp. Cambridge University Press. £3.25.

(b) MARY DOUGLAS (Editor): *Witchcraft Confessions and Accusations.* 387 pp. Tavistock. £3.15.

LUCY MAIR: *Witchcraft.* 256 pp. Weidenfeld and Nicolson. World University Library. £1.50 (paperback, 80p).

H. R. TREVOR-ROPER: *The European Witch-Craze of the 16th and 17th Centuries.* 144 pp. Penguin. 25p.

ALAN MACFARLANE: *Witchcraft in Tudor and Stuart England.* 334 pp. Routledge and Kegan Paul. £4.50.

C. L'ESTRANGE EWEN: *Witchcraft and Demonianism.* Facsimile of 1933 Edition. 495 pp. Muller. £3.50.

BARBARA ROSEN (Editor): *Witchcraft.* 407 pp. Edward Arnold. £3.25.

ROBERT MANDROU: *Magistrats et sorciers en France au 17e siècle.* 583 pp. Paris: Plon. 45.90 fr.

CHADWICK HANSEN: *Witchcraft at Salem.* 252 pp. Hutchinson. £1.75.

misadventures of the past it would be profitable for all concerned if the classicists and the social anthropologists could somehow manage to pool their resources. G. S. Kirk, yet another Cambridge don, is a half-convinced convert to this thesis. He is impressed by the relevance for classical studies of some of the threads of argument which are currently fashionable among the anthropologists and, up to a point, he is prepared to borrow their clothes. At the same time he displays a very obvious anxiety lest his dabbling in anthropology should lead his colleagues to think that he has fallen a victim to the lures of functionalist reductionism after the manner of Jane Harrison.

In many respects the problems of classical scholarship and of social anthropology are diametrically opposed. The classicist is stuck with a deficiency of fragmentary data all in the form of written texts. His problem, like that of the prehistoric archaeologist, is to reconstruct, to give flesh and blood to the bones of a very incomplete skeleton. The anthropologist, on the other hand, is plagued with a plethora of data, his problem is one of surfeit: how to cut down the available information to a scale at which analysis becomes possible. For the anthropologist words are secondary; whatever is recorded in writing or on tape is peripheral to the ultimate object of inquiry, the behaviour of human beings. In contrast, for the classicist, a meticulous study of the text is an end in itself. Paucity of material and the need to concentrate on words rather than actions help to explain several of Professor Kirk's most characteristic attitudes.

In a formal sense he would like to make the category 'myth' extremely wide. In the course of his argument he distinguishes various sub-categories of the genre under such heads as folktale, legend, fairy-tale and oral tradition; but in general he avoids definition. Everything is myth which anyone has ever described as such; the word is a box category which includes all kinds of traditional tale which contain any element of fantasy. With this point of departure, the destination is rather obvious: 'there is no single type of myth'; 'unitary theories of mythical function are largely a waste of time'. But what Professor Kirk seems not to understand is that he and the anthropologists (and the theologians) are not talking about the same thing.

The theological position, which is also that of the majority of anthropologists, is that myth is 'a sacred tale'; that is to say a story which is felt by the teller to carry moral implication for the listener. It is this moral implication, the reference to 'unobservable realities', which is crucial, not the element of fantasy. The sacredness is the definition. For a believing Christian the whole of the Bible is a myth; it is true because it is sacred. If some of it also happens to be true because it is history that is quite another matter. For the anthropologist-theologian, myth and history are not mutually exclusive categories; for Professor Kirk it seems that they are. This perhaps explains his fondness for the work of the anthropologist Lévi-Strauss, who has hedged the myth versus history controversy by confining his attention to the fantasy stories recounted by primitive peoples 'who have no history'.

The 'sacred tale' definition of myth is automatically functionalist since the significance of the story lies, in part, in the listener's reaction; thus, by their own criteria, the anthropological formulas, 'myth is a charter for social action' (Malinowski), 'myth and ritual are one and the same' (Leach), which Professor Kirk declares to be false, are simply tautologies. However, Lévi-Strauss has glossed this orthodox thesis by pointing out that any moral injunction presupposes a cosmological schema which is necessarily a simplification of any observable reality. Consequently, myths are not *only* concerned with expressing moral injunctions, they are also unconsciously designed to mask the regressive series of contradictions which result from the lack of fit between the logic of morality and the facts of experience. In the outcome, according to Professor Kirk, Lévi-Strauss holds that 'all myths are speculative or problem solving when properly understood'.

Professor Kirk, who first established his reputation as a specialist on the pre-Socratic philosophers, finds this Lévi-Straussian doctrine much more relevant to his own field than the simpler myth = ritual thesis of the Robertson-Smith/Frazer tradition, and much of the new book consists of tentative applications of Lévi-Straussian technique to certain selected themes in Greek and ancient Mesopotamian mythology. But Professor Kirk's approval of Lévi-Strauss's structuralism is highly selective, and in his presentation of the methodology he partly omits and partly rejects two of its primary features—first, the need to demonstrate the existence of a common schema (cosmology) in terms of which the categories of the mythology can be seen to make sense; and second, the claim that it is possible to pursue an examination of variations on a theme in such a systematic way that any implication emerges as an objective fact, rather than as the consequence of the repeated injections of intuition by the analyst.

One result of this selective attitude is that when Professor Kirk himself comes to apply structuralist method to the myths of the ancient world the product is just as superficial and arbitrary as the hunches of his predecessors, and this leads him to opt for a total eclecticism. The general conclusion of the book seems to be that those who want to understand Greek mythology can pick up hints all round—Max Müller, Jane Harrison, Otto Rank, Cassirer, Lévi-Strauss and the Stith-Thompson Motif-Index are all on a par, but none of them should be taken very seriously. Odd as it may seem, in Professor Kirk's own hands structuralist analysis becomes a highly conservative instrument which leads us right back to solar mythology and E. B. Taylor:

> Consideration of Mesopotamian myths suggested that the development of nature-gods into city-gods, although in one way a simple narrative reaction, may also have had special motives: to emphasise the limitations of human institutions and relate them to the natural environment as a whole, to establish the natural and social order as products of inevitability and divine mastery, and to elicit new conclusions about natural and human fertility, nature and culture, life and death by the juxtaposition of separate mythical episodes. . . . This restatement brings out the emphasis on the narrative and speculative aspects of myth at the expense of their practical and ceremonial ones. That is because I have consistently been concerned to show the error of universalistic theories, like those of the myth-and-ritual school, that deny any problem reflecting aspects beyond what is implied by trivial aetiology.

As can be seen, Professor Kirk's mythmaker is a primitive philosopher. But Professor Kirk has not understood Lévi-Strauss. For the latter, the words 'motives' and 'reflecting' in the above quotation would seem wholly out of place. Lévi-Strauss's thesis is that philosophical problems are posed by the structural inconsistencies of the mythology and that the problems are 'solved' by the operations of the myths themselves; it is not a matter of intellectual speculation at all. Of course, Lévi-Strauss may be talking nonsense, but if his methodology is to be tested it should be given a fair run and not be misrepresented.

The shape of the book is as follows. Chapter one reviews the past history of classicist-anthropologist relations since the beginning of this century and adopts the somewhat irritating stance that whereas the author knows what he is talking about, the anthropologists do not. A good deal of the argument is taken up with a criticism of the view that the word 'myth' is best reserved for 'sacred tales';

Professor Kirk here relies upon a distinction between the terms 'sacred' and 'secular' which no anthropologist could accept. The precise grounds for the author's hostility to anthropological orthodoxy in this matter are nowhere clearly stated, but they are not difficult to understand. Later in the book he is going to apply anthropological techniques to classicist materials. Before he can do this he must first establish the principle that anthropological techniques of myth analysis, in particular those of Lévi-Strauss, are not necessarily dependent upon the functionalist myth = ritual definition which presupposes an intimate understanding of the ethnographic background. We really know very little about the ethnographic context of the ancient world, and if, as Malinowski might have argued, the Gilgamesh epic is necessarily incomprehensible when it is divorced from its ethnographic context, then the whole of Professor Kirk's endeavour would be futile. So the Malinowskian position must be demolished. To this end Professor Kirk embarks upon a somewhat disastrous foray into his opponent's camp.

Having first poured contempt on attempts by anthropologists to apply structuralist procedures to the analysis of Greek mythology, he reverses the operation and stakes a claim to understand Trobriand mythology better than Malinowski, who, he declares, 'seriously misrepresented the tone of some of the tales that he himself had collected'. Professor Kirk knows better. 'It can be seen that' a tale listed by Malinowski as an entertaining folktale (i.e. as non-sacred) 'is a variant of a highly important myth'. Malinowski is long dead and fair game, and the story to which Professor Kirk draws our attention is certainly more interesting than Malinowski suggested; but, in fact, Professor Kirk quite misses the point. If he had understood his Trobriand ethnography he would have realized that the 'father and two daughters' are not kin but that they are an inversion of a real life 'father's sister and two sons' who would be in a sexual joking relationship. The explanation which Professor Kirk offers—'that these stories are concerned with the origin and functioning of the *kula*'—is borrowed from one which Malinowski himself applied to quite a different set of stories. The ogre who eats the father and then mates with one of the daughters is rated by Professor Kirk to be just 'an additional motif'. Others might feel that he was the central character. But, in any case, given its Trobriand context, the 'folktale' which he wants to reclassify as a 'myth' is an almost exact transformation of our own 'folktale' of Little Red Riding Hood. If

Professor Kirk's objective here was to show that stories can be evaluated by content alone without regard to context, he made an unfortunate choice. If the anthropologists want to rewrite their Malinowski they had better choose a different guide.

Chapter two is designed to give an outline of Lévi-Strauss's technique of myth interpretation. Anthropological professionals are again likely to feel embarrassed. The sources are *The Story of Asdiwal* and the first few myths from *The Raw and the Cooked*, but the result is only half-baked, or perhaps just smoked, like that unpopular wartime notability who was known as the Kipper—'a two-faced bastard without any guts'. Bits and pieces of the structural idiom come through reasonably well—all that stuff about binary oppositions—but the hard core of the matter, the crucial significance of a cosmological schema, the nature of structural transformations, the difference between metaphoric and metonymic symbolic associations (which was understood even by Frazer) are all missing, or at any rate so lost in fog as to be indistinguishable. If Professor Kirk's classical colleagues have got to suffer the indignity of being indoctrinated into structuralist theory they deserve better treatment than this.

Professor Kirk then goes on to explain why he feels he must in any case reject a number of key Lévi-Straussian principles, notably that which says that all discoverable versions in a set of stories are equally relevant for our understanding of the common structure. The argument here gives the impression that when Professor Kirk writes about the 'structure' of a myth he is referring to some quality of a very superficial kind closely linked with manifest content rather than to Lévi-Strauss's algebra of 'relations between relations'.

With Chapters three and four, Professor Kirk at last begins to mind his own business rather than the anthropologists' and immediately becomes much more interesting. He first applies his emasculated Lévi-Straussian technique to various Sumerian and Akkadian stories. The procedure brings to light a number of features which earlier commentators have overlooked, but suffers from the same defect as Lévi-Strauss's own work on South American myth. Professor Kirk necessarily works with English-language summaries of stories, derived originally from a totally alien culture, which have come down to us only in a severely mutilated form.

If one goes back to the original source material and takes note of the degree of uncertainty in the translations and also the large number of minor details which occur in the original text but which are ignored by the author, the area of doubt becomes enormous. It is again noticeable that the 'level' at which Professor Kirk claims to detect structural similarity is very superficial, so that the nature of the mythical paradox never comes into the open.

A case in point is the comparison between the story of Enki and Ninhursag and that of Enlil and Ninlil. Professor Kirk claims that 'the structural similarity between the two myths is really remarkable' and then proceeds to list six *similarities of content* in the two stories; for instance, 'in each case a very young goddess is instructed not to approach the water . . . in each case she does so and is immediately impregnated by the god. In each case the act of impregnation is repeated several times more . . .', and so on. But according to structuralist theory the interest should lie not in similarities of content at all but in contrasts of relationship, and though these are present in this case Professor Kirk fails to bring them out. Thus, if we confine our attention only to those details which the author himself has happened to stress, we might notice the following distinctions between the first story (A) and the second story (B):

A. Male God (X) prohibits child goddess to bathe
B. Goddess   urges   child goddess (Y) to bathe
A. Sexual acts are repeatedly incestuous—father with daughter
B. Sexual acts are all between man and wife
A. Female consort of X goes to underworld
B. Male   consort of Y goes to underworld

Professor Kirk himself concludes that the moral implication of these stories is that 'the pursuit of fertility can be carried to excess; if it is so carried, it tends to result in infertility'; a deeper-level structural analysis of the sort indicated above would certainly lead to quite different conclusions.

But even though Professor Kirk's brand of structuralism is very much a matter of 'Lévi-Strauss without tears', it remains interesting, and chapter four, which gives a relatively extended analysis of the Gilgamesh epic and stories relating to the Centaurs and the Cyclopes, is thoroughly worthwhile. Much more could be made of this material if the treatment were more systematic, but this is a valuable beginning.

Chapter five is a very crowded affair. Despite an innocuous title, 'The Qualities of Greek Myths', it in fact ranges over a vast area of Germanic, Egyptian, Hindu, Hurrian, Hittite and Canaanite mythology. However, the heart of the matter comes at the end, where Professor Kirk is addressing himself mainly to his professional colleagues. The orthodox view of Greek intellectual development is that Hesiod stood at the watershed of mythopoeic thought and modern rationalism:

The birth of philosophy in Europe consisted in the abandonment, at the level of conscious thought, of mythological solutions to problems concerning the origins and nature of the universe and the processes that go on within it. For religious faith there is substituted the faith that was and is the basis of scientific thought . . . that the visible world conceals a rational and intelligible order.

This goes along with the view that Greek mythology, as we now have it, is the folklore of an altogether special and superior people: 'Their legends are almost without exception free from the cloudiness, the wild grotesques and the horrible features which beset the popular traditions of less gifted and happy peoples.' Professor Kirk advocates a different theory to the effect that, in the terms of the development of Greek thought, Hesiod is late rather than early. We put him at the beginning simply because he is the earliest that we have. But in Professor Kirk's view the 'rational attrition' of Greek mythology may have begun 'centuries or even millennia before Hesiod'. In that case the emergence of philosophy was not a *bouleversement* which suddenly substituted rational thought for mythopoeic thought but a slow evolution in which the elements of deeply imaginative fantasy (which we must assume once formed a part of the proto-Greek mythical tradition) gradually became subsumed and replaced by the speculations of individual thinkers. The great tragedians of the fifth century were not, as Jane Harrison supposed, refashioning an active religious tradition; it was rather that they took the residue of a very ancient 'transitional and schematized mythology as a datum and with new techniques constructed out of it an erratic but vivid new world of myths'.

The final chapter takes us back to where we began. A myth for Professor Kirk is simply a traditional tale; and since there are all kinds of traditional tales, unitary theories about myth are a waste of time. The fact that the unitary theories about which he complains define myth in quite a different way is again ignored. He again misrepresents Malinowski and again concedes that there is some merit in Lévi-Strauss. The general drift of the argument is to persuade the reader that a myth can usefully be thought of as a thing in itself, a product of the creative activity of a long series of individual story-tellers, and that the ritual context in which these storytellers operated can safely be left out of the account. 'And in the end the firmest part of our study will continue to be the careful and sympathetic analysis of actual documents, surviving myths themselves'. That is, no doubt, a very proper attitude for a classical scholar to adopt; but if that is the classicists' last word, then the gulf between classics and anthropology will remain unbridgeable.

(b) WITCHES IN CONTEXT

THE BELIEF IN witchcraft has strong claims to be the most widespread delusion ever to trouble the human race. Few pre-industrial societies, in modern Africa and Melanesia, or in medieval and early modern Europe seem to have been free of it, and it is not entirely extinct even in the modern West. Until recently few historians have apparently regarded the subject as worthy of interest, and most of them have confined themselves to more or less dubious estimates of casualties by judicial murder. Even Professor Trevor-Roper's ingenious and wide-ranging essay, *The European Witch-Craze of the 16th and 17th Centuries*, is a history of persecution, not of witchcraft beliefs and their social significance. Only during the past decade have some historians begun to exploit the insights to be found in the studies of modern withcraft made by social anthropologists, and to show the subject in a radically new light.

The inspiration for almost all the anthropological work on the subject can be found in E. E. Evans-Pritchard's classic work, *Witchcraft, Oracles and Magic among the Azande*, first published in 1937. Few books can have had a comparable influence in a modern scholarly discipline, and it was a happy idea for the Association of Social Anthropologists to pay tribute to Evans-Pritchard, on the eve of his retirement, by holding a conference on the subject of witchcraft. The resulting volume is a notably successful festschrift for two reasons: it has a powerful unifying theme, and it fulfils Evans-Pritchard's long-standing ambition to bring historians and anthropologists together.

Perhaps because they are working a largely untilled field, it is the historians who make the most distinctive contributions to *Witchcraft Confessions and Accusations*, edited by Professor Mary Douglas.

I

Peter Brown's subtle and provocative essay on sorcery in late an-
tiquity, and Keith Thomas's brilliant analysis of English witchcraft in
anthropological terms are both very important and original pieces,
which deserve a wide public. Alan Macfarlane's summary of his work
on Essex is also valuable, but is naturally rendered less important by
the almost simultaneous publication of the full-length study, *Witchcraft in Tudor and Stuart England*, on which it is based. Only Norman
Cohn's brief essay on Satanism disappoints: it is little more than a
survey of well-known facts, and strikes a rather superficial note. It is
odd, in the context of his argument, that Professor Cohn does not
mention the book by Gougenot des Mousseaux, *Moeurs et pratiques
des démons*, which was published fifteen years before his well-known
anti-semitic treatise *Le Juif, le judaïsme et la judaïsation des peuples
chrétiens*, and makes the link between the witchcraft beliefs and the
fabrication of the Protocols of the Elders of Zion more explicit.

While historians are borrowing analytical tools from them, the
anthropologists themselves are beginning to question the assumptions
which have guided their work to date. Several of the authors in this
volume are attempting to find new approaches which could lead to a
greater theoretical sophistication. As Professor Douglas points out
in her stimulating introduction, the functional analysis of witchcraft
beliefs has not yet taken us very far beyond Evans-Pritchard's
pioneer work. Despite all the multifarious variations that have been
uncovered, the picture given remains that of a flexible response to
tensions within society and to individual misfortune. It is evident that
the lack of a temporal perspective has been a great handicap to the
evolution of any generalized explanation which could claim predictive
accuracy, and there has been some rather loose writing on the relationship between witchcraft beliefs and social change, plausible but
ultimately untestable.

These difficulties can clearly be related to an internal crisis affecting
the whole discipline of social anthropology, as it seeks to move beyond the ethnographical phase, in which the dynamics of individual
cultures and societies have been uncovered, towards a more synthetic
approach which would relate them to one another. The failings of
Lévi-Strauss's grand structuralist theories seem all too obvious to
Anglo-Saxon anthropologists, but perhaps it is a pity that he has not
spun one of his fanciful webs of sense and nonsense around the subject of witchcraft. For as Professor Douglas and many of the contributors to her collection recognize, witchcraft beliefs are not merely

instruments by which societies regulate their problems. They have a life of their own, and there is reason to suppose that they can profitably be approached from an individualist as well as a collectivist viewpoint. An analytical system which claims to reveal the hidden structures of the human mind which control our perception of the world, should have something to say about an illusion which even its advocates recognize as primarily a mental operation! The new generation of social historians will certainly be hoping that this crisis in anthropology will be speedily surmounted, and that a discipline which has provided so great a stimulus for other students of human society will continue to flourish.

It is a striking fact that there has been no serious attempt to date to assemble all the extant material on witchcraft in tribal societies, and to examine the overall picture it presents. Lucy Mair's short book, *Witchcraft*, therefore goes some way to plug a yawning gap, and it is likely to prove an extremely useful volume. The author gives a very fair and capable summary of existing knowledge, including a sensible account of European witchcraft which makes use of Dr. Macfarlane's new findings. But she does not attempt to impose any general interpretation on her material, confining herself largely to criticisms of the existing theories. Any radical reinterpretation would, of course, have been incompatible with the aims of a series of popular textbooks, and her book is an excellent one in its own terms. The evidence she uses is heavily biased towards Africa, but this is a reflection of the balance of anthropological field-work at present. What her book does suggest is that African evidence at least is now plentiful, and that a bold anthropologist might try his hand at a big and controversial general survey.

Such surveys have long been commonplace in the historical world, and have been based on notoriously flimsy and incomplete evidence. If anthropologists have been reluctant to generalize above the level of a handful of villages, few historians have bothered to think about rural society at all when they examine the so-called witch-craze of the sixteenth and seventeenth centuries. A prime example of this approach is provided by Professor Trevor-Roper's well-known essay— *The European Witch-Craze of the 16th and 17th Centuries*, now reprinted—which is so superbly self-confident that the unwary reader could be forgiven for thinking it the conclusive study of the subject, failing to notice the unknown gulfs he has been spirited over. As both Mr. Thomas and Dr. Macfarlane point out, his factual material is often extremely unreliable: second or third-hand accounts of hecatombs in distant towns, subject to all the vagaries of sixteenth-century arithmetic. But the actual number of victims is perhaps a minor question compared with his attempts to describe the ebb and flow of trials, and their relationship to economic and social factors. In the present state of the evidence such calculations are a waste of time, and perhaps dangerously misleading into the bargain. Very few good series of records exist for the early sixteenth century, so our ignorance in this area is likely to be permanent.

Unfortunately, Professor Mary Douglas has accepted a number of the dubious conclusions reached by Professor Trevor-Roper, and goes on to combine them with his interpretation of the 'General Crisis' of the seventeenth century.

She is therefore drawn on to picture the supporters of witchcraft persecutions as insecure intellectuals, competing for patronage in corrupt Renaissance courts. Even if this were true of most of the known enthusiasts for persecution, which it is not, the theory would still require that a much larger number of cases be produced. It is simply not sufficient to argue that because Jean Bodin, 'the Aristotle of the sixteenth century' (Trevor-Roper), was a fanatical witch-hunter, and because other well-known persecutors were inoffensive scholars in their private lives, the class to which they belonged shared their obsessions. On present evidence, it would be more accurate to suggest that most educated men believed in witchcraft, but that few of them regarded it as anything more than a remote threat to themselves or their society. Only in a few exceptional areas did the judicial authorities take the lead in seeking out witchcraft: most known cases were the product of accusations by peasants and by ignorant local officials. Professor Trevor-Roper never explicitly recognizes that he is writing about episodes which were exceptional even in their own time, and which call for very careful investigation. The explanations he proposes are intelligent and well worth consideration, but they are so generalized that they could account for far more persecution than is actually known to have occurred.

The appearance of two new works of research dealing with witchcraft in France and England is very welcome, and emphasizes the fact that serious work on the topic is only beginning. The authors adopt very different approaches: Robert Mandrou, in *Magistrats et sorciers en France au 17e siècle*, concentrates on the attitudes of the upper classes, whereas Dr. Macfarlane, in *Witchcraft in Tudor and*

Stuart England, conducts an anthropological investigation into the beliefs of the Essex peasantry. Both, however, arrive at conclusions which undermine substantial proportions of Professor Trevor-Roper's argument. Whatever the explanation for the relatively large number of accusations in Essex, there is no discernible connexion with either Puritanism or Catholicism. The positions adopted by French lawyers and clergymen are revealed as highly complex, with very substantial local variations, and again there seems to be little connexion with straightforward religious conflict. On one occasion when a Catholic-Huguenot confrontation did occur, the famous Loudun case of 1634, it seems to have encouraged scepticism, not renewed belief. Professor Trevor-Roper's attempt to link the persecutions of 1560–1630 with 'the intellectual regression of Reformation and Counter-Reformation, the renewed evangelism of the rival churches' is extremely difficult to square with the evidence provided by these two authors. It remains a plausible if partial explanation of the fantasies of Bodin and other demonologists, and it may still be applicable to the Rhineland and other areas of Germany, but it clearly will not do for Europe as a whole.

The great achievement of *Witchcraft in Tudor and Stuart England* is to put aside all existing generalizations, and concentrate on a manageable area with good records, establishing what actually happened. The result, as Mr. Thomas suggested some years ago, is a picture of a society which is strikingly similar to those described by modern anthropologists working in Africa and elsewhere. During the period 1560–1680 at least 290 supposed witches were put on trial at Essex Assizes, and the true figure is probably nearer 400. Seventy-four are known to have been hanged, and another thirty-six died in prison, but slightly more than half were acquitted or had their case dismissed: many of these acquittals were in the period after 1620, as the authorities became increasingly sceptical. With only two serious exceptions, the accusations were made by other villagers, and were based on the tensions and suspicions endemic in village life. Another 250 people appeared in the ecclesiastical and borough courts, showing only a very small overlap with the assizes: again the true figure may approach 400. Penalties here were milder, although a few of those who appeared in borough courts were put to death. Essex appears to have been more affected than any other English county, but there was a great deal of similar activity elsewhere, and more local studies are required before definite conclusions can be reached.

Even within the county of Essex, some areas were more troubled than others, and Dr. Macfarlane is very cautious in advancing explanations. The enclosed area of the county appears to have been more seriously affected, and there may be some connexion with customs of partible inheritance. But more probably there were random elements at work which distort the figures, for it is clear that many cases never came to court at all. 'Witches' might be under suspicion for years before a formal prosecution was brought, and if many of them were old women they had a good chance of dying unmolested. The first step against a supposed witch was commonly a consultation with a 'cunning man', who might help identify the suspect and suggest magical remedies for the evil attributed to him or her. Many complaints probably stopped at this point, and others may have been inhibited by fear of retaliation from the witch. As Dr. Macfarlane says:

> though it cannot be proved, it seems likely that villagers were constantly engaged in contending with, or discussing, witches. Through counter-action against witches, sufferers were united with their neighbours in a series of magical and other activities which not only brought present relief and some sort of explanation, but also hope of eradicating future misery.

As both Dr. Macfarlane and Mr. Thomas emphasize, the great majority of English witchcraft cases can be assimilated to a standard pattern. The suspect came to the victim's door to request some small neighbourly service (a gift of food or drink, the loan of some implement), only to be turned away empty-handed. Shortly afterwards some unexplained misfortune would afflict the victim or his household, and be attributed to the ill-will of the witch. It was clearly recognized that the basis of this malevolence was a real grievance: the victim had failed in his neighbourly duty, and his guilty conscience seems to have played a large part in his suspicions. The magical beliefs involved were often very clear: refusal to give butter, beer and similar substances might suddenly render their manufacture impossible, and to withhold milk could have disastrous consequences for cattle. Very frequently some form of counter-magic, such as dipping a red-hot horseshoe in cream which refused to churn, or burning a sick animal, would appear to bring relief. Dr. Macfarlane's evidence suggests that cases most commonly arrived in the courts when some lasting personal sickness or death was attributed to the witch's *maleficium:* the object of the accusation was to remove the witch and thereby obtain either a cure or revenge.

The analysis has the great merit of placing witchcraft firmly in its local setting, and employing the cases as a way to reveal the hidden tensions and pressures of village society. Although it is impossible to be certain until more evidence has been gathered, two broad causal factors do seem to be apparent behind the peak of accusations in the years 1570–1605. The first is the economic malaise which affected rural society and led to the establishment of the poor law system: the combination of a rising population with land hunger and a backward technology. The second is the replacement of the Catholic Church, with its arsenal of licensed counter-magical remedies, by Protestantism, which dismissed such useful public services as 'Popish superstitions'.

These two factors may also be connected with the decline in persecution during the seventeenth century, which remains extremely difficult to explain satisfactorily. The Poor Law and the rise of a new economic morality may have eroded the old notions of mutual help to the point where many members of the local community rejected them. The Puritan tendency to attribute misfortune to the sins of the sufferer or the inscrutable will of God may also have played a part. As Dr. Macfarlane very sensitively suggests, it would probably have been enough for a few influential members of the local community to adopt the new outlook. Suspicions quite plainly continued to operate at a local level, but there may no longer have been the consensus of village opinion which encouraged the instigation of a formal prosecution. After about 1650 the local gentry clearly became sceptical, and the very high proportion of acquittals may have made the assizes unattractive long before the final repeal of the Witchcraft Act in 1736. In this case the survival of the 'cunning men', who closely resembled African witch-doctors and diviners, was assured as long as the popular witch-beliefs endured, and both were to linger on well into the nineteenth century.

It will be evident from all that has been said above that Dr. Macfarlane has written a most admirable book, which could serve as a model for social historians undertaking local studies. Not least in brevity: there is far more in the book than it has been possible to discuss here, but it is written in a taut and economical style which makes it exceptionally stimulating reading. The author is attractively modest: he has been strongly influenced by the cautious approach to evidence taken by the social anthropologists, and distinguishes carefully between what he can prove and what he can only suggest.

Readers will be well-advised to turn to Keith Thomas's essay in *Witchcraft Confessions and Accusations* as a supplement to the book, for it takes careful account of Dr. Macfarlane's findings, but attempts to reach some more general conclusions, albeit on a tentative basis. They can also consult two recently published collections of documents, both of which provide excellent illustrations of the day-to-day reality of English witchcraft. One is a reprint of C. L. Ewen's valuable work of 1933, *Witchcraft and Demonianism:* it is to be hoped that his other major volume, *Witch Hunting and Witch Trials* (1929), will soon join it. The second is a new collection edited by Barbara Rosen, *Witchcraft*, which has a sensible introduction, more reliable and up-to-date than Ewen's, but is perhaps slightly less interesting as a collection of source material.

As has already been suggested, *Magistrats et sorciers en France au 17e siècle* is also an important book, although in some ways it is a disappointment. For a specialist in popular *mentalités*. M. Mandrou seems most curiously uninterested in the social reality of witchcraft, and his bibliography reveals no acquaintance with the anthropological literature. The founders of the *Annales* school, Marc Bloch and Lucien Febvre, were concerned to assimilate the methods of the social sciences into historical studies. Unfortunately French anthropological studies were then in their infancy, and had little influence. In recent years the many distinguished works by French historians of the school have turned the methods of demographers, economists and sociologists to good effect, but have paid virtually no attention to anthropology. It is also true that, under the influence of Lévi-Strauss, French anthropology has tended to move away from the detailed study of individual societies, which has become the preserve of the Anglo-American scholars. The effects of these cultural differences are very obvious in M. Mandrou's volume, which suffers from an undue degree of intellectual insularity. In a sense it is unfair to criticize the author for not discussing matters he has declared his intention of leaving aside, but many of the difficulties in his argument relate directly to these omissions. It is impossible to discuss the attitude of individual Parlements to witchcraft cases adequately without a good understanding of those cases which did come before them.

There is a good deal of evidence, both in M. Mandrou's book and in other printed sources, to suggest similarities between English and French witchcraft. The fantasies of the Continental judges, the confessions elicited under torture, are admittedly in striking contrast to the relatively sober crimes imputed to English witches. Against the Sabbat and the Satanic pact, England can only offer the use of 'familiars' in the shape of domestic animals as a contribution to esoteric demonology. But many of the known French cases exhibit the familiar pattern of the suspected witch, revenging some kind of ill-treatment by supernatural means. Cunning men and wise women are also important in France: M. Mandrou seems at times to regard them as prime targets for witchcraft accusations, but this must be a subject for further research. It is clear that in certain years persecution spread through areas of France in a manner only found in the Hopkins episode in England. But just as Hopkins and his assistants (very well described by Dr. Macfarlane) seem to have brought a whole mass of existing local suspicions to the surface, so many of the victims in France probably had a long history of local difficulties behind them. The parallel with some recent witch-finding movements in Africa is a suggestive one, and clearly the whole question of French witchcraft is wide open for the kind of investigation Dr. Macfarlane has pioneered in England.

The chief interest of M. Mandrou's book lies in his attempt to explain the change in the official attitude to witchcraft, culminating in the stern measures taken by Colbert to end persecutions in 1670–72. His argument has two main aspects. First, he seeks to demonstrate that certain famous cases of demonic possession—Gaufridy at Aix, Urbain Grandier at Loudun, Madeleine Bavent at Louviers—stimulated a debate on the whole issue of Satanism, and gave new arguments to the sceptics. Secondly, he examines the judicial standpoint adopted by the Parlements, particularly that of Paris, in order to reveal the gradual development of a more cautious attitude to witchcraft cases. It is this second line of approach which produces the most interesting results, for M. Mandrou is able to show that as early as 1601 the Parlement of Paris outlawed the water ordeal, and that in 1640 it effectively ceased to punish those accused of witchcraft. In 1641 three officials of a subordinate jurisdiction were condemned to death and executed for the murder of a suspected witch. Several other Parlements, including those of Dijon and Toulouse, also showed an increasing caution at this time, and only those of Pau, Bordeaux and Rouen remained relatively unshaken until they were brutally coerced by Colbert and the King in 1670–72.

While it is evident that the new world-view exemplified by the scientific revolution finally destroyed the intellectual basis for the witchcraft persecutions, and to this extent both Professor Trevor-Roper and M. Mandrou are correct, it is difficult to believe that this was the whole story. Attitudes in both England and France seem to be changing during the first half of the seventeenth century before the new cosmology was much more than another speculation. It could perhaps be argued that M. Mandrou is on the right lines, but has not taken his argument far enough. The grotesque exaggerations of the demonologists had never won complete acceptance, although at first the premises on which they rested went almost unchallenged. As the persecutions spread, so they provided the very evidence necessary to discredit them, even in the eyes of men who never read Spee or Weyer. The application of the common-sense rules of evidence to witchcraft accusations was the essential step, and it seems to have taken place within a couple of generations after the beginning of serious persecutions in many areas. The more experienced and sophisticated members of the judicature might be persuaded at first, but many of them were likely to develop doubts in time. Even the notorious Henri Boguet seems to have repented of his witch-hunting before his death, and sought to prevent the reprinting of his treatise on the subject.

There was repentance in New England, too, in the aftermath of the famous Salem trials of 1692. None of the existing accounts of this episode is entirely satisfactory, and it is easy to understand why Professor Hansen decided to attempt a reappraisal. Many of the ideas which lie behind *Witchcraft at Salem* are good: he recognizes the power of popular fear and suspicion, and makes effective use of medical evidence. His efforts to rehabilitate the reputation of Cotton Mather are also a useful corrective to prevailing opinions. But although the book's detailed argument will be of considerable interest to scholars, it is a very unsafe guide for the general reader. Professor Hansen seems unable to resist the temptation to sensationalize his material, and writes in an unnecessarily provocative style. His use of evidence is extremely loose, and he too often cites his own unverifiable speculations as if they were hard facts. His treatment of European witchcraft is not calculated to inspire confidence: he takes the absurd theories of Margaret Murray far too seriously, and treats his readers to a quite irrelevant and very dubious account of the *affaire des poisons* at the court of Louis XIV. If there is one thing that is borne out by the writing of historians of witchcraft, it is that large and hasty generalizations represent the road to ruin, and that only patient and thoughtful scholarship, in the style admirably exemplified by most social anthropologists, is likely to advance our real knowledge.

II

THE DEFINITIVE PEPYS

ON MAY 21, 1662, Samuel Pepys took a holiday from the office, and went walking with his wife in Whitehall Garden. 'And in the privy Garden', he duly noted in his *Diary*, 'saw the finest smocks and linen petticoats of my Lady Castelmayne's, laced with rich lace at the bottomes, that ever I saw; and did me good to look upon them.' After dinner he and his wife went to a theatre, and there in the audience was Lady Castlemaine herself, 'and with much pleasure we saw and gazed upon her'. When Pepys reached his office next morning, he found an order from the principal Secretary of State calling on him to produce all the papers he could find relating to the younger Sir Henry Vane's term of office as Treasurer of the Navy; and Pepys duly dug out the evidence that led to the trial of Vane ten days later for high treason, and his execution on June 14. Having produced the Vane documents Pepys went off to the theatre to see Shirley's *Love in a Maze*, and in the evening he was pleasantly surprised to learn that a naval captain was sending him 'some anchoves, Olives and Muscatt; but I know not yet what that is, and am ashamed to ask'. On May 23 he was at his office again 'good part of the morning', but after dinner he and his wife 'slunk away' to another theatre, and topped off the evening at a puppet play:

Here among the Fidlers I first saw a Dulcimore played on, with sticks knocking of the strings, and is very pretty. So by water home. And supped with Sir W. Penn very merry; and so to bed.

Those are three fairly typical days in the life of Pepys as recorded in the famous *Diary* from January, 1660, to May, 1669. If they are not quite typical, that is because in May, 1662, he was having one of his periodical bouts of social gaiety; but those are always followed in

---

The Diary of Samuel Pepys. A new and complete transcription edited by Robert Latham and William Matthews. Volume I: 1660. 348 pp. Volume II: 1661. 266 pp. Volume III: 1662. 328 pp. G. Bell, £10.50 the set.

RICHARD BARBER: *Samuel Pepys Esquire*. 64 pp. G. Bell, £1.25 (paperback, 75p).

due course by periods of hard work and deliberate self-control. On May 31 he notes that he has 'obliged himself [i.e. taken an oath to abstain] from wine and playes', and on June 30 he is able to record with satisfaction: 'Into a good way; fallen on minding my business and saving money, which God encrease: and I do take great delight in it and see the benefit of it.' Yet he never ceases to enjoy life, and his ability to find innocent pleasure and to indulge his curiosity in un-promising circumstances is endless: if not a dulcimer being played at a puppet show or Lady Castlemaine's snow-white undies bleaching in the privy garden, then something else equally unexpected. On May 4, 1662, he was distressed to see a dead man floating in the Thames, 'and had done (they say) these four days and nobody takes him up to bury him, which is very barbarous'. No less barbarous was the scene Pepys had witnessed some eighteen months earlier when he went to Charing Cross to see Major-General Harrison hanged, drawn and quartered; but on that occasion he contented himself with the com-ment: 'he looking as cheerfully as any man could do in that con-dition'.

Wacthing executions was, in fact, one of Pepys's special ex-periences, and one that was enjoyed a century later by James Bos-well. Pepys had started his own collection as early as 1649, when, as a fifteen-year-old schoolboy, he contrived to be present at the execution of no less a celebrity than Charles I. Not that he was hard-hearted: he had a good deal more than the average sensibility in an age that was accustomed to the sight of daily suffering in the streets of Lon-don, and in which much was calmly accepted that we think, or would like to think, intolerable today. But Pepys was always avid of ex-perience, or, as he puts it in his own natural way, he was 'with child to see any strange thing'. In his excellent discussion of the *Diary* as literature William Matthews rightly defines him as 'a typical seven-teenth-century virtuoso, a man who justified himself by the diversity of his interests'; and he points out how frequently the *Diary* is peppered with such spontaneous comments as 'fine', 'rare', 'brave', 'mighty pleasant', 'exceeding good'. He further suggests that Pepys's catholic interests and love of experience for experience' sake 'proceed from one single comprehensive quality, vitality'. In a final analysis it is his love of life, his childlike concentration on the passing object or event, that must account most satisfactorily for the enduring (and endearing) interest of Pepys's diary.

But of course there is much else. Like Boswell, Pepys was deeply interested in his own reactions, and much given to self-analysis. Unlike Boswell, who usually seems to view himself in the mirror of society and to be conscious of the sort of impression he is making on other people, Pepys comes near to achieving a scientific impartiality in his self-observation. When he jots down that he doesn't know what Muscat is and 'is ashamed to ask' he is recording a private finding about himself. When, in 1665, he goes to collect his new watch from the watchmaker, he makes a characteristic observation:

> But, Lord, to see how much of my old folly and childishnesse hangs upon me still, that I cannot forbear carrying my watch in my hand, in the coach, all this afternoon, and seeing what o'clock it is one hundred times, and am apt to think with myself, how could I be so long without one; though I remember, since, I had one, and found it a trouble, and resolved to carry one no more about me while I lived.

In the prose fiction of the period there is almost none of this close observation of human behaviour, and comparatively little in the drama. Whether (as Professor Matthews suggests) we are to attribute these frank and often piercing revelations to Pepys's confidence in the obscurity of his shorthand, or to the puritan habit of self-examination, or merely to 'a book-keeper's ordinary honesty', they give the *Diary* a very special quality: the diarist is at once 'the observer and the observed, the penitent and the priest, the patient on the couch and the psychiatrist too'.

While Pepys presents himself in the *Diary* with a Richardsonian fullness, we also become familiar in varying degrees with his family, his naval colleagues, his maids, his cronies, and above all with his wife. When he began to keep his diary Pepys was almost twenty-seven, and had been married for about five years. Elizabeth Pepys, an Anglo-French girl, was seven years younger than himself, and the marriage had proved childless. By 1660 the first raptures were clearly over: there had even been a short separation, but the matrimonial boat was now settled on a fairly even keel. Yet Pepys had always had an eye for a pretty girl and a fondness for the snatched kiss, and as the years passed the status of Mrs. Pepys dwindled to that of a wife in Restoration comedy. Amateurs of the erotic, however, will be disappointed with these first three volumes of the *Diary*: their chance will come later. For the most part the years 1660–1662 show Pepys living on affectionate terms with his wife. An entry in the *Diary* for October 24, 1662, is fairly typical of this period:

After with great pleasure lying a great while, talking and sporting in bed with my wife (for we have been for some years now, and at present more and more, a very happy couple, blessed be God), I got up and to my office. . . .

Of course they had their off-days. There was the morning when they set out together for church, and his wife not being dressed to his liking he was angry with her, 'and she, when she was out of doors in her way to church, returned home again vexed'. When he was having another storey built on to his house in Seething Lane, the workmen made such a mess that he arranged for his wife to go and stay with his parents. Pepys consoled himself in his bachelor existence by drinking a good deal more than usual, and there was a business trip to Rochester lasting for several days, during which he danced and flirted with the pretty daughter of the Clerk of the Ropeyard at Chatham, and could not get her out of his head—all in all 'the pleasantest journy, in all respects, that ever I had in my life'. Back in London, he called one day later on his wife, and they had a misunderstanding: Pepys apparently pretended in the course of the evening that he wanted to go home, and his wife pretended that she was willing to let him go, and he left the house in anger.

But she, poor wretch, fallowed me as far, in the rain and dark, as Fleete brige to fetch me back again; and so I did, and lay with her tonight—which I have not done these eight or ten days before.

Sadder still is a much later entry, for February 27, 1668, which Professor Matthews appropriately quotes to illustrate Pepys's 'intense attraction to beauty'. He had been with his wife to a performance of Massinger's *The Virgin Martyr*, and had enjoyed it.

But that which did please me beyond anything in the whole world was the wind-musique when the Angell comes down, which is so sweet that it ravished me; and endeed, in a word, did wrap up my soul so that it made me really sick, just as I have formerly been when in love with my wife.

Pepys adds that he 'remained all night transported', but it was no longer, as it once had been, with his young wife. A good deal had happened in the intervening years, and the diarist had moved on from harmless flirtations to those more serious lapses and liaisons that we encounter in the later pages of the *Diary*, but that were never more than rather discreditable incidents in the life of a busy public servant. But the pretty child he had fallen in love with when he was twenty-two and she was fifteen could hardly be expected to see it like that. Pepys took a considerable interest in the lukewarm relationship

between Charles II and his young Portuguese Queen, and in some
ways Elizabeth Pepys was a middle-class Catherine of Braganza to
her own husband's Charles II (Pepys had an unbounded admiration
of Lady Castlemaine, and even wrote in the *Diary* that he 'loved'
her); but their married life remained full of interest, unpredictable,
often unsatisfactory, but just as often irradiated by a genuine and
touching affection.

If it is as a personal document that the *Diary* appeals to most
readers, Robert Latham is there to remind us, in an able discussion of
the *Diary* as history, that it is also an important chronicle of public
affairs. But that chronicle, as he points out, gains greatly in significance from the fusion of a private life with public events; what we
are seeing is what one man saw in the early years of the Restoration
from 'a private window giving out to a broad and varied external
view'. Pepys has much to tell us about the cultural and religious and
political life of the period, about the English Navy and its administration; but because his information is filtered to us through his
personality and his contacts with great men and little men, we can
more easily absorb it, and more completely imagine ourselves in
his situation. As Mr. Latham puts it: 'We are more easily interested
in a man's politics or religion if we know what he had for dinner.'
More interested, and better able to realize how the issues appeared
to the men and women who were living through them.

Up till now the *Diary* has never been satisfactorily edited. Lord
Braybrooke, working with the transcript made by the Rev. John
Smith, printed only about two-fifths of the text, and made many
minor editorial changes. The next editor, the Rev. Mynors Bright,
made a fresh transcription and published about four-fifths of the
Diary (six volumes, 1875–79), leaving out such passages as he
thought 'would be tedious to the reader, or that are unfit for publication'. In 1885 Messrs. George Bell reached an agreement with the
owners of the *Diary*, Magdalene College, Cambridge, for a new
edition, and Henry B. Wheatley was appointed editor. His edition
appeared in eight volumes (1893–96), followed in 1899 by an index
volume and a volume of commentary entitled *Pepysiana*, supple-
menting the footnotes. For the first time an editor had printed almost
the entire text, except for some erotic or scatological passages; but,
where those were left out, editorial dots indicated the omissions.
There was, too, a certain amount of bowdlerization; for instance,
when Pepys told his wife that he 'would fling the dog which her

brother gave her out of the window if he pissed the house any more', Wheatley's Victorian dog only 'dirtied' the house.

The least satisfactory part of Wheatley's edition was the text; he had no knowledge of shorthand himself, and his text was based on that of Mynors Bright, with some further transcriptions and revisions by a Fellow of Trinity. The text of the new Matthews–Latham edition is based on a transcription made in the course of several readings by Professor Matthews, an expert in shorthand, scrutinized at various stages by his fellow editor, Mr. Latham, an expert on the history of the period covered by the *Diary*. Their text includes 'all words and passages omitted from previous editions, whether by accident or design'. What Wheatley would have been execrated for printing in 1893 our two modern editors would be rebuked for leaving out in the permissive climate of 1970. The editorial problems posed by establishing a text written in shorthand (with occasional words and passages in longhand and the *lingua franca* used by Pepys for the 'unprintable' bits) are truly formidable; but the editorial decisions are judicious and sensible, and we have now got as near as we are ever likely to get to the *Diary* as it might have been written by Pepys himself if he had ever transcribed his own shorthand.

Equally commendable is the annotation. Previous editors were obviously appalled by the proliferation of names (both of persons and places), and did little to enlighten the curious reader. Lord Braybrooke waved the problem aside with a well-turned sentence:

It is indeed obvious that, in a work throughout which so many names occur, there are some of whom nothing can be said, because nothing can be discovered, without an amount of labour wholly disproportionate to the result; and there are others of whom little need be said, being already well known.

Mr. Latham, who is mainly responsible for the explanatory footnotes, has not shirked that disproportionate labour, and must have spared himself no pains to illuminate those names about whom 'nothing can be discovered', for he rarely leaves us uninformed.

Each volume contains a 'Select List of Persons' and a glossary, both of which help to relieve the pressure on the footnotes. When the text is completed in nine volumes, we are promised a tenth volume of commentary containing 'the information which the reader may well find it necessary or desirable to have but which (in the judgment of the editors) he does not need to have immediately under his eye as he reads the pages of the diary'. Some readers may take exception to this

K

arrangement, but the alternative—to include all such information among the footnotes—would have left many pages with too little of Pepys and too much of his editors. Such frustration as the reader may experience should be largely dissipated when the final index volume appears; but for the present anyone who just dips into the *Diary* here and there (as most readers of Pepys do) must often find himself at a loss, since cross-references have been cut to the bone, and in a text so crowded with names it would be impracticable to supply them. So, too, one must wait for Volume X to find out the locality of the 'Half-Moon' or the 'Dogg', where Pepys ate or drank with his friends. The remaining volumes are promised in instalments over the course of the next few years: it is to be hoped that they will keep moving steadily off the assembly-line.

It was a wise decision to call upon the assistance of specialist editors: for the theatre (William A. Armstrong), music (Macdonald Emslie), pictures and works of art (Oliver Millar), and London topography (the late T. F. Reddaway). Their annotation is uniformly well-informed, pertinent, and precise. Mrs. Lois Matthews, who has been for so long closely associated with her husband's work on the text, completes this highly competent team as Text Assistant. With only three volumes so far published it may be premature to say 'And so to bed'; but it is not too early to say that when this edition of the *Diary* is completed it will take its place among the outstanding contributions to literary scholarship in the twentieth century.

12

TO RATIONALIZE WAR

Sir Basil Liddell Hart's *History of the Second World War* was finished only shortly before his death. The simultaneous publication of a new edition of his *History of the First World War* provides a valuable opportunity to survey his life's work and compare the attitudes and contents of the two volumes.

The same method was employed in the compilation of both. His first volume was built up from a series of monographs on particular aspects and episodes of the First World War and published in 1930 as *The Real War 1914–1918*. This was enlarged four years later under the title *A History of the World War 1914–1918*. His new book has had a similar patchwork origin. It draws heavily on *The Other Side of the Hill*—his record of discussions with several German generals who were prisoners of war—and on the research he undertook as author of *The Tanks*, the regimental history of the Royal Tank Regiment, and as editor of *The Rommel Papers*. Preparation for lectures, particularly in the United States, and discussion with a very wide range of military experts, uniformed and civilian of many different countries, provided much of the raw material. They also absorbed much of his time and effort. The price paid for this piecemeal approach is a weakness in the general design of both volumes. The balance is uneven and there is some repetition. The reader finds himself switching in scale and retracing his steps in time.

Let it be said at once that to attempt to deal with the vast field of the operations of the Second World War, and all that lay behind them, in one volume—even one of more than 700 pages—is a task of the greatest difficulty. The author is faced with an inescapable dilemma: whether to provide a summary of all the moves and decisions, which has already been done by others; or to concentrate on some of the major issues, assuming that the reader is conversant with the general story. The latter was the pattern chosen for the first

---

B. H. Liddell Hart: *History of the First World War*. 635 pp. Cassell. £4.20. *History of the Second World War*. 768 pp. Cassell. £5.25.

history, and on the whole it is a more satisfactory approach than the more diffuse story of the Second World War. Understandably the operations in which the British were engaged are dealt with in greater detail than all the others, but the attempt to cover the whole wide field has led to insufficient space being devoted to some of the major issues of policy and strategy which Liddell Hart was so eminently well qualified to discuss.

If there is some criticism of the general design, there can be none of the artistry of detail. Liddell Hart has no rival in the literary skill with which he describes and comments on military operations. Both in his new book and in the *History of the First World War* he exercises an economy and felicity of phrasing that makes the complicated scene intelligible to the reader with the minimum of effort, and yet incorporates an apt and telling comment at almost every turn.

The Sage of Medmenham rightly gained a high reputation as an historian, but it is as a military critic that he is likely to be best remembered. As he himself made clear in a note on why and how he wrote his *History of the Second World War*, the one activity led to the other and the two became merged:

When exploring the events of the First World War, in the 1920s and 1930s, I came to realize how much history was handicapped because no independent and historically minded enquirer had been able to ascertain and record what the military chiefs were actually thinking at the time—as a check on their subsequent recollections. For it became very evident that the memories of the participants in dramatic events are apt to become coloured or twisted in retrospect, and increasingly as the years pass. Moreover official documents often fail to reveal their real views and aims, while sometimes even drafted to conceal them.

All those who have set their hands to write works of military history will echo these sentiments. Liddell Hart goes on to explain that, when visiting British and Allied senior officers during the war, he made copious notes on what they had revealed to him and that much use had also been made of his conversations with German generals in captivity. One gains the impression that, valuable as these sources were, he leans too heavily on them. This distorts the picture in areas which he was unable to visit. In such cases he relies largely on those for whose accounts or personalities he had a personal sympathy, and as a result he is vulnerable to the accusation of falling below his own high standards of objectivity. One also feels that he is much more inclined to accept a German general's version of events than a

British, unless the latter is one of the favourites, like Dorman-Smith.

Liddell Hart's whole life was a reaction to his experiences on the Somme in 1916. His sharp, analytical and iconoclastic mind was concentrated on the search for some better way to conduct affairs—and particularly military ones—than the senseless, direct head-on attack after long preparation, which proved both so expensive and so ineffective. He therefore set himself to study in detail what methods could be effective and how military affairs, and the policy which they support, should be conducted. The first step in this examination was to analyse what really happened and what actual effect it had. A lot of myths and fancies had to be cleared away in the process, resulting in some conclusions unpalatable to the orthodox. His study led to the assertion of a number of general principles or maxims, which emerge at intervals in his *History of the First World War*. Part of the interest of reading his new work lies in seeing to what extent events in the Second World War proved the soundness of his conclusions and how much his own writings had influenced them.

What were these maxims? The first emerges from his account of the Battle of the Marne in 1914:

The profoundest truth of war is that the issue of battles is usually decided in the minds of the opposing commanders, not in the bodies of their men. The best history would be a register of their thoughts and emotions, with a mere background of events to throw them in relief.

By this standard his *History of the Second World War* is a disappointment. With the exception of some discussion of the thoughts of opposing commanders in the Pacific theatre, there is very little of what went on in the minds of the opposing commanders. How indeed is one to discover it?

The next important maxim is that of the indirect approach, in its most extreme terms expressed by the phrase: 'In strategy the longest way round is often the shortest way there.' Emphasis on this led him in the earlier work to support the Eastern school and to stress the strategic effect of the campaigns in the Dardanelles, Salonika, Palestine and Mesopotamia and of the naval blockade. But in the Second World War the application of this on the level of Grand Strategy is not apparent. In the naval war in the Pacific, in the re-entry into Europe and in the application of air power the implication is that dispersion of effort on anything that did not directly affect the main issue was a contravention of the principle of economy of force. In the actual conduct of major operations—in the great spaces of the Pacific Ocean and of the Russian steppes, as well as in more constricted theatres of war—the value of the indirect approach, the baited gambit and other Liddell Hartian maxims is rightly given full play. To the uninitiated it is perhaps more easily understood as an element of that most important factor—surprise. 'Time and surprise are the two supreme factors in war', he wrote in describing the German breakthrough to the Marne in 1918—and all that he writes in both volumes bears this out to the full.

Although some of the major policy and strategic issues of 1939–45 are not dealt with in as much depth as might have been wished, one fundamental and very controversial issue is given prominence in both the first and the last chapters of the new volume, that of the origin of the war itself. He lays the blame squarely on the shoulders of the British Government, primarily on Chamberlain and Halifax. This appears to be the only occasion in the Second World War when he agrees with Churchill. In contrast to the tribute paid to him for his mobilization of the Fleet, his support of the invention of the tank and his 'strategic insight' over the Dardanelles in the earlier work, there is not a word of praise in *History of the Second World War* and much implied criticism. But they are at one on the issue of the folly of the guarantee to Poland without any change in the frigid attitude to Russia, after having led Hitler to believe—whether correctly or not— that, provided he restricted his adventures to a Drang nach Osten, he would not be opposed. Nevertheless, Liddell Hart cannot refrain from pointing out that Churchill's wisdom was that of hindsight, as he had himself supported Chamberlain's offer to Poland at the time. He lays the blame very largely on the ignorance of the statesmen of the day not only about current military affairs, such as the relative value of the German and Polish forces, but also of the permanent factors of policy and strategy which should guide the conduct of affairs.

In contrast to his implied denigration of Churchill he gives Hitler several good marks, principally for a better appreciation of strategic realities in the earlier part of the war (and before it) than his generals. Liddell Hart reserves his criticism for the 'no retreat' orders of the later phases, but even in that case he admits that the sacrifice of von Paulus's Sixth Army at Stalingrad saved Kleist's and Manstein's Army Groups. He shows very clearly his liking for his faithful disciples, the German generals, and one begins to hear an echo of the final sentence of *History of the First World War*.

Whatever be the verdict of history on her policy unstinted tribute is due to the incomparable endurance and skill with which Germany more than held her own for four years against superior numbers—an epic of military and human achievement.

If only, one can almost hear him say, the British and their allies could have been such good professional soldiers. Perhaps it is this sympathy for them which, in spite of his own constant stress on the importance of ensuring that military operations are subservient to policy, leads him to gloss over—indeed never to mention—the basic difference between the two world wars: the moral issue and its effect on public opinion. This is relevant both to his criticism of the origin of the war and of the policy of unconditional surrender.

In 1914 patriotism, the violation of Belgian neutrality, the need to bring to an end the Kaiser's militaristic posturings were enough to provide a moral foundation for engaging in a war, which, as Liddell Hart pointed out in his study, came almost as a relief to the tensions of the preceding years. Rupert Brooke was certainly not alone in feeling this. As the war progressed, atrocities were made much of; but it had been and remained acceptable to go to war as part of the general play of international politics.

The realization that the ghastly slaughter of that war had resulted largely from the irresponsible manoeuvrings of the kings and so-called statesmen of that time meant that the very opposite held good in the 1930s. It was the revulsion of the British, French and American peoples from the thought of a repetition that was responsible for the apparently craven attitude of the French and ourselves and the isolation of the United States from 1935 onwards. To lay the blame for the sudden reversal of our attitude with the guarantee to Poland in 1939 on Chamberlain and his colleagues is to underrate the feeling of moral indignation in the whole British Commonwealth at our betrayal not only of the Czechs and Slovaks, but of all those within Germany as well as on its borders who were being treated not as civilized human beings but as animals.

Even though the full horrors of the concentration camps and the Final Solution were yet to come, the public had finally woken up to the fact that all that European civilization stood for was at stake. It is surely not right to call the Second World War, as Liddell Hart and Churchill did, 'the unnecessary war'. It should have come earlier—

in 1935 or 1938—but somehow or other Hitler and all his works had to be defeated, proved as evil and wrong as they were, and eliminated if European civilization was to survive.

In his avoidance of this issue Liddell Hart assumes that there were forces within Germany, especially among the generals, who, given a modicum of encouragement from the Allies, would have overthrown Hitler and Nazism from within. It is on these grounds that he condemns so harshly the policy of unconditional surrender. But anybody who knows the story of Dietrich Bonhoeffer will realize that the true tragedy lay in the fact, which that saintly man saw so clearly, that this was not so: that almost to the end Hitler and his henchmen were more popular in Germany than was the potential resistance; that at almost no period, and certainly not in 1939, would a revolt against Hitler—especially one supported from abroad and thus appearing to be treasonable—have any chance of winning popular support.

It was not just the guarantee to Poland that was so foolish, but the refusal to accept an alliance with Russia to restrain Hitler's Ostpolitik. This nation would not have tolerated appeasement of the ogre any longer.

It is only too evident that in 1939 he [Churchill] like most of Britain's leaders, acted on a hot-headed impulse—instead of with the cool-headed judgement that was so characteristic of British statesmanship.

are the concluding words of Liddell Hart's opening chapter; but to imagine that the affairs of the world are not largely dictated by emotional impulses, in which moral issues play a large part, is to be blind to a whole area of policy. It may be reprehensible and shortsighted, but it should not be overlooked in a history which claims to be objective.

Liddell Hart, as one would expect, is not afraid to take an original or unpopular line in some of the major controversies. Over the campaign in Greece he agrees with the view that Hitler's decision to invade Yugoslavia, after the unexpected coup d'état and the subsequent campaign in Greece, delayed the date of his invasion of Russia and perhaps forfeited victory there; but he maintains that the British intervention in Greece did not provoke Hitler's decision. The fear of it had already led Hitler to plan to occupy Thrace as a defensive measure before launching his forces into Russia—to prevent another Dardanelles or Salonika campaign. He also maintains that the heavy losses of Student's parachute forces in their attack on Crete were a critical factor in deterring Hitler from using them against Malta. Liddell Hart's general conclusion on the ill-fated campaign in Greece and Crete is therefore less unfavourable than one would have expected.

His criticisms of the handling of the British forces in the Libyan campaign are all that one would have expected from the editor of *The Rommel Papers* and such a staunch friend of Dorman-Smith, who was as prejudiced a source of both John Connell's *Auchinleck* and Corelli Barnett's *Desert Generals* as he was a disastrous principal staff-officer to Auchinleck himself. Ritchie is by inference condemned for withdrawing from the Egyptian frontier to stand at Mersa Matruh after the fall of Tobruk; but when Auchinleck, as soon as he took over in the field there from Ritchie, himself decided to retreat even farther and fight 'a more mobile battle in the Alamein area', he is described as

showing a cool head and a strong nerve. Although a further withdrawal could not be justified by the balance of material strength, it was probably wise in view of the weaknesses of the Mersa Matruh position, which could be easily by-passed, and of the balance of morale.

If that was true of Matruh, which was a prepared position largely occupied by fresh troops, it was far more true of any other position further west, where Ritchie might have tried to hold Rommel, including the frontier itself.

Montgomery throughout receives low marks for caution, but is praised for his flexibility in being prepared to change his plans and strike elsewhere as soon as one thrust lost impetus, in the manner of Foch in 1918. Liddell Hart rightly points out that Montgomery's claim that everything always went according to plan has detracted from the credit due to him for this flexibility, a notable feature both of El Alamein and Mareth.

In describing Operation Torch, the Allied invasion of North Africa from the west, he underlines the paradoxical strategic value of Eisenhower's failure to reach Tunis in the early phase. Had he done so, the Germans would never have poured so many troops into Tunisia only to lose them all, as well as those already there with Rommel's army, thus making easier the subsequent invasion of Sicily. Indeed throughout *History of the Second World War* Liddell Hart points out the advantages that accrued in the longer run from defeats and failures in the early stages. One almost gains the impression that the enemy should be invited to overrun large areas and thus suffer from 'overstretch'—as happened so significantly to the Japanese as well to the Germans in Russia—in order to render their subsequent defeat the easier: one version of the indirect approach.

The conduct of the campaign in Italy is criticized principally on the grounds of 'no advance without security': the failure to take risks by operating beyond fighter cover in the early stages, to exploit the amphibious capability later, and the general insistence on overwhelming fire-support. Alexander's project to drive through the Ljubljana Gap on a thrust to Vienna is seen as unrealistic. In the controversy over the part the campaign played in the general strategy of the war, Liddell Hart takes a balanced view: that it did not draw any German forces away from Normandy; but that without its pressure, German strength on the Channel coast could have been increased and that the use in Normandy of the German forces detained in Italy might have been fatal to the success of the landing, which was a close-run thing in any case. The release of Allied forces from Italy would not have added to our own strength, as the limitation lay in landing-craft and the subsequent maintenance of the forces ashore.

In the fierce Eisenhower-Montgomery argument over the strategy to be pursued after the break-out from Normandy, Liddell Hart again takes a line between the two extremes. Eisenhower's broad-front strategy would have been suited, he believes, to the situation it was designed to meet—a withdrawal by a strong and unbeaten enemy; but the conditions of collapse after Falaise required the single and concentrated thrust demanded by Montgomery. But Liddell Hart does not lay the blame, as Montgomery did, on the priority given to Patton. He pins a good deal of it on Montgomery himself for delays in the pursuit and in opening the port of Antwerp; for the resources devoted to a whole series of airborne operations which never took place; the diversion of the Americans to objectives too far south; and, generally, on the slowness of the Allied war-machine to adapt itself to exploit the favourable situation, and the relaxed and optimistic attitude of almost everyone except Patton.

The German counter-offensive in the Ardennes at the end of 1944 is given a whole twenty-page chapter to itself, in contrast to the fighting in Normandy which rates about a page and the Arnhem operation which gets three fleeting references. No doubt the reasoning is that the German Ardennes offensive is not well known to the

English-speaking public, while the others have been described in detail, in many other books; but it illustrates the imbalance of scale and the bias towards interest in the German point of view.

Sailors and airmen alike will complain that, with the exception of the Pacific campaign in which the Royal Navy played very little part and the R.A.F. none, far too little space is devoted to the war at sea and in the air. In terms of space this is so; but their effect on land operations is not neglected and the chapters on the Battle of the Atlantic and the 'Crescendo of Bombing' are masterpieces in summarizing complicated subjects.

In general the broader the brush the more satisfactory the picture. Liddell Hart's accounts of the Russian and the Pacific campaigns are perhaps the best chapters, particularly the latter. The space is vast, the movements large and, on the few occasions when the reader's attention is focused on detail—such as in the Battle of the Leyte Gulf —the story is enthralling. It is a pity that the maps are not of the same high standard as the text.

At the end, fittingly, falls the atom bomb. Why was it used? The answer is cynical—to justify the expenditure of effort in developing it and to avoid dependence on help from Russia in finishing off Japan. 'A generation later', writes Liddell Hart, 'it is all too clear that the hasty dropping of the atomic bomb has not been a relief to the rest of mankind.' Is it clear? Did not the revelation in human terms of the horrifying effects of even such a limited-yield bomb just before the end of the war preserve us from the likelihood of its use in some later conflict? Had it not been used on Japan in 1945, it would almost certainly have been used in Korea less than ten years later. Has it or has it not kept the peace? Liddell Hart rightly devoted much of his efforts in the 1950s to fighting against the view that it should be regarded as a military vade mecum and the danger that our civilization might be destroyed in a fit of nuclear absent-mindedness.

Although he has earned undying respect as an historian who sought after truth in order to protect future generations from the senseless slaughter of *Oh! What a Lovely War*, his greatest contribution will have been as a critic who did his best to convince his fellow-men that wars, which are probably an inevitable result of our human weakness or of our cultural and genetic heritage, should be fought in a rational way for rational purposes. An emotional man by nature, he had a Voltairean passion for the virtues of reason. If we have to err, it is better to do so in his direction than in that of the blind direct approach.

13

DIALECTICAL METHODOLOGY

FOR THE PAST two decades the German Federal Republic has figured in the consciousness of the English-speaking world primarily as the residuary legatee of Bismarck's vanished Reich: a truncated body abruptly and permanently severed from its grandiose but catastrophic past. The severance, so far as an outsider could judge, extended to the country's intellectual life no less than to its somewhat parochial politics: so reassuringly humdrum by comparison with the ceaseless turmoil of the Weimar Republic.

Of late, however, there have been signs that this quiescent phase is coming to an end. Not only has the long reign of conservative somnolence in Bonn been terminated by the unexpected formation of a liberal–labour coalition. There have also been echoes of the American and French student revolts, and—at a considerably higher level—public debates between Marxists and theologians. Now, to confirm the worst fears of American pragmatists and British empiricists, there is a new *Methodenstreit*, or methodological dispute, at an intellectual altitude so elevated as to make structuralism or neo-Cartesian linguistics seem positively commonsensical. Just what one might have expected from the Germans; and to make matters worse, some of the participants are in the tradition of the Frankfurt school of sociology: in plain language, they are Marxists steeped in Hegelian logic. It is enough to make any decent empiricist despair; and to judge from some of the contributions to this debate, despair is indeed uppermost among the sentiments with which the disciples of Karl Popper have greeted the new phenomenon.

THEODOR W. ADORNO: *Stichworte.* 193 pp. Frankfurt: Suhrkamp. DM 3.

THEODOR W. ADORNO and others: *Der Positivismusstreit in der deutschen Soziologie.* 384 pp. Neuwied: Luchterhand. DM 28.

ALFRED SCHMIDT (Editor): *Beiträge zur marxistischen Erkenntnistheorie.* 265 pp. Frankfurt: Suhrkamp. DM 5.

ALBRECHT WELLMER: *Kritische Gesellschaftstheorie und Positivismus.* 160 pp. Frankfurt: Suhrkamp. DM 3.

MAX HORKHEIMER and THEODOR W. ADORNO: *Dialektik der Aufklärung.* 275 pp. Frankfurt: S. Fischer. DM 24.

The roots of course go back to Weimar days, and indeed to the first great *Methodenstreit* around the turn of the century, when Max Weber's sociology was taking shape as part of an attempt to overcome the cleavage between scientific rationalism and romantic intuitionism. But after 1945 it was assumed—among liberals anyway—that the issue had been settled for good. West Germany having purged itself (or having been purged by the Allies) of its demons and having adopted the Enlightenment tenets so long and obstinately spurned by its educated elite, the metaphysical blight cast by Hegel and his successors must surely be seen by all as an aspect of the great catastrophe the country had twice suffered in this century.

But somehow the message did not sound wholly convincing to Germans otherwise disposed to make an entirely fresh start. Marxism-Leninism indeed might be (and was) ignored: it was too rigid, as well as being associated with—to put it mildly—unpopular regimes in Eastern Europe. The ancient conservative ontology descended from Schelling and the Romantics likewise did not suit the new positivist temper and was quietly consigned to the attic. Nietzsche too went unread among postwar students—this was progress indeed—and Heidegger was generally thought to have displayed the cloven hoof too plainly in 1933, when he hailed the Führer in language not usually employed by academic philosophers. But scientific empiricism of the Anglo-American type continued to encounter obstinate resistance even among former emigrants, from the conservative Karl Löwith to the radical Theodor W. Adorno. Indeed it was just these returned exiles who perversely insisted upon the enduring relevance of the great tradition of German idealism—a tradition extending from Kant, via Hegel and his pupils, to Marx.

Having spent long years abroad, for the most part in the United States, these exiles had acquired a profounder understanding of the democratic process, a circumstance that facilitated their reintegration within the new society of postwar Germany. The old arrogance which counterposed German *Kultur* to Western *Zivilisation* was gone —it had indeed been discredited among Germans generally. But neither gratitude for hospitality received nor admiration for democratic folkways unknown in Central Europe had blotted out the unshakable conviction that positivist scientism in all its forms— including those originally evolved in the Vienna of the 1920s—was philosophically sterile.

How is one to account for this perversity? Is there some mysterious entity at the centre of the collective consciousness—a soul, an essence, a spiritual trait securely anchored in the very structure of the German language that resists the beneficent effects of an Anglo-American environment? Yet Central Europe too has produced radical critics of traditional speculative thought: indeed, the most radical of them all, Wittgenstein, was a native of Vienna. Or is there perhaps an obscure link between Wittgenstein's unexampled analytical rigour and his unmistakable yearning for veritable insight into the nature of ultimate reality? The final message of the *Tractatus* after all is that science tells us nothing we really want to know. In another context and employing different language, Weber made a similar point some years earlier, when he said there was no bridge between science and faith (*Wissenschaft als Beruf*). To Weber this was a true but tragic insight into the condition of modern man. In general, German thinkers, including those who have stoically accepted the dissociation of thinking from being, do not seem able to endure the resulting disillusionment with anything like the composure to which the denizens of more fortunate lands have become accustomed.

This can be illustrated by considering Adorno's posthumously published collection of essays issued by Suhrkamp under the title *Stichworte*, only a few weeks after his sudden death last August, with an author's preface dated 'June, 1969'—a philosophical testament if ever there was one. There is a sense in which Adorno, like the Frankfurt school in general, stood for a specifically modern kind of rationalism: that represented by T. H. Green's dictum that 'every form of the question why the world as a whole should be what it is . . . is unanswerable'. This is to make short work of an entire mode of thought ultimately rooted in the pre-Socratics, dominant in European philosophy until the eighteenth century, and influential in Germany down to our days—witness the sensational success of Heidegger's *Sein und Zeit* in the 1920s. It is to acknowledge that questions of this sort are not, properly speaking, a theme for rational discourse at all.

To that extent the logical positivism of the original Vienna Circle— of which Wittgenstein was not, in the strict sense, a member—did not conflict with the basic assumptions of those Hegelian Marxists who in the 1930s grouped themselves around the *Zeitschrift für Sozialforschung*. Where then lay the crucial difference, and why do we now have before us a volume of essays labelled *Der Positivismusstreit*, with a lengthy polemical introduction by Adorno, an important contribution by Sir Karl Popper, and a fascinating dispute between Professor Hans Albert and Professor Jürgen Habermas? Principally, it seems, because the kind of rationalism to which Adorno and his colleagues were committed had never cut its connexion with the tradition of German idealism. That is to say, it aimed at something over and above the *Wissenschaftstheorie* of logical positivism, without for that reason yielding an inch of ground to ontology. The case is best stated in Adorno's own words:

With Kant, thinking . . . makes its appearance under the term of spontaneity. Reasoning is *prima facie* an activity of the sort registered by the naive consciousness when it distinguishes the sensations, the impressions apparently made available to the individual without any exertion on his part, from the experience of laborious activity inseparable from thought. However, Kant's greatness . . . manifests itself not least in the fact that . . . he does not simply identify the spontaneity which, according to him, constitutes thought with conscious activity. For him, the basic constitutive operations of thinking were not the same as acts of reasoning within a world already constituted. [They] are barely noticeable to self-awareness. . . . *The Critique of Pure Reason* is already a phenomenology of Mind in the sense of Hegel's analysis of consciousness which later bore that title. . . .

Implicitly, Adorno, and with him the Frankfurt school in general, adheres to the Kantian distinction between a sensible world of appearances and an intelligible world that lies open to rational knowledge. On this assumption the empirical sciences deal with mere appearance while philosophy has to do with *Wesen* (Being), that is to say, with transempirical reality. *Wesen* is not to be understood as a supersensible realm of being in the traditional metaphysical sense. The distinction between reality and appearance relates solely to the circumstance that philosophy transcends the horizon of the sciences, in as much as it is not bound by the instrumentalist character of the scientific process. The latter presupposes a particular way of investigating an object whose existence philosophy takes for granted. The philosopher for his part subjects this object-world, and its scientific correlative, to a critical investigation whose standards are indeed meta-scientific, but by no means speculative or ontological. They are 'critical' in the twofold sense of being descended both from Kant's *Critique* and from its materialist antipode; the 'critical theory' of Marxism.

This appropriation of the Kantian heritage by the Marxist Adorno is mediated by the fundamental pre-supposition of the entire Frankfurt school: Marxism is rooted in German idealism—not in the trivial biographical sense familiar to every student of the subject, but in the sense that Marx's 'materialist' inversion of Hegel conserved the problematic enshrined in Hegel's earlier critique of Kant. The thesis is briefly expounded in Alfred Schmidt's preface to the volume of studies he has edited for Suhrkamp: *Beiträge zur marxistischen Erkenntnistheorie*:

The specific epistemological approach of dialectical materialism arises from the fact that Marx and Engels accept Hegel's critique of Kant without being able to accept its speculative foundation. With Hegel they affirm the cognoscibility of being [des Wesens der Erscheinungen]; with Kant (albeit without invoking the *Critique of Pure Reason*) they insist upon the non-identity of form and matter, subject and object of cognition.

Another contributor to the same volume, Jindrich Zeleńy, makes a related point:

Marx proceeds critically from the theorizing about the ontological structure of reality which German transcendental philosophy, notably Hegel, had worked out in opposition to the scientism of Galileo-Descartes and their conception of movement and causality. The starting-point is the materialist interpretation of Hegel's concept of Spirit.

Albrecht Wellmer, who suspects Marx of positivism, none the less comes to similar conclusions concerning his relationship to Hegel in his *Kritische Gesellschaftstheorie und Positivismus*.

It is perhaps as well to bear in mind that the distinction between appearance and reality is not as such peculiar to transcendentalists, let alone to Hegelians. In a sense it may be said to be as old as science. Certainly the Baconian or Newtonian understanding of scientific method operated with some such contrast, as did Ricardo's analysis of the economic process (a point rightly stressed by Zeleńy).

Common sense here inevitably prompts one to ask the irritable question: 'Why then all this fuss about Hegel?' Because (replies the Frankfurt school) positivism and Marxism differ about the meaning to be imputed to the notion of reality or *Wesen*. Ever since Comte began to extrapolate the method of the natural sciences, sociology has been in search of invariant structures underlying the surface play of historic change. The latest and most ambitious attempt in this direction is associated with the structural anthropology of Claude Lévi-Strauss and its various offshoots—including the quasi-Marxism of Louis Althusser, for whom a genuinely scientific theory of society remains to be worked out after the unfortunate Hegelian heritage has been shed.

Anyone who imagines that this standpoint is compatible with Marx's own interpretation of historical materialism is advised to read Alfred Schmidt's essay 'Der strukturalistische Angriff auf die Geschichte' in *Beiträge zur marxistischen Erkenntnistheorie* (which ought to be translated for the benefit of British and American students of the subject who in their enthusiasm for Lévi-Strauss may have missed Sartre's and Lefebvre's devastating attacks on Althusser and his school). What we have here is a discussion whose significance far transcends the silly dispute between Western empiricists and Soviet Marxists: a quarrel which has now gone on long enough and should be quietly terminated before the audience dies of fatigue.

To avoid a possible misunderstanding which may easily creep in at this point: in the context of the recent German *Positivismusstreit* the 'positivism' of Comte and his school is not particularly relevant, except that the heirs of logical positivism frequently tend to be positivists (in the nineteenth-century sense of the term), in matters political as well. Whether this is purely fortuitous is perhaps open to doubt. Equally one may suspect that the prevalence of empiricist and pragmatist ways of thought among contemporary Anglo-American liberals is more than a coincidence, even though empiricists are notably reluctant to flaunt a political banner in public. Anyone who has attended a gathering of Continental European philosophers will have noticed that whereas Marxists and Thomists make no bones about their respective political orientation, it is remarkably difficult to get their empiricist critics to take a stand on political principles. Somehow or other they are not anxious to advertise their faith in New Frontiers, Great Societies, Alliances for Progress, and similar slogans of the Kennedy-Johnson era. Even when the debate ranges over strictly academic topics—say, the uses and misuses of sociology—they can rarely be induced to abandon the security of their methodological shelter.

Can we at last confront this latest *Methodenstreit*? Alas, not yet. We still have to surmount one more preliminary hurdle: Albrecht Wellmer's onslaught on the Vienna Circle and its heritage. But perhaps 'preliminary' is not quite the word. *Kritische Gesellschaftstheorie und Positivismus* appeared in 1969: twelve years after Adorno had opened the debate with a lecture titled 'Soziologie und empirische Forschung' at the Frankfurt Institut für Sozialforschung; eight years after Karl Popper had restated his well-known doctrines at a Tübingen session of the Deutsche Gesellschaft für Soziologie in October,

1961; and six years after Jürgen Habermas, in an essay titled 'Analytische Wissenschaftstheorie und Dialektik' (now reprinted in the *Positivismusstreit* volume) had unlimbered the heaviest artillery at the disposal of the Frankfurt school. Perhaps Wellmer's little volume should rather be regarded as a postscript to a controversy which has now raged for more than a decade. It is, however, an extremely learned postscript, and for good measure it carries a punch that lifts the debate well beyond the range of polite academic disputation. A brief quotation will suffice:

> In contrast to the belated liberal Popper, Carnap represents unreservedly the technocratic consciousness of his age. One might even say that he has carried the language-critical approach of the youthful Wittgenstein to as radical a conclusion as Wittgenstein himself. If the late Wittgenstein deciphers the meaning of language in its practical functioning, Carnap rejects as senseless any language which does not function properly; if Wittgenstein affirms the unity of language and existence, Carnap apprehends the residual difference between them; his aim is to eliminate it.

Wellmer, it might be added, is a pupil of Habermas.

To the battlefield then. *Allons marcher aux canons.* After all this distant gunfire the reader is entitled to an account of the actual slaughter. But of course no one was killed or even seriously injured. When the smoke had lifted, all the contending parties were seen to be securely in possession of their ground. The great contest had ended in a draw: or perhaps one should say the rival armies never really came to grips. In the end they did not perhaps have enough in common to make a genuine engagement possible. Certainly Professor Albert's 'Kleines verwundertes Nachwort zu einer grossen Einleitung' gives the impression that its author was somewhat put off not merely by the excessive length of Adorno's introduction to the volume (more than seventy pages), but also by its philosophical sweep. The positivist has some trouble with the Hegelian who *will* insist on talking about everything at once, as though it were still possible to carry on in the ancient holistic manner. And it is undeniable that Adorno's reckless cavalry charge across the entire field of debate, from metaphysics to linguistics, carried its own dangers.

Albert is not alone in feeling that the grand manner is no substitute for the kind of rigorous analytical reasoning which became the hallmark of the Frankfurt school once younger men—Habermas above all, closely followed by Schmidt and Wellmer—had taken over from the veterans Horkheimer and Adorno. All the same, if someone had to meet Popper head on, Adorno was not a bad choice: the more so since in the 1920s both men inhabited that specifically Viennese intellectual world from which logical positivism, psychoanalysis, musicology, linguistics and neo-Marxism were shortly to radiate outwards.

Yes, but what is *Der Positivismusstreit in der deutschen Soziologie* finally about? Well, to put it as briefly and unfairly as possible, it is 'about' the ancient quarrel between the disciples of Marx and those of Max Weber. Of course this was not quite how it was put (except when Albert and Habermas briefly lost their tempers and clashed over a corner of the field recently brought into prominence by the neo-Marxist revisionism of Leszek Kolakowski, whose earlier work Habermas had already criticized in his 1963 essay collection *Theorie und Praxis*).

For the most part, the contestants avoided political topics and stuck to their methodological guns. Even so, the spectre of Marxism raised its head when Habermas observed: 'I am concerned to question . . . the separation of science from ethics.' This was followed by a brief reference to 'the dialectic' which, to cite Habermas once more, 'figures as a scarecrow in the unbuttoned Weltanschauung of certain positivists'. These positivists currently employ Popperian language, but no German would dream of denying that the sociologists among them are the spiritual heirs of Weber.

Now it so happens—another coincidence?—that Weber was the most important and consistent theorist of liberal imperialism in Wilhelmine Germany. That is to say he was the intellectual leader of a school which stood for a very definite political orientation. This circumstance carries awkward implications for theorists who insist that sociology to be genuinely scientific must be 'value-free': Marxism being unscientific by definition because it makes no secret of its commitment to certain values. But did Weber not espouse a value system of his own? Yes indeed, but he had the honesty to affirm that his beliefs were unrelated to his real work as a scholar. His values, that is to say, were grounded in purely personal decisions not anchored in a speculative philosophy or Weltanschauung. It was just this which to his followers made his approach seem responsible and scientific: his methodological assumptions were divorced from his private desiderata. This radical disjunction of science from ethics was and is the pride of the school. It also represents what its critics regard as a confession of intellectual bankruptcy.

Here then is the link, or a link, between the earlier *Methodenstreit* and its present-day sequel. Now as before the positivist school conceives itself to be defending the autonomy of science against assailants stemming from the Romantic right or the Marxist left, both in the last resort invoking arguments derived from speculative metaphysics. The rationale of this two-front war, whether stated in Weberian or Popperian language, is always the same: science in general, and social science in particular, needs to be *wertfrei* (value-free) so as to perform the task of exact empirical description. In so far as the scientist gives his allegiance to religious, philosophical, political or artistic values, he does so in his personal capacity.

While not disputing the theologian's belief in a divinity, or the artist's right to embrace the Romantic creed—the latter being a kind of metaphysical inflation of the artistic view of the world—the scientific investigator in his professional role eschews these temptations. Likewise he departs from the older positivist tradition associated with Comte, for he does not regard it as his task to prescribe the aims which rational understanding of the world, or the social whole, is destined to serve. Lastly, he abandons the search for 'laws' of historical development therein following a line of thought inaugurated by Weber's neo-Kantian contemporaries, notably Dilthey and Rickert, and brought to perfection in our own days by Karl Popper. As far as sociology is concerned, this restriction of the field results in the detailed elaboration of formal systems of 'social relations' (Tönnies) or 'social action' (Weber, Talcott Parsons). In Weber's system rational behaviour counts as the 'ideal type' of social action, with the obvious proviso that ideal types are not actually encountered in empirical reality. None the less the course of Western history, down to and beyond the industrial revolution, is interpreted in terms of a general theory of social action; as against the historicism of the Marxists, for whom bourgeois society represents a transitory phase of societal evolution, to be succeeded by the 'truly rational' order of socialism.

Finally, and this is where the current debate becomes overtly political the 'technocrats' of the New Right (Hans Freyer, Arnold Gehlen) have stepped in with a theoretical model of their own which is no more to the taste of liberals like Popper, Albert, and Ralf Dahrendorf, than the romantic Rousseauism of Marcuse and the New Left. Technocracy has been described (by Habermas) as the doctrine that the social order can be consciously adapted to the requirements of contemporary science and technology. To put it in language familiar to Marxists, the 'superstructure' no longer needs to be reshaped by social revolutions stemming from the familiar contradiction between 'relations of production' and social relations. Instead of these convulsive eruptions from below—which admittedly still do occur in the more backward regions of the globe—what we now have is a deliberate rearrangement of the socio-cultural sphere, brought about by the managers of the new technology and their political allies or masters.

This point does not emerge clearly from the *Positivismusstreit* volume, but then Gehlen's followers—like those of Herbert Marcuse —were not invited to contribute. The academic establishment in the Federal Republic is indeed split down the middle, but at the professorial level the only really significant confrontation opposes the left centre (Habermas) to the Weberian or Popperian liberals (Albert). The extremes are excluded. Freyer and Gehlen were too deeply involved with the Third Reich to be acceptable among liberal or socialist humanists; and the romantic mysticism of the aged Ernst Bloch, with his rather endearing faith in Schelling's *Naturphilosophie*, appeals only to that section of the New Left which is eternally in search of a Weltanschauung to bolster its instinctive rejection of the modern world: a very Germanic trait this, at one time suggestive of fascist tendencies, nowadays fortunately transmuted into a rather harmless kind of anarchism.

From the positivist standpoint the foregoing remarks introduce extraneous considerations having to do with the more or less accidental political positions of some of the participants in the recent German discussion. To the dialectician they are of the essence, and this is just where the debate between Albert and Habermas runs into the sands. Albert explicitly subtitles his first section 'Dialektik contra Positivismus', thereby incidentally pulling the rug from under certain learned bystanders who dispute the legitimacy of this terminology. For good measure he introduces his critique of the Frankfurt school with a brief retrospective glance at Weber's heritage. This approach has the merit of enabling the reader to grasp the intimate connexion between *Wissenschaft* and *Wertfreiheit* in the sense usually given to these terms. Albert, whose *Traktat über Kritische Vernunft* was dedicated to Karl Popper, makes no bones about his dislike of the Hegelianism implicit in the publications of the neo-Marxist school. At the same time he sees clearly enough that the positivist disjunction of technical rationality and normative ethics leaves a gap between theory and practice. His solution of the problem has a neo-Kantian ring:

It is . . . possible to overcome the positivist resignation in questions of moral philosophy without lapsing into the existentialist cult of *engagement* which replaces rational discussion of such problems by irrational decisions. The criticism which opens up this possibility before us has . . . itself a moral content. Whoever adopts it thereby commits himself not to an abstract principle without existential significance, but to a way of life. Among the direct ethical consequences of criticism there is the conclusion that the unshakable faith . . . upheld by some religions is not a virtue but a vice.

In his epistemological study *Erkenntnis und Interesse* (reviewed here June 5, 1969) Habermas proposes an alternative solution by postulating an inherent union of cognition and interest: likewise at the level of 'criticism', but in a sense plainly derived from Hegel and Marx rather than from Kant and Weber. What he terms 'Kritik als Einheit von Erkenntnis und Interesse' is not *Erkenntniskritik*, but something a good deal more practical. Both books were written, or at any rate published, after their distinguished authors had fired prolonged salvoes at each other during the debate over the methodology of the social sciences. They help to explain the fundamental standpoints underlying the essays reprinted in the *Positivismusstreit* volume, an English translation of which is now rumoured to be in progress not far from the London School of Economics. It will be interesting to see how the translators deal with Adorno's lengthy introduction; they should have less trouble with the polemic between Albert and Habermas, or with the brief contributions made by Ralf Dahrendorf and Harald Pilot.

However unbridgeable the gulf between Albert's empiricism and the neo-Hegelianism of the Frankfurt school, all concerned express themselves with a clarity and precision not universally common in earlier and stormier days. When Habermas gets down to the business of explaining the difference between the functionalist (Weberian or Parsonian) notion of 'system' and the dialectical concept of 'totality', even the reader not initiated into the mysteries of Hegelian logic can easily follow his train of thought. With Albert's exposition of Popper's positivism, there is of course no problem at all: the English-speaking world is thoroughly familiar with it.

We are now in a better position to answer the question what the whole argument is 'about'. As far back as 1963, when Habermas fired the opening shot in his critique of Popper (see 'Analytische Wissen-schaftstheorie und Dialektik'), he spelt out a number of propositions which, whatever one might think of them, are plainly incompatible with the scientist credo. Dialectical theory, he wrote, 'questions whether science is entitled to proceed in regard to the world of men with the indifference successfully practised in the natural sciences'. And again, dialectical thinking 'overcomes the separation of theory and history'.

In his 1964 rejoinder, Albert described the purpose of the enterprise as a 'practically orientated philosophy of history dressed up as science'. By the conventional standards of the academic world this was plain speaking, and there was to be a lot more on both sides. The basic issue emerged almost incidentally when Albert registered astonishment at the sight of a colleague in search of a legitimation of practical action. 'He [Habermas] looks for an objective legitimation of practical activity through meaning in history, a legitimation which naturally cannot be provided by a scientific sociology bearing a realistic character.' Well, at any rate there is no dispute about the normative incompetence of this kind of positivist sociology.

If one adopts the criterion of *praxis*, two rival but interrelated standpoints are automatically excluded: the dogmatic crucifixion of the individual in the name of God, the World Spirit, or Being; and the empiricist conviction that anyone equipped with a normal dose of intelligence can make sense of the world simply by applying ordinary moral criteria. As regards the former there was no dispute among the participants, although matters might have become awkward if the debate had been joined by a theologian. The difference related to the latter, and it did so because empiricists proceed from the nominalist assumption that the social whole is made up of individuals who have to learn rational behaviour if they are not to get in each other's way.

In a sense this is obvious, but it is the kind of truth that blurs the perception of what is really at stake in this sort of controversy. For a society in which individuals are held together by nothing but their manifest self-interest is precisely the target of critical theorizing on the part of the dialecticians. The latter need not be orthodox Marxists —Habermas at least is a revisionist even by the tolerant standards of the Frankfurt school—but they have inherited the basic insight of the 'critical theory' into the problematic nature of contemporary society. What if this society increasingly becomes a deliberate artefact produced by the technocratic managers of the new order? Then a philosophy which in the name of empiricism excludes every kind of transcendence must inevitably turn into an apologia for the status quo.

One may also put it differently: the logical status of value judgments has become a practical problem not just for a few reflective individuals, but for everyone. Weber was able to ignore this circumstance because the society of his age was still autonomous vis-à-vis the state, and because the kind of liberal Protestantism on which he had been brought up was adequate for the educated German middle class to which he belonged: a stratum that has since undergone catastrophic upheavals, and incidentally shown itself helpless, to say the least, when confronted with the monstrosities of the Third Reich. *Der Positivismusstreit* is among others the record of a spiritual crisis brought about by the unprecedented collapse of German liberalism in 1933. It is true and important that enlightened rationalism has now, at long last, become the creed of the German educated world. It is likewise important that the romantic undercurrent, which for so long nourished the politics of the extreme right, has been diverted leftward by the student movement. But welcome though these changes are, they do not dispose of the dangers arising from the technocratic model—and anyway the new mood cannot validate the empiricism of the positivist school. So far as sociology is concerned, the school appears to be operating with equipment which was already inadequate in Weber's day. Its notion of rational behaviour is too formal to constitute an effective barrier against irrationality.

This is not to say that the debate can be written off as an academic dispute—another *Methodenstreit*. The issues at stake in the Albert–Habermas controversy, and in the antecedent duel between Popper and Adorno, concern us all. It is perhaps worth emphasizing once more that the discussion cuts across the East-West antagonism to which we have all become habituated. In so far as politics enter the matter, they relate to the functioning of a democratic order in a free society. None of the participants would want to be seen in the company of Spanish generals, Greek colonels, or East European bureaucrats. In short, this is a thoroughly civilized debate between the representative thinkers of a leading European country, now for the first time fully integrated within the general orbit of what is vaguely known as Western civilization. As such it merits attention irrespective of the intricate logical and philosophical topics at the centre of the dispute. In the long run, though, what counts is the core of the argument. It is just conceivable that this generation of German philosophers is going to make up for the misdeeds of its predecessors by helping the rest of us to find a way out of the maze into which the uncontrolled explosion of scientific technology has led us.

In the light of the foregoing remarks we may now conclude with a brief reappraisal of a work which for many years led an underground existence among the homeless left of the Federal Republic: the joint study of modern culture by Max Horkheimer and Theodor W. Adorno, entitled *Dialektik der Aufklärung*, originally composed by its two distinguished authors during their Californian exile in 1944, first published in 1947 by Querido in Amsterdam, repeatedly pirated, and finally re-edited and re-published by S. Fischer in 1969 with a joint preface dated 'Frankfurt am Main, April, 1969'. The book can stand as a monument to the intellectual trajectory described by two eminent representatives of the Old Left during the quarter-century separating one age from another. There is no hyperbole involved in speaking of an 'age' dividing the present generation from its fathers; it is only since 1945 that modern society has begun to assimilate the technological upheaval associated with nuclear fission, computerized knowledge, lunar rockets and so on. The concurrent transformation of the sociopolitical 'superstructure', although dimly visible since the day the first atom bomb fell on the unsuspecting inhabitants of Hiroshima, is now sufficiently far advanced to lend point to the gloomy analysis Horkheimer and Adorno placed at the opening of their joint enterprise in 1944:

Historically the Enlightenment, in the most general sense of progressive thinking, has aimed at the goal of delivering men from fear and making them masters of the world. But the wholly enlightened globe radiates triumphant disaster.

The theme has become rather tediously familiar, and signs are not lacking that what was new and original around 1945 is now turning into a litany of cut-price apocalyptics—what the eponymous hero of Saul Bellow's *Herzog* called 'the commonplaces of the Wasteland outlook, the cheap mental stimulants of Alienation, the cant and rant of pipsqueaks about Inauthenticity and Forlornness'. For all that, the book is still worth reading as an introduction to the peculiar synthesis of Marx, Freud, Nietzsche and Heidegger commonly associated with the name of Herbert Marcuse, and innocently popularized by a rising generation of intellectuals to whom the violent death of the Weimar Republic, and the concurrent collapse of the Old Left, signify no more than a particular bloodstained episode in the recent history of Continental Europe. Few of them are likely to respond favourably to the 1969 preface, with its disillusioned side-glance at 'the conflicts in the Third World, the new growth of totalitarianism' as the legitimate prolongation of the age of Hitler and Stalin. 'Critical thinking . . . today demands that one should side with the residues of freedom, with tendencies towards real humanism.'

Where then is the rising generation to look for guidance? To the ultra-left? But Maoism for practical purposes has a following—in Europe and America anyway—only among the lumpenproletariat and the lumpenintelligentsia, those ancient reservoirs of anarchism. Can one seriously build upon such foundations?

The pseudo-intellectuals of today cannot tell the difference between Marx and Mao, or between Freud and Timothy Leary, or between Beethoven and the Beatles. Many believe that the enemy is not the technocratic ruling stratum of the new order, but civilization itself— any civilization. What can one do with such human material? Make a revolution? But the working class loathes the very sight of them, and the cry 'kill the pigs' testifies only to the mental sickness of those who utter it. People who invent such slogans are themselves part of the disease they talk of curing.

The *Dialektik der Aufklärung*, then, has itself become an illustration of the dialectical interplay between the critique of 'mass culture' and the utilization of this critique by the leaders of a new generation of infuriated telly-watchers who rush into the streets whenever their blood boils over at the sight of yet another massacre in some far-away country of which, alas, we know only too much. It has become a commonplace that the driving force behind this non-stop protest is the cleavage between the omnipotence of the new technology and the felt impotence of the individuals who service it and are served by it. The diagnosis is true and apposite. Its current exemplification in the chaotic politics of the United States—at once the most advanced and the most conservative country of the Western world—bears out the statement that the Enlightenment has turned into its opposite. Only —and this is where the two authors felt obliged in 1969 to modify their original prospectus—this particular dialectic is not confined to the Western world, let alone to the collapsing culture of European bourgeois society. It applies to the 'socialist camp' as well. For proof one need only consider the current state of relations between Moscow and Peking.

On dialectical principles this outcome was to be expected. The universality of the crisis testifies to the effective unification of the world by the new technology let loose by the second industrial revolution. The fact that this revolution takes place over great areas of the planet under the banner of socialism or communism is historically significant when viewed from an authentically global standpoint. It then becomes apparent that the dichotomy capitalism/socialism is on the point of losing its former significance. What it portends is no longer a fundamental choice between alternative modes of existence, but a convergence towards a point where both systems disclose their common descent from principles held in common since the Enlightenment triumphed over its enemies: the defenders of the pre-industrial order. The socio-political cleavage symbolized by the effective partition of Europe in 1945 falls into place as an important but subordinate aspect of the global transformation in progress since that date, and the divergence between the 'two camps' loses its relevance in the measure in which both sides in this global contest for preeminence confront the threat of instant annihilation, and the subtler menace of technocracy: the latter signifying the conscious adaptation of the 'superstructure' to the new technological 'base'. Hence the *Methodenstreit* between the heirs of Marx and Max Weber occurs within a dimension of experience where the secret of the new order is at last out in the open: the social structure has become malleable on both sides of the political divide, and it has done so because the original Baconian vision is now close to fulfilment: science has become the instrument of total reconstruction. On what principles? In the name of what aims and values? Science as such has no answer to this question. Nor will it ever have one.

14

CAREERS IN PHILOSOPHY

(a) A. J. AYER

THE PHILOSOPHICAL scene in this country in the mid-1930s was respectable but not inspiring. Bertrand Russell had withdrawn from the subject into educational experiment and writing for a wide public in the 1920s, although a philosophically creative period still lay ahead of him. G. E. Moore, the senior figure in Cambridge, still dealt in the ideas he had expounded to the students of Morley College just before 1914. Wittgenstein had returned to Cambridge and philosophy but the striking new thoughts of his second period were carefully confined to a small inner circle, and his sole publication of the decade was a letter to *Mind* reproving a colleague for unauthorized mention of some of his ideas in an article.

In Oxford a mild reign of terror was administered by those two able, but resolutely negative, adherents of Cook Wilson: H. A. Prichard and H. W. B. Joseph. R. G. Collingwood, as a kind of English Santayana, propounded an idiosyncratic version of the local idealism that the school of Cook Wilson had displaced, but very much as a licensed and neglected irregular beyond the fringe of the main operation. Some may have read him for his style, cultivation and width of allusion, but his ideas were not to receive any serious attention for another twenty years. Only H. H. Price's magisterial *Perception* of 1932 and a steady flow of vigorous articles by Gilbert Ryle testified to anything in the way of lively philosophical innovation, and their work was limited in its appeal to professionals.

In 1936 A. J. Ayer's *Language, Truth and Logic* came out, explosively, in this somewhat frozen setting. Appropriately enough it was

(a) A. J. AYER: *Metaphysics and Common Sense*. 267 pp. Macmillan. £2.90. *The Origins of Pragmatism*. 347 pp. Macmillan. £3.50.

(b) W. V. QUINE: *Philosophy of Logic*. 109 pp. Prentice-Hall. £2.50 (paperback, £1). *Ontological Relativity and Other Essays*. 165 pp. Columbia University Press. £2.60.

not published by a university press or the more traditional publisher of philosophical books, Macmillan, who has published all Ayer's subsequent writings. The handsome little blue volume—whose nearly square, wide-margined and typographically severe pages had a distinctly progressive, Bauhaus quality—was brought out by the firm of Victor Gollancz, to take its place in a list where George Orwell, Prince Mirsky and the latter's white hope of the English intelligentsia, John Strachey, were still to be found, before the Moscow trials and the Nazi-Soviet pact, in plausible apposition.

This brief and crystalline volume—it is not much more than 50,000 words long—must have been the most widely read work of serious professional philosophy in English since the date of its publication. (Russell's engagingly personal *History of Western Philosophy* is too popular and desultory to qualify for comparison.) It was calculated to appeal to two audiences: to professionals as a brilliantly lucid and systematic presentation in English of the body of ideas elaborated by the Vienna Circle from the profound, elusive suggestions of Wittgenstein's *Tractatus*; to a larger public interested in general ideas as a uniquely accessible account of the seismic implications of recent developments in technical philosophy for habitually revered modes of thought in the domain of morals and religion.

With this book Ayer established himself as the chief active continuator of the national tradition of secular empiricism whose leading members are Hume, J. S. Mill and Russell himself. Like them Ayer has always upheld the methodological claims of natural science and mathematics, with their rigour and explicitness, against alternative paths to knowledge: intuition, feeling, authority, tradition, even that most traditional of authorities—common sense. Like them too he has always been concerned for the relevance of philosophy, narrowly conceived, to the stock of general ideas and beliefs current in the thinking, but not strictly philosophical, public. If his interests and extra-philosophical expertise have not been quite as wide as theirs (he has not written a massive history of England like Hume, engaged in organized movements for social reform like Mill or revolutionized the foundations of mathematics like Russell), this is because, unlike them, he has been continuously engaged in university teaching. He has been effectively engaged too: his transformation of the philosophy department of University College, London between 1946 and 1959 from a very modest undertaking to one of the liveliest philosophical centres in the English-speaking world made it a fit receptacle for the many applicants who were drawn by his personal fame to study there.

To the generally interested public and to the popularizers who directly serve it, *Language, Truth and Logic* was, reasonably enough, the authoritative exposition of 'logical positivism'. If it was less correct to suppose that logical positivism was identical with analytic philosophy in general, the fault lies with the failure of analysts less convinced of the pre-eminent status of formal logic and natural science to get their dissenting opinions across. What mainly shocked or excited the book's first readers was its uncompromising insistence that judgments of value were not statements, true or false, but propositional-looking expressions of emotion, gestures of applause or condemnation presented in words, and that the utterances of metaphysicians and theologians, attempting to demonstrate some harmony between the universe at large and human wishes, were empty word-play, a kind of talking in the dark.

Since 1936 the reflective public has become used to the ideas that there is no royal road to the elimination of diverse moral convictions and that religion cannot, in concrete, practical terms, guarantee eternal life and the rectification in it of the injustices of the world. The dominating tendency in theology itself is to dilute the claims of religion: the legalistic definiteness of the traditional moral law has given way to the idea of the moral sufficiency of love, amorphously conceived; and the old paternal God, ordaining and sanctioning the moral law, has been replaced by an object of Ultimate Concern, at times honorifically described as the Ground of Being. Thus, nearing sixty, Ayer finds himself in a situation where the general system of ideas and beliefs has more or less caught up with him, a fact symbolized by his knighthood in this New Year's honours list, a form of public recognition that would have seemed exceedingly improbable thirty-four years ago. Indeed, as the recently retired president of the British Humanists, he has become something of an established religious leader himself, alongside the Archbishop of Canterbury, Cardinal Heenan and the Chief Rabbi.

There were three main doctrines in *Language, Truth and Logic* and they correspond to a threefold distinction between types of thought or utterance which has served as an essential background to a great deal of subsequent philosophizing; the distinction between empirical statements of fact, analytic statements of necessary connexion, and a substantial residue of utterances that look like statements but are not and serve some other function, the content of our evaluations and the speculations of metaphysics and theology. The first doctrine, verificationism, maintains that a sentence can make a statement of fact only if it is associated by rule with a range of experiences which verify, or at least confirm, it. Secondly, there is conventionalism, which holds that necessary truths, in particular the propositions of logic and mathematics, are really definitional truisms, however hard to discover this may be on account of their complexity of structure, true (or false) in virtue of the meanings assigned by linguistic convention to the terms of which they are composed. Emotivism, finally, ascribes the function of expressing the speaker's feelings to the residue of utterances that are neither empirical nor analytic, in particular to judgments of value, somewhat more off-handedly to metaphysical utterances.

For Ayer an experience was, and has remained, the immediate awareness of a current state of mind, sensory or introspective. It followed from this that any statement which claimed to be factual and yet did not simply report an experience of this elementary kind can make good its claim only if it can be translated into a set, perhaps very complicated, of such experiential reports. From the outset he applied this principle of reduction to beliefs about material things, which he interpreted, in accordance with Mill's phenomenalist slogan, as 'permanent possibilities of sensation'. The full development of this theory about material objects was provided in *Foundations of Empirical Knowledge* in 1940. Since that time he has progressively qualified his claim that our beliefs about the external world can be reductively analysed without remainder in terms of the experiences observers would have in various circumstances, first in a chapter of his *Philosophical Essays* (1954), then in the chapter on perception in *The Problem of Knowledge* (1956) and, most recently, in the final chapter on radical empiricism of *The Origins of Pragmatism*. All he is now prepared to assert is that 'our conception of the physical world can be exhibited as a theory with respect to our experiences'. This, as it stands, is too weak to count as any sort of phenomenalism at all, for it applies as well to a causal account of our perceptual knowledge like Locke's as it does to the position of Mill or Ayer's earlier self.

The reductive interpretation of our beliefs about the mind has proved an even more refractory undertaking and has continued to occupy Ayer's attention. There are two main problems here. First, there is the task of accounting for the enduring identity of a person through time in terms of the relations between his experiences and without reference to any pure or transcendental Ego, a non-empirical mental substance. Ayer has continued to worry at this since he became dissatisfied with the blunt position he adopted in *Language, Truth and Logic* by which experiences are linked together by the enduring human body which manifests them. The chapter on 'Myself and Others' in *The Problem of Knowledge*, the title essay of *The Concept of a Person* (1963) and the radical empiricism chapter of *The Origins of Pragmatism* record the stages of this preoccupation.

The second problem about our knowledge of mind is that of what we can mean by what we say and believe about the minds of other people, to which we have no direct, experiential access. Ayer began by taking the view that 'I am in pain' is a direct report of experience, while 'he is in pain' is a complex remark about my experience of that behaviour in another which is all that my belief in the pain of another could, verifiably, amount to. This asymmetrical theory came to grief on the fact that 'I am in pain' said by me and 'he is in pain' said at the same time about me are the very same statement made in different ways and yet, on Ayer's analysis, one could well be true when the other was false. Unwilling to restore symmetry by Ryle's heroic device of interpreting autobiographical assertions in behavioural terms, Ayer has ingeniously revived the traditional analogical theory, by which I ascribe experiences to others in virtue of the analogies between their bodies and that ubiquitous body which I come to regard as my own.

A large part of Ayer's philosophical work since 1936, then, has been concerned with the implications of the verifiability requirement for the central problems of traditional epistemology. Not that his attachment to verificationism has been altogether unyielding. The most forcefully critical essay in his recent collection *Metaphysics and Common Sense* (unless that description should be reserved for the vigorous and uncompromising rebuttal of J. L. Austin's *Sense and Sensibilia* in the same volume) is his lethally effective handling of Professor Norman Malcolm's crudely verificationist theory that, since dreams cannot intelligibly be reported by the dreamer when they are supposed to occur, they cannot be experiences that one has when asleep; to have dreamed is to wake up disposed to tell stories about what seems to have happened but has not.

The other two main doctrines of *Language, Truth and Logic* Ayer has done little to develop. The chapter on the a priori in that book, endlessly anthologized, has been by far the most influential presentation of the conventionalist view about necessary truth. Every university student whose course contains the smallest tincture of philosophy must have at least been invited to read it. The view Ayer presents has been subjected to a sustained and fundamental criticism by Professor W. V. Quine of Harvard in an extended series of publications; and of all currently active philosophers Quine is the one for whom Ayer would seem to have most respect. But he has published no answer to Quine, even parenthetically. Quine argues that there is no sharp duality—as the conventionalists and their ordinary Kantian opponents assume—between analytic and synthetic statements. Our beliefs form a continuum in which are to be found only differences of degree in our unwillingness to abandon them. At the root of Quine's objections lies a serious doubt about the explanatory power of the concept of meaning in terms of which the distinction he criticizes is always defined.

The negative aspect of Ayer's emotivism—the thesis that it is not the function of judgments of value to state facts—has been more influential than the evaluation of them as philosophically fairly uninteresting which this thesis seems to have led him to make. It has given rise to a whole school of ethical theorists concerned to articulate the special peculiarities of evaluative discourse whose most dogged member is Professor R. M. Hare: and, more generally and more indirectly, it must have played some part in encouraging that insistence on the large multiplicity of non-fact-stating uses of language, characteristic of the later Wittgenstein and partially systematized in Austin's *How To Do Things With Words*, which sometimes suggests that the communication of beliefs is one of the rarest and least significant purposes that language can serve.

All the same Ayer's philosophical repertoire remains very large. He covers a much wider field of problems than most of his more specialized juniors. Besides a good deal about perception and the philosophy of mind, his two new books contain extended treatments of numerous topics in philosophical logic (truth, meaning and reference, the elimination of singular terms, intentionality and the analysis of such abstract entities of semantics as propositions) and in the philosophy of science (chance and probability, the justification of induction, the nature of theoretical entities, space and time and the susceptibility of human action to causal explanation). These

M

interests are intimated in, and so entirely continuous with, his first book.

Other items in the essay-collection *Metaphysics and Common Sense*, which is at once more popular and miscellaneous than his two previous collections, can be attributed to the nature of the occasions that evoked them. The first essay, which was a Granada lecture, 'Making Philosophy Intelligible', and 'Philosophy and Science', a contribution to a Russian philosophical periodical, are lucid defences of the type of philosophy he practises against common or communist preconceptions about what he ought to be doing. There is an admirably compact and sympathetic survey of Russell's philosophical career. Political philosophy is put in the modest place his fundamental emotivism would allow it in a cheerfully mischievous Eleanor Rathbone lecture. Bad old metaphysics, the dragon that has still not succumbed to the vorpal blade of the verification principle, is set about with gusto in 'Reflections on Existentialism'.

What is new, perhaps, is that instead of galumphing back from this exemplary task Ayer has stood awhile in somewhat uffish thought on the subject of ontology. The kind of radical, reductive empiricism that Ayer derived from the Vienna Circle did not infer from the reducibility to experiences of everything that actually exists that experiences alone really exist in some pre-eminent or ultimate way. Both Schlick and Carnap carefully disowned any such inference from their reductions. Schlick said 'we do not hold that nothing but the given exists'; and Carnap, more formally, distinguished between the empirical problem of reality—where the question of whether some thing, mind or social institution exists, is to be settled by seeing if the order of experience is what the concepts of these entities prescribe—and the vacuous and unsettleable metaphysical problem of reality.

But earlier radical empiricists, in particular William James and Russell (who was much influenced by James in this matter), had been less ontologically chaste. James's manifesto of radical empiricism was called 'A World of Pure Experience', and when he gave a negative answer to the question 'does consciousness exist?' he did not deny that there are states of consciousness; he denied only that substantial conscious entities are part of the ultimate furniture of the world. Russell concluded his lectures of 1918 on logical atomism with one called 'Excursus into Metaphysics: What There Is' in which he identified logical constructions, things like physical objects and human minds which could be reductively analysed into series or systems of experiences, with logical fictions and roundly proclaimed the unreality of such entities.

A neutral monist ontology of this kind is intimated in the later chapters of *Language, Truth and Logic*, though by no means explicitly affirmed there. It is a natural enough implication of reductive analysis. If Xs are logical constructions out of Ys, then Xs are really nothing but Ys; there is nothing more to an X than the Ys that constitute it. Ayer takes the subject up in Chapters Four and Five of his essay collection ('What There Must Be' and the title essay) and again at the very end of *The Origins of Pragmatism*. He admits that philosophers have generally taken reductive analysis to have ontological implications. But he is held back from neutral monism by a number of considerations.

In the first place the reducibility of the philosophically important cases (material objects, mind, propositions) is much more questionable and certainly much looser than that of such exemplary specimens as the average plumber. Secondly, he takes refuge to some extent behind a distinction Carnap draws between two ways of interpreting questions about the existence of entities of a given broad category, a distinction reminiscent of his earlier separation of empirical from metaphysical problems of reality. 'Are there numbers?', for example, may be construed 'internally' as arising for someone who already accepts the numerical vocabulary, in which case the answer is, trivially, yes. It can also, however, be construed 'externally' and in that event it is not a theoretical question the answers to which are true or false at all but a request for a decision: 'Shall we use the numerical vocabulary?' One objection to this has been put by Quine: how are we to distinguish between the categories of things questions about whose existence can be given such an 'external' interpretation from those lesser, empirical classes of which this is supposedly not true? A more fundamental objection is that conceptual frameworks are not matters of absolutely free choice: at least the world has to be such that the concepts in question can find an application in it.

In the final section of his book on pragmatism Ayer makes two further points. One is that, although experiences (or qualia as he now calls them) are the terminus of epistemological analysis, they cannot be the real stuff of the world because the thesis that they are provides us with 'no viable picture of the world'. This is a surprisingly aesthetic, or at any rate emotional, requirement for Ayer to lay down, not unlike F. H. Bradley's demand that a valid conception of truth and reality should 'satisfy' all sides of our nature. His other, more definite point is that experiences, or qualia, can find a place in an objective time-order only by way of their connexion with the bodies of the persons who experience them. A resolute neutral monist would ask why, if the objective time-order is a logical construction, a *façon de parler*, a symbolic convenience, it should be enthroned as an ontological criterion.

At all events Ayer concludes that the neutral monism of James and Russell is a non-starter and that the choice must lie between the kind of naive realism that attributes reality pre-eminently to perceptible material things, including human beings, and a scientific realism which attributes it to the fundamental particles of physics. Along with Professor Wilfrid Sellars and Professor J. J. C. Smart, Ayer here resurrects Eddington's notorious two tables which had long been supposed to have been indestructibly reunified by the counter-arguments of Susan Stebbing. Ayer's total detachment of ontology from reductive analysis does not testify only to his doubts about the thoroughness of his reductions. The neutral monism that he is anxious to avoid is very hard to keep neutral. As W. T. Stace argued in his critique of Russell's version of the theory thirty years ago, it slides very easily into idealism. Every actual experience is part of some mind; many are logically independent of matter; most matter is only potential with respect to actual experience.

It would be wrong to end a discussion of these books having treated their contents only in a dismembered way. *The Origins of Pragmatism* is a unitary design and by a considerable measure Ayer's longest book. In it he gives equal and equally sympathetic attention to both Peirce and James. But he applies his attention in a different way in each case. For all his anfractuosities of vocabulary Peirce writes in the idiom of a present-day philosopher. By comparison James is windy, rhetorical and desperately imprecise. In consequence Ayer's study of Peirce stays close to the detail of Peirce's arguments. This is possible because the arguments are actually there. In James's case there is a lot of admirable psychological description (a family trait, no doubt), but the philosophy is by comparison a matter of hopeful gesturing. Thus Ayer is able to use James's lively but argumentatively undernourished suggestions as opportunities for independent discussions of the topics at issue. The result is philosophically lively and interesting (among many other things a notable clarification of James's concept of the specious present is to be found), but it does not amount, in the case of either philosopher, to a full-blooded commentary of the usual scholarly sort. Ayer neither cites nor debates with other interpreters of his two pragmatists. But Peirce and James have stimulated him to enough original thought for him to leave the task of commentary to more pedestrian spirits.

(b) WILLARD V. QUINE

THE DEATH OF Bertrand Russell has deprived the philosophical world of its greatest contemporary figure. Of those who remain perhaps no one has a higher professional reputation than the American philosopher, Willard Van Orman Quine. Professor Quine, who is now in his early sixties, is most closely associated with the University of Harvard where he has been teaching since 1936, but he has been a visiting professor at a number of universities outside the United States, including the University of Oxford, from which he this year received an honorary degree. He started his career as a mathematical logician and of the twelve books which he has so far published, beginning with *A System of Logistics* in 1934, seven, including one that he wrote in Portuguese, are devoted to logic in the technical sense. Of these perhaps *Mathematical Logic*, of which the first edition appeared in 1940 and a revised edition in 1951, and *Set Theory and Its Logic*, of which the first edition appeared in 1963 and a revised edition in 1969, are the most important.

While Quine has few if any equals as an expositor of logic, and while in the development of his own logical system he has displayed original and fruitful ideas, he cannot be said to have made such far-reaching discoveries as are owed to contemporary logicians like Gödel, or Tarski, or Church. The field in which he has made himself pre-eminent is that of the philosophy of logic, to which his latest book, entitled *Philosophy of Logic*, provides a short but brilliant introduction. It is a subject which he has extended so that quite a wide range of philosophical questions, including questions which textbooks might classify as metaphysical, comes within its scope.

Two of the earliest papers in which Quine developed some of the characteristic features of his philosophical position were an essay 'On What There Is', which appeared in the *Review of Metaphysics* in 1948, and one entitled 'Two Dogmas of Empiricism', which appeared in the *Philosophical Review* in 1951. They are both reprinted in his collection of essays, *From a Logical Point of View*, which was published in 1953. It was in the essay 'On What There Is' that Quine coined his well-known slogan that to be is to be the value of a variable.

To understand what this means, it is necessary to know something about Russell's Theory of Descriptions. Russell had been concerned over the fact that nominative expressions, like 'The present King of France', could occur in meaningful sentences, even though there was no object which they were being used to denote. His response was to treat all definite descriptions of this sort as disguised predicates, whether they denoted anything or not. Thus, to take his own favourite example, the sentence 'Scott was the author of Waverley' was equated with the conjunction of the sentences 'For some x, x wrote Waverley', 'For all y, if y wrote Waverley, y is identical with x' and 'x is identical with Scott'. In the same way, the sentence 'The present King of France does not exist' simply became 'It is not the case that for some x, x now reigns over France'.

The letters x and y, as they occur independently in these sentences, were said to designate variables, and when the letters occurred in such expressions as 'for some x' or 'for all y', the variables were said to be quantified. Expressions like 'x is wise' or 'ϕ Socrates', the Greek letter ϕ being one of those used by Russell to hold a place for predicates, were said to contain free variables, and to designate propositional functions. These functions became propositions when the variables were quantified. So, 'For some x, x is wise' expresses the proposition that someone is wise: 'for some ϕ, ϕ Socrates' expresses the proposition that Socrates has some property. The values of a variable, over which the variable is technically said to range, are then simply those objects, or those properties, of which the function in which the variable occurs is true or false.

Now Quine's procedure has been to extend Russell's treatment of definite descriptions to the point of eliminating all singular terms. Proper names succumb to the device of treating 'being identical with so and so' as a unique descriptive predicate, and pronouns and other demonstratives are replaced by individuating descriptions, selected in accordance with the context. It is not claimed that this regimentation, as Quine puts it, of our ordinary way of speaking yields perfect translations of the sentences to which it is applied, but it is said to yield paraphrases, which are adequate in the sense that they comport no loss of information. The result is that we have a language in which the only way of referring to objects is indefinitely, through the use of signs which stand for quantified variables. It follows that the things over which the variables of such regimented discourse range are the only ones that it allows any title to existence, and the question what particular things there are is turned into the question what things actually satisfy the predicates with which the signs for quantified variables are coupled. This, then, is the point of Quine's saying that to be is to be the value of a variable.

As Quine himself recognizes, this is not so much an account of what there is as of what there is said to be: it is, as he puts it, a criterion of ontological commitment. A theory, in the broad sense used by Quine in which any set of assertions and their logical consequences is said to constitute a theory, is ontologically committed to the sorts of entities over which its variables range, and this will be determined by the predicates which it contains. Now clearly there may be things which fall outside the range of any given theory in this sense. All the same, we shall see that in his book *Word and Object*, which was published in 1960, and still more in one of his most recent books, a collection called *Ontological Relativity and Other Essays*, Quine takes a position which implies that although the question what there is does not exactly coincide with the question what there is said to be, nevertheless the two are not entirely separable.

A consequence of Quine's view of ontological commitment is that the range of entities to which a theory is committed will depend upon the way in which the theory is formulated. In some cases the avoidance of commitments which one finds undesirable will be a more or less simple matter of reparsing, but in others, the more interesting cases, it will turn on the question whether one can find a means of reducing one type of entity to another. Thus, if someone wishes to renounce abstract entities, as Quine once said he did, in a paper called 'Steps toward a Constructive Nominalism' which he and Nelson Goodman published in the *Journal of Symbolic Logic* in 1947, he will have to avoid quantifying over properties or classes, and then, as this paper showed, he will need considerable ingenuity in order to be able to make the rough equivalent of even so humdrum a statement as that there are more dogs than cats.

In his more recent writings, Quine has given up this austere nominalism on the ground that it does not allow for the amount of classical mathematics which one is obliged to accept if one wishes to do justice to contemporary science, and he now admits a hierarchy of classes into his ontology. He believes that classes can do all the respectable work for which properties might be thought to be needed, and he thinks that classes are to be preferred to properties because, unlike properties, they are subject to a clear criterion of identity, a class A being identical with a class B if and only if A and B have the same members.

Since Quine conceives of quantification as ranging over objects rather than linguistic expressions, except in the cases where linguistic expressions are themselves treated as objects, it is important for his purposes that the functions which take these objects as values should be well-behaved, in the sense that they do not allow anything to be true of an object under one designation which is not true of it under another. But notoriously there are areas, both of ordinary and of philosophical discourse, in which this condition is not satisfied.

One conspicuous class of instances results from the use of modal operators like 'it is necessary that'. To take one of Quine's own examples, the number nine is identical with the number of the planets, but while '9 is necessarily greater than 7' would commonly pass for a true statement, 'the number of the planets is necessarily greater than 7' would commonly be thought to be false. More familiar instances are supplied by indirect discourse and by the use of words which stand for what Russell called propositional attitudes. Thus, to take another of Quine's examples, I may believe that the man who stole such and such secret documents is a spy, and yet not believe that my respectable neighbour is a spy, though in fact it was my respectable neighbour who stole the documents. Consequently, 'being believed by me to be a spy' is true of this man under one description and false under another.

The difficulty about modal operators does not greatly trouble Quine, since he is quite content to do without them. For a reason which we shall come to in a moment, he thinks that the distinction which philosophers have drawn between necessary and contingent propositions is neither requisite nor properly made out: and while he does countenance talk about possibilities, in that we can speak significantly, not only about what does happen but also about what would happen if the appropriate conditions were realized, he holds that such conditional statements can be resolved into statements about dispositions; and, less plausibly, that statements about dispositions can be resolved into statements about the structure of the objects to which the dispositions are ascribed, these attributions of structure being themselves derived, in many cases, from theories about the constitution of 'natural kinds' to which the objects belong.

On the other hand, Quine admits the obligation to accommodate talk about propositional attitudes, and he has not yet found a satisfactory way of bringing it into line. He hopes that it can be resolved into talk about the constitution and behaviour of the persons who have the attitudes, where the references to behaviour must be taken as implying no more than that the persons in question make, or are disposed to make, certain physical movements. But any programme of this kind is exposed to obvious difficulties which no one has yet seen the way to overcome.

The basis for Quine's avoidance of modal concepts is already to be found in the essay 'Two Dogmas of Empiricism'. The empiricist dogmas which he rejects are, first, that there is a tenable distinction between analytic and synthetic propositions, and, secondly, that every empirical proposition has definite truth-conditions, in terms of the experiences that would confirm it, which fix its meaning independently of other propositions. Traditionally, the mark of an analytic proposition has been taken to be that it owes its truth solely to the meaning of the sentence which expresses it; and this also has been given as the explanation of its necessity. In the case of a synthetic proposition, on the other hand, the meaning of the sentence which expresses it has been thought to yield no more than its truth-conditions, but not to determine its truth.

It has been disputed whether all necessary propositions are analytic, but it has been generally agreed that there is a valid distinction to be drawn between necessary propositions, which are not at the mercy of empirical matters of fact, and contingent propositions which are at their mercy. The difference between empiricists and, say, Kantians, in this regard, is simply over the question whether necessity extends beyond analyticity.

Quine does not share in the agreement which underlies this difference, and his reason for not sharing in it is partly allied to his rejection of the second empiricist dogma. In his view, the propositions or, as he would prefer to say, the sentences which make up a given theory do not confront the facts singly; the theory presents itself for judgment as a whole, and when it conflicts with our experience, there are various ways in which it can be modified. Admittedly, we are more ready to modify some parts of the theory than others. The whole corpus of a man's beliefs can be likened to a sphere in which reports of observation lie on the periphery and logical, semantic, and mathematical principles are at the centre. Reports of observation, being, as it were, forced on us by our experiences, are relatively secure, and so are the principles at the centre. If repairs are called for, they are nearly always undertaken somewhere in between.

Nevertheless, there may be times when we choose to reject the verdict of our senses, rather than give up a set of well-entrenched hypotheses, and there might be circumstances in which we should find it expedient to recast our mathematics or our logic. As Quine characteristically puts it, 'the tail thus comes, in an extremity, to wag the dog'. Quine is very much given to quoting Neurath's simile of our being like sailors in a ship which never puts into port. We cannot get outside the ship to reconstruct it as a whole, but even while we remain on it there is no part of it that we cannot undertake to repair.

It might be thought that we could accept all this and still uphold the distinction between analytic and synthetic propositions. If analytic propositions are those that are true solely in virtue of the meaning of the words that express them, then to renounce an analytic proposition will be to alter our linguistic usage, which we are indeed free to do. This will, however, still be different from the case where we change our view about some empirical matter of fact.

Quine's answer to this is that the concept of meaning which is thus made to enter into the definition of an analytic proposition is not sufficiently clear for the purpose. He is willing to employ the concept of logical truth, since a logically true proposition can be defined as a true proposition in which only logical constants occur essentially, the list of logical constants being given by enumeration. But not all propositions thought to be analytic are logically true: to turn a would-be analytic proposition like 'Bachelors are unmarried men' into a logical truth, we need to assume that the word *bachelor* is a synonym for *unmarried man*, and the concept of synonymity does not meet Quine's standard of clarity.

Moreover, even if all propositions said to be analytic could be shown to be instances of logical truths, the claim that logical truths themselves are analytic would still have to be justified. The justification usually given for it is that the propositions of logic are made true by linguistic convention, but this answer has never satisfied Quine. In an essay called 'Truth by Convention', which he first published as early as 1935 and has recently reprinted in his book *The Ways of Paradox*, he admits that one could formulate conventions which would govern any known systematization of logic, but argues that this is true of any systematic body of doctrine: there is no ground here for distinguishing between the allegedly a priori sciences and the rest.

A further difficulty arises from the fact that the truths of logic are infinite in number, from which it follows that we cannot establish them severally by fiat. But if we have to derive groups of them en bloc from our definitions, then we shall be using logic to infer logic from the conventions which are supposed to govern it. One can, indeed, try to meet the charge of petitio principii by maintaining that the conventions are operative before they are formulated, but Quine's comment on this is that it is only if the conventions are taken to be explicit that the thesis that the propositions of logic are true by convention has any interest.

It can be objected that Quine's distaste for the concept of meaning is excessively puritanical. The fact that he was not able to give a definition of synonymity in other than semantic terms would not ordinarily be regarded as a fatal disqualification for the compiler of an English dictionary. But Quine's position here reflects a wider philosophical standpoint. He holds that there is bound to be a radical indeterminacy in any translation from one language to another, or even from one sentence to another within the same natural language.

The argument for this view was first set out in the opening chapter of *Word and Object*. A linguist, studying a native language, notes that a native says 'Gavagai' when a rabbit runs past. He carries out his usual tests and finds them all favourable to the hypothesis that *Gavagai* is the native word for a rabbit. But this hypothesis must always remain conjectural. Even if it could be established that this was not a case of what Quine calls indirect ostension, that is, a case where the word refers not to something X which is observably present but to something else which is associated with X, any evidence which went to show that 'Gavagai' referred to a rabbit would be equally consistent with its referring to rabbithood or to rabbit, where *rabbit* is construed as a bulk term, or to a rabbit-stage, a temporal slice of a rabbit, or to an undetached rabbit part. The linguist would, indeed, try to remove these uncertainties by asking questions about number and identity, but in order to interpret the answers to these questions he has to form what Quine calls analytical hypotheses about the semantical structure of the language which he is investigating; and a different choice of such hypotheses would still lead to different interpretations of his subjects' meaning, which would be equally in accordance with all his data.

It might be suggested that the linguist's difficulties were simply due to his having to penetrate the native language from the outside. If he were bilingual there would be no problem. But Quine will not accept this easy way out. He argues that the same problem arises in interpreting the utterances of those who speak the same language as oneself. We assume a community of meaning, because we assent to the same sentences in the same observable situations: but, this leaves as much room for radical differences as in the case of the native's 'Gavagai'.

At least, it may be said, one knows what one means oneself, but Quine seems unwilling to concede this, since he speaks of semantics as being 'vitiated by a pernicious mentalism so long as we regard a man's semantics as somehow determinate in his mind beyond what might be implicit in his dispositions to overt behaviour'. This leaning to behaviourism might well be questioned, but it is a side-issue, since it is enough for Quine's purpose that communication between different speakers should be indeterminate for the reasons that he gives.

The indeterminacy of translation goes together, in Quine's view, with what he calls 'ontological relativity'. What there is may not be what there is said to be, both because we may be mistaken about the objects which satisfy certain functions, and because there may be things which have not come within our ken. Nevertheless the only existential statements that are operative for us are those relating to the satisfaction of predicates which enter into our theories, and whatever does come within our ken must be covered at least by some enlargement of our stock of concepts for the question of its existence or non-existence to have any significance.

But then the considerations which dictate the indeterminacy of translation come into play. Since our theories are always underdetermined by the experiences which give rise to them, quite different accounts of what there is, each with its own way of interpreting the evidence, may be equally in accord with our experiences. This applies even in mathematics. If we ask what a natural number is, we get three different answers, according as we adopt Frege's or Zermelo's or von Neumann's method of reducing numbers to sets. Though these answers are not equivalent, any arithmetical statement which comes out true in one system has a true counterpart in the others, and for this reason there is no sense in asking which is right.

Similarly, we may have physical theories which are radically different, although each of them accommodates all the relevant observations that have been or will be made, and here again there is no sense in asking which of them represents the world as it really is. We cannot even compare them except in terms of a common background theory and to this theory also there will be alternatives, though to see them as alternatives we have to set them against a further background. The relativity is inescapable.

But surely physical objects must figure in all our theories in one guise or another, if they are to do justice to our experiences? Quine's answer seems to be yes, in practice, though he makes it a matter of convenience. He speaks of our positing physical objects, as a way of organizing our experiences, with the implication that other courses are open to us, but he does not treat any other course as a serious option. Thus, he denies that we can manage with sense-data on the ground that 'immediate experience will not, of itself, cohere as an autonomous domain'. So 'the positing of physical objects must be seen not as an *ex post facto* systematization of data, but as a move prior to which no appreciable data would be available to systematize'.

This is all a sophisticated form of pragmatism, with the difference that Quine, unlike the earlier pragmatists, does not treat theories as equivalent when they have the same observable consequences. But if, in the last resort, I cannot find out whether my neighbour is referring to rabbits, or to rabbit-stages, or to rabbit-parts, or to regions of space-time with rabbity properties, and if the truth value of his statements remains the same, under each of these interpretations, then the fact that I am theoretically able to differentiate between them is not of much consequence. The moral, which Quine himself does not explicitly draw, is that ontology is unimportant, except as raising the question whether, and if so how, one type of entity is reducible to another. What matters is not what there is but what is true and how different sorts of truths are mutually related.

The title essay of *Ontological Relativity and other Essays* reproduces two lectures which Quine delivered at Columbia University in 1968. They constituted the first of the John Dewey lectures which are to be given biennially and they set a standard which it will be hard for subsequent lecturers to maintain. There are other good things in the book including some reflections on Pythagoreanism, a discussion of the status of propositions, and a fresh attempt on the problem of induction, and it is written with Quine's usual incisiveness. He has a style which is very well adapted to the display of his philosophical qualities: a happy combination of technical expertise, inventiveness and wit.

I5

FICTION OF I97O

(g) IRIS MURDOCH
A Fairly Honourable Defeat

MORGAN, a lady philologist, arrives back from the States in a state and in a mess. Her love affair with Julius—allegedly a biochemist of distinction—has ended abortively in more senses than one, but she is not interested in going back to her husband Tallis, who lives an apparently hopeless life in Notting Hill surrounded by good causes and piles of old washing-up. She makes for her sister Hilda, who lives prosperously and with a liberal conscience in S.W.10. and who is ostentatiously happily married to Rupert, a thoroughly sound civil servant who is also a Sunday metaphysician. Hilda is extremely fond of and feels very close to her sister, about whose situation she is determined to do something constructive. It will come as no surprise to Miss Murdoch's regular readers that, in the end, it is Morgan's crisis which disintegrates Hilda's and Rupert's stability; as the title implies, the end of the book has its tragic aspect. Others closely involved include Simon, Rupert's younger brother—unable continuously to believe his good fortune in loving and being loved by Axel—and Peter, Rupert's and Hilda's son—who has given up Cambridge in disaffection and dropped out.

It is often easy to make the plots of Iris Murdoch's novels sound, in summary, as if an operatic arbitrariness of motivation has been

(g) IRIS MURDOCH: *A Fairly Honourable Defeat*. 402 pp. Chatto and Windus. £1.75.

(h) DAN JACOBSON: *The Rape of Tamar*. 183 pp. Weidenfeld and Nicolson. £1.50.

(i) DAVID LODGE: *Out of the Shelter*. 303 pp. Macmillan. £2.10.

(j) JOHN UPDIKE: *Bech: A Book*. 206 pp. André Deutsch. £1.50.

(k) PATRICK WHITE: *The Vivisector*. 642 pp. Cape. £2.

(l) JOSEF ŠKVORECKÝ: *The Cowards*. Translated by Jeanne Němcová. 416 pp. Gollancz. £2.20.

IVAN KLÍMA: *The Jury* and *A Ship Named Hope*. Translated by Edith Pargeter. 255 pp. Gollancz. £1.80.

yoked to a choreographic rigidity of execution. It is perhaps fairer to her remarkable narrative ability to ask whether, in a given case, her pace and her personalities are such as to overcome any resistance there may be to patent if not flagrant authorial manipulation. *A Fairly Honourable Defeat* could only have been written by the immensely practised novelist that Miss Murdoch has so industriously become, and it has many of her characteristic qualities. The actual story is at least intermittently inventive—there is a particularly engaging sequence which begins with Julius effectively imprisoning Morgan in his flat by cutting up all her clothes into small pieces, and then leaving her naked, and alone. The dialogue—of which there is a great deal—is inevitably intelligent, although it often rehearses in an academic manner problems of morals and notions of reality that have frequently been discussed in Iris Murdoch's work before. The author's feeling for the King's Road/Fulham Road/Boltons area of London is adequately in evidence. And, most of all, there are moments when a human capacity for loving other people despite their otherness is touchingly embodied.

The character who most demonstrates this in the new novel is the apparently pathetic Tallis. His care for his cantankerous and cancerous father and his clear-sightedness about his wife is good, even though he is too hamstrung by his feeling for both of them to help them much. It is significant that during an unpleasant scene in a Chinese restaurant in which a Negro is being beaten up, Tallis is the one who effectively intervenes. His opposite is the much more dynamic Julius, who is the most powerful agent in *A Fairly Honourable Defeat*. The fact that he is also its least plausible character gives the novel a central and disabling weakness.

The danger signs appear early: Julius is introduced as having a faintly central European accent, and is said (admittedly by the impercipient Morgan) to be 'mythical'. He is the latest in what is becoming a long line of enchanters. Julius takes a reductive view of human nature, and seeks to prove that people are puppets by manipulating them himself. He aims to expose the well-meaning idealism of Rupert's philosophy by demonstrating that Rupert's trust in the power and sensible clarity of love is an illusion. He makes Rupert fall in love with Morgan, and then alerts Hilda (Rupert's wife, Morgan's sister) to the situation. He is no doubt evil, but—human inadequacy being what it is—his arguments are to some extent justified, or at least borne out, by the results of his experiments.

However, his capacity to make others believe what is not true, and to coerce them into acting in ways which they would not otherwise do, is fictively dependent on his plausibility as a personality capable of keeping others in thrall. Many readers are likely to feel that the guarantees behind Julius are not solid enough for them to credit the power over the other characters with which he is endowed. And if his power remains implausible or theoretical, then those who are made to capitulate to it will seem uncritically and even inexplicably vulnerable.

In a way Julius is a demonic alter ego of the novelist, and perhaps by the same token he is insufficiently distanced from her. But none of the characters in *A Fairly Honourable Defeat* has the density of the dying protagonist of her last novel *Bruno's Dream*. It may be that such an effect is not aimed for, and certainly the new book is one of those novels where Miss Murdoch gives more of her mind to the web than to the transubstantiating spider. All the same, between the long and diffuse stretches of chatty and even jolly dialogue, apparently authoritative analyses of the characters are given. And the tone of these passages seems to imply that the author has thought of and thought about her creatures carefully, but that she has not lived them or been possessed by them.

They are treated with the interested, speculative, but ultimately neutral attention that is given to acquaintances about whom one gossips but about whom one does not really care. However much the sympathies of the novel's total design are, as we should expect, on the side of love and intelligence, the quality of the author's absorption in the individual case lacks creative enthusiasm.

Such handicaps are too fundamental to be compensated for by the kind of tit-bit snapped up by explicators. With one's eyes firmly on the subtext, one can probably do a good deal with a heroine called Morgan who at times could be said to be fey. Malory is in fact mentioned briefly, but there is also a curious scene in which Morgan has a moment of panic in a dell near Cambridge which makes one wonder if there is not at least a fleeting allusion to the author of *The Longest Journey*. There are, too, some discussions about the morality of stealing which it would not be too hard to relate to the main plot. The tearing up of the manuscript of the father's book of philosophy by the son is surely significant, and the late revelation of the fact that Julius was once in Belsen must clearly be allowed to count for something. But however energetically such details of reference and such

N

figures in the carpet are picked out and deployed, they seem unlikely
to accumulate sufficiently to bring round the unconvinced reader.

(*h*) DAN JACOBSON

The Rape of Tamar

IT'S STIRRING STUFF, 2 Samuel 13—loads of sex and violence, battle
and intrigue, codes cruelly broken, revenges mercilessly wreaked and
the lot of it almost exclusively incestuous. Enter the screen-hungry
Historical Novelist? Not a bit of it. Dan Jacobson has spotted something odd in that Old Testament account of David's erring sons. The
oddity is the character of Yonadab, 'a very subtil man'. It is
Yonadab, he has noticed, who is approached by the love-lorn
Amnon and who advises him to lay the fatal trap for Tamar. And it is
also Yonadab who, when the deed is done and after Absalom has
murdered Amnon, is mysteriously on hand to assure David that
(contrary to spectacular and ill-informed reports): 'Amnon only is
dead, for by the appointment of Absalom this hath been determined
from the day that he forced his sister Tamar.' From this point on, we
hear no more of subtil Yonadab; we can safely assume, though, that
he, if anyone, survived the ensuing conflict.

Two obvious queries have occurred to Mr. Jacobson. Why was
Yonadab so helpful to Amnon in the first place, not only telling him
what to do but how to do it? And how is it that he alone seems to
have known about Absalom's plans for revenge? In short, whose
side was he on? And what did he expect to gain? *The Rape of Tamar*
authoritatively clears up all these mysteries by inviting Yonadab
himself to provide his version of the whole affair.

Yonadab is readier to accept such an invitation today than he
might have been, say, a hundred years ago. He feels that he can trust
us, and that we will find it easy to sympathize and even identify with
the actions of a man paramountly motivated by intense boredom, a
man who 'sees vanity where others see prowess, meaninglessness
where others see divine purpose, theatricality and role-playing where
others see fate and passion; farce where others see tragedy'.

A modern man, a cynic and manipulator, a mischievous ironist,
Yonadab—he confides in us—acknowledged only two necessities: the
need to survive, and the need to make survival at least entertaining.

And what entertainment could be had from the daily rituals of David's sycophantic court? Engulfed in 'the unending nausea of repetition'. Yonadab could hardly be blamed for welcoming the spicy confidences of Amnon, nor for encouraging them towards some interestingly calamitous conclusion. Friendship? 'I never knew anyone in whom I was tempted for a moment to put an absolute trust', and anyway Amnon was a feeble figure, privileged son of a king whom Yonadab's own father spent his whole life crawling to.

And so the plot unfolds. 'I can't pretend to be one of your anonymous narrators', Yonadab warns us. His tone throughout is matey, conspiratorial, and as he tells the tale he keeps up a steady flow of amused, even contemptuous, self-analysis. At one point he confesses to having been 'overcome with an emotion that surprised me disagreeably: it was remorse', but such moments are few and far between. He was the clever one in a world of fools; so why be modest?

In attempting to present Yonadab as a man of our world while maintaining a convincing sense of his presence in the world he is describing, Dan Jacobson set himself a difficult task. He brings it off superbly. His simple strategy is to hand the task to Yonadab:

> O dear, it seems that we are faced here with what the anthropologists call a culture gap, which can be crossed only by a certain stretching of the imagination on your side, a certain amount of deliberate explication on mine.

Thus, Yonadab (speaking throughout in witty modern colloquialese) is able to make easy use of words like 'psychosomatic', 'ethnographical', and so on, without seeming fake, and yet still leave himself lots of scope for the 'deliberate explication' of, say, court procedure, of how people dressed and furnished their houses, how David's harem operated. Warning us not to be carried away by Hollywood-induced preconceptions, he goes on:

> Put out of your mind those portraits of languid houris lying about in attitudes suggestive of inner heats; forget those eunuchs in baggy silken pants brandishing scimitars outside mysterious ogee-arched doorways. It wasn't like that. The women's quarters of David's palace were quiet, domestic, respectable. Indeed, almost suburban. After all, your suburbs, too, are pretty much inhabited by women and children only during the daylight hours.

This is a delicate balance to sustain, but only rarely does Mr. Jacobson allow himself to slip into the obvious pitfall and overplay the up-to-date deglamorizing ('Christ!—if I may call on the name of the most famous of my family connections' gives a brief indication of just how the book might have turned out had his approach been less scrupulous and tactful). And it is from the interplay between old dignities and fresh debunkeries that the book's funniest and most compassionate effects derive; compassionate because, absurd as that old world is shown to be, we also know it to have been momentous. The irony of Yonadab, though it familiarizes and downgrades, does not finally destroy. And here again, Mr. Jacobson has had to call on the most fragile of skills. *The Rape of Tamar* is a tight-rope triumph; you are never sure it's going to keep its balance until it's over—and then you can't imagine how he managed it.

(i) DAVID LODGE
Out of the Shelter

IN HIS NEW NOVEL David Lodge returns to the setting of his first book, *The Picturegoers*, published ten years ago: shabby-genteel Catholic family life in South London. His first treatment of this milieu was warm and even sentimental; now he regards it with a cool though not contemptuous eye. At the beginning, the hero, Timothy Young, is five years old; London is undergoing the Blitz, and Timothy enjoys the snug warmth of the Anderson air-raid shelter where the family sleeps at night. A bomb destroys a neighbour's house, killing his little playmate and her mother, and the shelter is half-buried in rubble; even so Timothy doesn't want to leave: 'In the end, one of the men carried him, kicking and screaming, out of the shelter, into the open air.' The implications of this sentence resound throughout the novel.

This opening section is evocative and moving, and though Mr. Lodge frankly relies on the first part of Joyce's *Portrait of the Artist* in presenting Timothy's developing consciousness, the substance of the story is firm enough to prevent one having any sense of obtrusive mannerism. Timothy shows every sign of growing up into a latter-day Stephen Dedalus; he is a timid but brainy lad and goes to the local Catholic grammar school where he is hard working and priggish, though in a more human way he is obsessed with sex and football. Mr. Lodge skilfully sketches in the multiple influences at work on Timothy: a narrow maternal possessiveness, the primness of self-conscious suburban respectability, and a rigid, somewhat superstitious form of Catholicism. In the background, half-perceived by the growing boy, the war moves to its conclusion and dismal aftermath: D-Day, V.E. Day, the sudden mysterious replacement of the great war leader Churchill by the colourless Attlee, and the advent of Strachey, Shinwell and Cripps as current demons, instead of the grosser bogeymen like Hitler, Goebbels and Goering. The bringing together of individual consciousness and public history is extremely well done, in a way that is rare in contemporary fiction. Mr. Lodge shows a keen sense of place as well as time; at the age of sixteen, on the way to Victoria to embark on his first trip abroad, Timothy looks with fresh eyes at the dreary region where he has grown up:

From the window of the bus the familiar streets took on a strange visual clarity and resonance of association. He felt that he was seeing them for the first time as they really were, that he was responding with all his senses to the special character of South-East London, its soiled, worn textures of brick and stone, its low, irregular outline, its odours of breweries and gas and vegetables and tanneries. He noticed how old and neglected it all was: if you raised your eyes above the modern shop-fronts you saw that they had been pasted on to buildings crumbling into decay, with cracked, grimy windows and broken-backed roofs and chipped chimney-pots. The predominant colours were black, brown and a dirty cream. Guinness tints.

Stephen Dedalus would have been capable of such acute and painful observation, but this epiphany is more than a revelation of Timothy's agonized sensibility; it provides, in its context, a metonymic image of the drab England of the immediate postwar period, recorded at a point when Timothy is about to leave it and, temporarily, to move out of the stifling shelter of family life.

Kate, his elder sister, has already moved out. During the war she hitched her waggon to the Americans' star, and in 1951 she is working as a secretary with their army of occupation in Germany. She has not been home for several years, though she keeps the family well provided with goodies from the PX and has invited Timothy to spend a holiday with her in Heidelberg where she works. The greater part of *Out of the Shelter* is a detailed account of Timothy's German holiday, most of which he passes in a state of marked culture shock. Much of the account is discreetly funny: by degrees Timothy comes to seem less like Stephen Dedalus and more like Jim Dixon. David Lodge has remarked in *Language of Fiction* that he has a 'strange community of feeling' with Kingsley Amis, and Amis's influence is better assimilated here than in *The British Museum is Falling Down*; mostly it takes the form of a steadily maintained awareness that

Timothy is an absurd figure as well as a sympathetic one, not least in his own eyes; the contradictions of adolescence are convincingly enacted. There are, however, one or two patches of crude atavistic farce, as when Timothy gets locked in a wardrobe in a girls' hostel where he is clandestinely staying to save money.

Germany is not much more than a background to Timothy's experiences, compounded of impressions of Old Heidelberg, plus a sense of Wagnerian menace and wartime nightmares about Hitler. The real impact is made by the brash and luxurious culture of the American occupying forces: the conspicuous consumption, whether of Hershey bars, or huge steaks, or big cars with automatic transmission, or the bewildering and seductive variety of ice-cream sodas in a drug-store. In every sense this is rich fare for the naive schoolboy just emerged from the physical deprivations and imaginative poverty of post-war England: even Timothy's sexual frustrations are somewhat relieved by a high-school girl who initiates him into that well-established American activity, heavy petting to climax. At the end of the novel, fifteen years later, Timothy, having moderately made it in academic life, is travelling through America at the expense of a Foundation, and visits Kate who has long ago emigrated to the United States. He is still marvelling, at the comfort of the motel, at the ice in the drinks and the heated swimming pool, though he remains too English to accept it all without question, like Kate. Mr. Lodge has brilliantly dramatized a kind of Anglo-American encounter very remote from anything ever envisaged by Henry James, yet central to the English experience of the past twenty-five years. To have grasped it so firmly in its historical and cultural dimensions, and to have made so well-ordered and humanly engaging a work of fiction in the process, is a striking achievement.

(j) JOHN UPDIKE

Bech: A Book

JOHN UPDIKE permits the hero of his enjoyable new book to write its Foreword. Henry Bech, famous novelist and critic, doesn't mind being made the subject of a novel—after all, the most recent critical appraisal of his work had been titled 'Whatever Happened to Henry Bech?'—but he can't help wondering if Updike hasn't merely *used* him to typify a general plight. He rightly points out, for example, that there is a bit of Mailer, a flash of Bellow, a whiff of Malamud in the fictionalized Bech; indeed, there is even 'something Waspish, theological, scared, and insulatingly ironical' that seems to him pure Updike. Even so, he doesn't really mind, because in the end all American writers, at any rate the celebrated ones, are in the same, gradually sinking, boat.

Updike's novel, or linked collection of short stories, is as much about the boat as it is about any individual passengers. It's about

. . . the silken mechanism whereby America reduces her writers to imbecility and cozenage. Envied like Negroes, disbelieved in like angels, we veer between the harlotry of the lecture platform and the torture of the writing desk, only to collapse, our five-and-dime Hallowe'en priests' robes a-rustle with economy-class jet-set tickets and honorary certificates from the Cunt-of-the-Month Club, amid a standing crowd of rueful, Lilliputian obituaries. Our language degenerating in the mouths of broadcasters and pop yellers, our formal designs crumbling like sand castles under the feet of beach bullies, we nevertheless and incredibly support with our desperate efforts . . . a flourishing culture of publishers, agents, editors, tutors, *Time*niks, media personnel in all shades of suavity, *chic*, and sexual gusto.

The paranoia is elegantly packaged, but then Bech is writing to the elegant John Updike, and is deliberately (?) over-playing the insulating irony. The book itself shows his response to the cultural machine to be somewhat more ragged, self-pitying and eagerly collaborative. Presented as a series of 'adventures' it discovers Bech at a low point in his career. He made his name, we are reminded, with a book called *Travelling Light* in 1955 (a novel about the motorbiking young, it enjoyed an immense campus vogue); *Brother Pig*, a novella, and *When the Saints* (a book of essays, remaindered in England) followed, but had nothing like the same success. Then, in 1963, had come his big book, his *Letting Go*, his *Herzog*, his *Couples*. Called *The Chosen*, it had been a resounding flop ('Who Did the Choosing?', *Time*, 'More in Sorrow', *Partisan Review*, 'Bech's Mighty Botch', *Reporter*, and 'So Bad It's Good', *New York Review of Books*, are just a few of the reviews listed in the lengthy bibliography). That was five years ago, and Bech has written nothing since; if he were to die tomorrow, he would certainly get 'Best Remembered for his Early Work'-type obituaries. Far from fleeing the cultural machine, he is in urgent need of it—to reassure him that, whether or not he's writing, he's a Writer.

Hence, most of his adventures, as a cultural emissary behind the Iron Curtain, as the guest of honour at a publisher's party in England, as a speaker at a girls' college in the Deep South. He even takes his holidays on a stretch of notedly literary beach, where he knows he will be recognized:

Bech moved off a few strides and stood, bare-chested, gazing at his splendid enemy the sea, an oblivious hemisphere whose glitter of whitecaps sullenly persisted without the sun. Shortly, a timid adolescent voice, the voice he had been waiting for, rustled at his shoulder. 'I beg your pardon, sir, but by any chance are you. . . .'

Just as he goes from gathering to admiring gathering, to keep up the essential supply of boost, so he goes from girl to girl—loathsome the machine may be, but it doesn't leave its victims short of sex (and nor, it should be said, do the victims usually fail to repay what they are loaned). Bech is unmarried, and though now and then as whimperingly in need of true love as he is of his next novel, means to stay that way; an ego so soaring and voracious has no room for family matters. Ultimately Bech is his (now declining) career.

The notorious difficulty of writing about a writer is shrewdly skirted by John Updike; believing in Bech's talent isn't really necessary—all we need to accept is his fame, and his bygone seriousness, and his present inability to separate the impulse to write from the impulse to make a killing on the literary market (his next book, he has pathetically decided, will be called *Think Big*). But what Updike hasn't been able to skirt is his own fondness for his hero, a fondness which will not permit Bech to come across as pitiful or powerful or maimed but which—although these aspects *are* signalled to us throughout—persistently promotes him as witty, laconic, self-aware, cleverer than anyone he meets, and genuinely lovable. The victims in the book are the victims of Updike's often devastating (but just as often too thinly playful) satiric barbs—precisely the functionaries, the hangers-on, the band-waggoners, the entrepreneurs who are collectively supposed to have reduced our Writer to his current plight. Bech emerges more as the agent of a gleeful revenge fantasy than as a wounded hero.

(k) PATRICK WHITE

The Vivisector

JUST AS THE COURTROOM SCENE is a natural for drama, so the *Bildungsroman* is a natural for narrative: with a convincing character to educate, and some convincing details of his education, even the least ambitious writer can hardly miss. Patrick White's large new novel *The Vivisector* unfortunately does miss, although in the biggest possible way. The central character is not especially convincing. The details of his formation as a painter are skimped. Finally, and decisively, the author is the most ambitious writer in the world: it is hard not to admire the aggressive strength with which he attempts to club the reader into numb submission. Hard, but very necessary.

The Vivisector is a book about a Great Artist—a painter called Hurtle Duffield. Since the viewpoint is mainly Duffield's, the writing can legitimately (Mr. White supposes) seize every opportunity to be painterly: we are precipitated willy-nilly into the midst of a vision. Need one add that the vision is impulsive, irrational, tangled, obsessive, paranoid, pulsating, elemental, holy? *Can* one add it, or indeed get a single word in edgeways?

In *The Horses's Mouth*, a novel which in many ways is the proto-type for the work under discussion, there was always the doubt (and the doubt was the saving grace) whether Jimson was really all that good. Duffield is assumed by his creator to be the greatest—so great that even the poor damned fools who presume to understand his paintings can only momentarily sustain themselves on such a dizzying spiritual peak before tumbling back into the common pit of mortality. By the end of the novel Duffield has become one of Australia's national institutions, a fact Mr. White makes great game of, in his plodding satirical manner. But throughout the novel there is not a single trustworthy independent voice responding to the products of Duffield's demonic creative drive—with the possible exception of Katherine Volkov, an incredible girl genius who makes love to Duffield across a fifty-year age gap before departing to conquer the world as a pianist. What the reader has to do, from square one, is accept Duffield's unique talent simply on the strength of the language employed to communicate his vision. It would be easy here to mistake the intention for the deed. Certainly there can be no quarrel about the level of the intention—it was a hugely ambitious thing for White to try to do. But as for the deed . . . well, it would take great solemnity to swallow it whole.

To take only a small sample, the effectiveness of a sentence like the following is absolutely dependent on the reader brushing by it with-out thinking—dependent, that is, on a willingness to be abstractly impressed: 'Soso pursed up her face into the shape of a doughnut.'

Writing of that type is neither reality concentrated nor reality intensified, nor even reality circumvented. It has nothing to do with
reality at all. It has no relevance to anything except Writing—its effect
depends on the reader being vaguely aware of what modern writing
has been made to do, and might conceivably in this novel be doing
again. And in this novel, as in all White's previous novels, it is this
art-writing that commingles with his true power of observation and
quite literally mucks it up.

Consider this momentary impression of Duffield's patroness,
Olivia Davenport (née Boo Hollingrake):

. . . and her face which that evening had shed its van Dongen chic for the
gas-lit concavities of a Greco Christ, was further transformed, by strain,
into a large, costive, powdered arse.

Now what is going on here, except a glaring attempt to up the
ante by piling on the effects? The phrase about 'van Dongen chic'
conveys something, both in absolute terms and in terms of the preparation White has given it in his earlier descriptions—Olivia's
elegant surroundings have been established with a suggestive lushness
which demonstrates admirably White's power of evocation and historical recall. Similarly the bit about the gas-lit Greco concavities
transmits something. But what does the large, costive, powdered
arse convey except (a) White's fascination with the word 'costive',
which makes several other appearances, and (b) *convexities*, which
are extraordinary things for gas-lit concavities to be further transformed into, even by strain?

It is characteristic of White to have no style, but rather a manner—
an inflated manner. And it is characteristic of an inflated manner
that you cannot ease off without lapsing into a *de*flated manner, as in
the following example:

She was wearing that slightly cold, expressionless expression some children
can put on, and which is the most complete of all disguises.

But such passages are rare in *The Vivisector*, which has the special
task of transmitting a burning visual intensity from first to last, and
whose language is consequently inflated to and beyond bursting
point. So there is very little expressionless expression. Instead, there
is a plenitude of powdered arse.

Evoked in such a manner, the paintings themselves are a bit hard
to take. The obsessive vision which enables Duffield to get the top
end of Olivia mixed up with the bottom end leads him to produce a

corpus of work which seems on the whole to resemble the early efforts of James Gleeson. No doubt the Tom Adams painting on the jacket—a toothily sub-Baconian caprice tarted up along the bottom edge to look like a poor Drysdale—also has its relevance. There is no reason, except the awed numbness induced by a relentless black-jacking from the author's prose, for taking these evocations as representing anything else than run-of-the-mill surrealist confec-tionery.

Sad to say, a judicious disinclination to be overwhelmed by the trans-figurative urgency of Duffield's interior workings also entails a certain scepticism about the characters on the feature list. Nance Lightfoot is the wonderfully generous whore who obligingly writes herself off when no longer necessary. Hero Pavloussi is the Greek lover who is better than anybody else at eating the hero alive (Duffield's is an ingestive and excretory vision) but never really *understands*. Not even his foster-sister, the hunchbacked dwarf Rhoda who is there at the beginning and in at the death, genuinely grasps what Duffield is getting at. That privilege is reserved for the fellow-artist, Katherine Volkov, and even she has her own life to lead. What else is there for Duffield to do, in the finality of his giant loneliness, except to paint God and die in the attempt? Did any other critic ever count?

As a painter, Hurtle Duffield is a writer's fantasy—*this* writer's fantasy. Alone, misunderstood on all but superficial levels, piling on his effects in a divine scramble, and always trying for the big one. You suspect him of not realizing his own true virtues. In the end he goes down in a flurry of language which may have been inspired by *Finnegans Wake* but which unfortunately recalls *A Spaniard in the Works*. It is an appropriate end for a hero whose whole existence was in language. For all the novel's innumerable gestures towards con-crete detail, the business of Hurtle Duffield's actually *learning to paint* is got over in a paragraph. The solid hero of the book is the city of Sydney.

(*l*) JOSEF ŠKVORECKÝ

The Cowards

and IVAN KLÍMA

The Jury and *A Ship Named Hope*

TWENTY-ONE YEARS after it was written and twelve years after it was first published in Czech—only to be banned a week later at the start of an incredible campaign of vilification against the author, which spread into a large-scale purge of Czech culture—Josef Škvorecký's *The Cowards* is at last available in English. And despite the writer's explanatory introduction, written when times in Czechoslovakia had changed sufficiently to allow a second edition, many people will be puzzled what all the fuss has been about; no one probably will be ready to believe that this book was once even denounced as pornography.

It describes an eventful eight days at the end of the Second World War in a small town in north-east Bohemia, as seen through the eyes of twenty-year old Danny Smiřický, zoot-suited tenor-saxophonist, sentimentalist and self-styled lover of all the beautiful girls in the world, including Judy Garland. An artfully protracted (and mostly imagined) unhappy love affair is of more consequence to him than the antics of the local bourgeoisie, who are busily organizing a last-minute orderly 'revolution'. Although they would prefer to be liberated by the Americans, it is the Russian guns whose rumble can be heard just over the horizon. So, having reached an understanding about a peaceful takeover with the retreating German Wehrmacht, they prepare to welcome the Slavic brothers with a brass band, flags, speeches by the town dignitaries and dressed-up little girls with bouquets for the Soviet heroes.

Before the celebration can start, however, a lot of unexpected things happen. Instead of the victorious Red Army, withdrawing SS troops turn up first, savagely shooting at everybody in sight; Communists emerge from underground and take charge of the revolution which has suddenly become real and bloody; and even Danny gets involved before he can return to his dreams of girls and Louis Armstrong.

An important piece of history is marvellously recorded here, and anyone who wants to know how it felt to be young, idealistic and innocent at the end of the war in what then was Reichsprotektorat Böhmen und Mähren, should read *The Cowards*. He would also learn something of the indefinable sense of impending change which at that time pervaded this part of Europe, tenuous at first, but growing stronger with the advance of the Soviet armies; and understand, too, what Marxists mean when they speak of the 'bourgeoisie leaving the stage of history'.

It was ironical that when *The Cowards* appeared in 1958, history had been rewritten and the author was faced with a barrage of critical and political attacks from a strange alliance of enemies: some were simply shocked by a book that did not conform to the prevailing dogma of socialist realism; others were party hacks who had themselves taken part in the 'correct interpretation of historical events' and would not tolerate any suggestion that there may have been some less glorious sides to the revolution of May, 1945. Curiously enough, the latter were supported by members of the propertied class most ridiculed in the novel; by now they had found a place in the new power structure and did not wish to hear of their true past. The novel turned out to be anti-Party and anti-God at the same time; everybody felt himself a victim of the author's satire. Those who would have stood up for him, including many Communists, had either been silenced or were freshly released from Stalinist prisons and not yet able to speak up.

In spite of all the suppression *The Cowards* became a milestone in Czech literature and Josef Škvorecký one of the country's most popular writers. Reading the novel today, one cannot help wondering what direction Czech fiction would have taken had it been allowed to develop freely in the 1950s. Although this is, first of all, a major Czech novel, as profound and self-derisive a study in national character as Hašek's *Schweik*, in 1948 its author was, like many young writers all over Europe, under the influence of American prose. There are passages which betray immediately who his mentor was:

Then I carried my tea out of the kitchen and into my room. I put the tea on a chair next to the bed, went over to the cupboard, opened it and took out a tube of aspirin, closed the cupboard and opened the inside window. It was pouring outside again. A white curtain of rain veiled the river with a thin mist. I closed the window and pulled down the blinds. Now it was dark in the room and the window gleamed a yellowish brown. I went over to the door and closed it.

Besides Hemingway, there are traces of sentimental irony and detachment reminiscent of Scott Fitzgerald. And the youthful drive of Mr.
Škvorecký's writing, as well as the aching nostalgia which has subsequently become the hallmark of his prose, bring him close to another
author, who was also writing his first novel at about the same time
and had to wait seven years to see it in print: the late Jack Kerouac.
After all, they both, though worlds apart, started from the same
point in literary tradition.

The American translation, for once appropriate, by Jeanne Němcová, enhances these aspects of *The Cowards;* on the other hand, it
inevitably effaces the novelty of the use of slang; in English the
dialogue sounds quite natural, but in 1958 the re-introduction of slang
into Czech fiction was considered scandalous.

Ivan Klíma's two short novels are in many respects the very opposite of Josef Škvorecký's book. They do not refer directly to any
events that actually occurred, were published in Czechoslovakia only
last year and, as for literary tradition and influences, Mr. Klíma
remains on home ground. Like some other contemporary Czech
writers, Jaroslav Putík for instance, he has evidently found much of
his inspiration in Franz Kafka.

The first novel, *The Jury*, is about a group of ordinary citizens
called upon to pass a verdict on an alleged murderer. During the
trial it becomes obvious, however, that a verdict of 'Guilty' has
been taken for granted and the accused in fact already executed. The
jurors react in different ways to the pressure to which they are
exposed. In the end, only one of them dares to maintain his view that
the defendant is, or rather was, innocent, but finds out that even this
is part of the game and that his dissent merely helps to keep up the
semblance of the jury's independence.

While Mr. Škvorecký is mainly a story-teller, Ivan Klíma's aim is
to convey an idea. *The Jury* is an allegory based on the Stalinist
trials, which provides a unique insight into the moral and psychological problems faced by people caught in the judicial trap set up by a
totalitarian system, from which there is no escape. The theme of
nightmarish helplessness recurs in the second novel, *A Ship Named
Hope*, another highly complex allegory about people being taken to
their death in the name of hope. Mr. Klíma's writing is admirable, as
is Edith Pargeter's translation. It seems, though, that the second
novel is slightly overburdened by symbolic details, which get more and
more involved, until a baroque structure is built up that tends to

obscure rather than clarify the original statement. On the other hand, this may well reflect the nature of contemporary totalitarianism, which is more sophisticated than that once described by Arthur Koestler.

Between them, these two books span twenty years of Czech fiction and tell much about the difficult path it has travelled. Equally revealing are the personal circumstances of their authors: Mr. Škvorecký now lives in Canada, while Mr Klíma, true to what he writes in *The Jury*, has decided to 'get away inside' and has returned from America to Prague (the blurb is wrong in this respect). Both continue to write novels, without much hope of seeing them published in Czech in the foreseeable future.

A word about the presentation. Although one must be grateful to the publisher for having ventured to bring out anything so exotic as two Czech novels at once, the way Czech words and names (particularly in *The Cowards*) have been handled is atrocious. Only the authors' names have been allowed the luxury of diacritical marks, but then only on the title pages, not on the jackets. Perhaps it should be pointed out that these marks designate phonemes.

16

BANDIT HEROES

IT WOULD BE difficult to write a dull book about bandits. Sociologists might have a try, but Dr. Hobsbawm is not a sociologist and, when dealing with such extreme individualists, such puritans of violence and eccentricity as are most of the heroes of *Bandits*—for they *are* heroes, both according to their own lights and in the eyes of the poor—he has had the wisdom to check in at the cloakroom his sociological laws. He writes of them in their own right, without attempting to subject them to general concepts; and he writes of them as a historian—and as all historians should, and some do, write—that is, with great elegance, a constantly renewed and often startling insight, compassion, and a sympathetic humour. The result is a wise as well as an exciting book, a very valuable addition to the history of mentalities and to that of popular protest (a field in which the author is one of the leading European experts), and a stimulus to further research, particularly at the regional level.

Dr. Hobsbawm has rediscovered and reconstructed the submerged and often largely mythical history of the bandit with as much success and flair as he displayed previously in the rescue from oblivion of 'Hodge', the English farm labourer of the early nineteenth century. There was, it is true, little danger of the Bandit Hero ever being so entirely forgotten as poor Hodge—he is too strongly entrenched in rural, and even urban memory—but the author has reduced him to human proportions; and while stripping him of something of his swagger and glamour, he has succeeded in relating him to his social background, to the particular conditions of the period in which he operated and to the collective assumptions of primitive, simple and often wildly optimistic communities.

The main themes of the present book are those that run through all popular history—poverty and violence: in this instance, rural poverty, the problems of the rootless, the landless and the dispossessed; and violence often of hideous, unbelievable savagery,

---

E. J. HOBSBAWM: *Bandits*. 128 pp. Weidenfeld and Nicolson. £1.50.

partly as an instrument of terror and vengeance, partly as an end in itself, as a form of enjoyment and personal self-expression. Other themes more particular to the subjects are physical courage, self-dramatization, the love of display, extreme individualism, and a primitive egalitarianism.

Dr. Hobsbawm, in *Primitive Rebels*, a pioneering work written ten years ago, had already prospected some of the terrain so masterfully covered in *Bandits*. He had then confined himself to forms of social banditry, secret societies and primitive protest commonest in the poorest rural areas of Southern Europe: Sicily, Apulia, Andalucía. In the present book he ranges, with apparent ease, from Europe to China, Indonesia, India and the Americas. One of his most interesting sections concerns Brazil. But he is equally at home with the bandoliered, heavily-moustached Balkan bandit smelling of goat's cheese, his legs criss-crossed with leather thongs. His most surprising figure is the bespectacled Lampião, from the Brazilian north-east, a man of intense cruelty who enforced on his followers a form of sexual puritanism and whose activities were only brought to an end, after twenty years, in 1938; his most endearing is that of the Catalan plumber, Francisco Sabaté, 'El Quico'.

The author sees rural bandits as an already extinct breed, save in Sardinia, so that his book might be taken as an epitaph on a form of social protest that has long been overtaken by the sophistication of economic organization and of political action and revolutionary technique. The bandit is an individualist who, operating only in very small groups—fifteen to twenty men—can subsist only in areas of geographical isolation and can expect to stay alive, at least as an activist—he may, of course, retire or even take employment with the forces of repression—for two or three years at the most. Lampião's run was altogether exceptional.

Banditry probably had its heyday, at least in France, the Netherlands and the Rhineland, in the anarchic conditions of 1795 to 1802 or so. But it flowered, in the Balkans, in Italy and Hungary, throughout the second half of the nineteenth century, and in parts of South America, Spain, Sicily, Southern Italy, Sardinia and Corsica, until quite recent times. The last Corsican bandit, Dante Spada, disappeared in 1935, Giuliano was shot down in 1950, Sabaté just reached the 1960s, though by then he was already an anachronism.

Bandits are probably the last of the individualists; this no doubt is the reason they have tended to become the object of such nostalgic

o

interest on the part of intellectuals and of the urban population as a whole, for whom they represent an escape back into a simple, generally sunny—the author has a splendid phrase about the old gunfighters of the West: 'silent in the white sunlight of their empty midday streets'—back-to-the-land romanticism. Their naivety is endearing, their optimism unbounded. Sabaté is an extreme example—he took on a whole régime, a social order, almost single-handed—but most of the others had an almost unlimited belief in the power of individual example, in the proselytizing value of individual heroism or individual terror. They were like the lusty champions of the Muslim villages of Montenegro, described by Djilas, who would stand on the bridge and hurl abuse and challenges to the menfolk of the Orthodox communities on the other side of the valley. They stand little chance in an age of collectivities.

Dr. Hobsbawm rightly stresses the connexion between banditry and dearth. We hear for instance, in the French context, of a sudden increase both in rural banditry and in urban crime, in the country round Marseille and in the port itself, during the two consecutive summers of 1788 and 1789. There are similar reports from the Gard during the terrible winter of 1782–83. But the greatest opportunity came with the famine of 1795, and during the subsequent years, 1796 and 1797, the 'chauffeurs du Nord' were in full activity both sides of the old border; the celebrated 'bande d'Orgères'—one of the largest bandit groups ever to operate in modern France: 109 persons were identified and arraigned before the Chartres court—was in operation from 1791 to 1799, but its most spectacular and most sanguinary outings were in 1795 (twelve operations), in 1796 (twenty-eight operations) and 1797 (forty-three operations), years which also witnessed the largest number of attacks on mail coaches in the Lyon area and the largest number of political assassinations in the river valleys from Mâcon to the Mediterranean.

In France there was a fairly widespread recrudescence of banditry, especially in the Somme and the Norman departments, in the spring and early summer of 1812, at a time when the dearth panic was at its height. The author's insight into this subject can thus be amply illustrated by French regional examples from the period of the Year III, the Directory and even the beginning of the consulate crisis in northeast France in 1801.

Dr. Hobsbawm has a telling point to make too with regard to the principal weakness of peasant protest: the peasant's immobility

('The peasant's back is bent socially, because it must generally be bent in physical labour in his field'). Even if he takes to the hills, sooner or later need will drive him down; even the shepherd, so often the archetypal bandit in the Balkans and in Italy, has to come down from the mountains with his flocks; and in most of Europe at least, banditry is subjected, like the peasant's year, to the implacable dictates of the calendar; we hear of the Bulgarian haiduks' annual season, from April 23 (St. George's Day) to the Day of the Cross (September 27).

Banditry could hardly compete with snow; though, in more temperate French conditions, the 'bande d'Orgères', the gangs round Lyon and in the Rhône Valley, and the 'chauffeurs du Nord' were operating throughout the winter months, thanks to a whole network of friendly inns in which they could sleep (and in which many of them were taken, in between two operations). The bandits' calendar would be further influenced by such fixed dates as annual fairs; those of the 'bande d'Orgères', over a period of nine years, scarcely ever miss the fairs of Ventôse, of St. John's Day and St. Andrew's Day, when horse-dealers and fatstock merchants congregated at the markets of Chartres and Pithiviers, returning to their village full of good cheer and with bulging purses. Scouts are often sent ahead, to the fair itself, to report on those who made the most profitable sales.

Dr. Hobsbawm is equally acute on the subject of the age and social origins of full-blown banditry. In primitive peasant societies the bandit is a young man, unencumbered with wife or children. In the Balkans, marriage generally means an end to the wild ways and a return to the village. A Colombian priest describes how the participants in the 'violencia' are uprooted and unloved young men who, while avoiding the well-trodden paths used by peasants over the mountainside, can only satisfy their sexual appetites by rape, often followed by murder; they can no more afford love, a permanent relationship, than allow themselves to remain in one place long enough to acquire habits and to become recognizable.

There are, however, instances of female bandits in the Balkans; a third of the members of the 'bande d'Orgères' were women, some of them outstripping their men in savagery. There existed in this gang relationships as secure as those of marriage, though some of the leaders passed on their women from one to another; the presence of women was indispensable to this particular group for the disposal

of stolen goods, particularly clothes and fabrics that had to be un-
stitched and sewn on other cuttings, to make them difficult to identify.
The Orléans group even employed large numbers of children, both
to scout and to enter buildings and open doors from inside. It also
had its schoolmaster, the 'père des mioches', as well as a few very
old men, survivors of previous *bandes*, whose function was to keep up
morale by evening tales about the heroic exploits of semi-legendary
bandits who had operated at the mid-century. Sabaté was married,
had two daughters, and enrolled two of his brothers.

The groups draw heavily on shepherds, drovers, carters, smugglers,
as well as on ex-soldiers and sailors and deserters (on these Dr.
Hobsbawm makes the perceptive comment: 'men who came back
from afar, masterless and landless, are a danger to the stability of the
social hierarchy', a point amply borne out by the composition of the
murder gangs of the first French White Terror in the Midi)—all
categories that figure largely in French banditry between 1795 and
1802. Equally common are horse-dealers (so often also horse-thieves).
In Germany, he mentions knife-grinders and rag-and-bone men ('les
terribles chiffonniers', as Mercier calls them, the child-slaughterers
of popular imagination, as well as the allies of receivers).

But bandits cannot operate in a vacuum; they need the help of
middlemen who will dispose of the goods that they have stolen, they
have to be fed, clothed and sometimes even housed; hence such
allies as old-clothes merchants, inn-keepers, junk merchants, fair-
ground people, pedlars, the ubiquitous *revendeuses*, and an army of
roving people, unknown locally. In more sophisticated societies they
would likewise need engravers to supply them with papers. The
'bande d'Orgères' even carried its own cooks—male and female—
and many completed operations were celebrated by nocturnal feast-
ings and collective orgies in forest clearing and welcoming glade.
The movements of this particular group could often be traced by the
piles of bones and feathers left behind by the redoubtable picnickers.
Many bandits were the sons or grandsons of bandits; and in the
'bande d'Orgères' we find three generations of one family, a trio of
brothers, two pairs of brothers, three pairs of sisters.

Dr. Hobsbawm refers on several occasions to the physical deformi-
ties of many famous bandits. Lampião wore glasses; many were not
at all physically strong, a number were lame or had only one arm; in
the 'bande d'Orgères' there are two one-eyed men ('le borgne du
Mans' and 'le borgne de Jouy'). This last disability, though it made

recognition rather easier—there were, however, a great many people in eighteenth-century France in this condition—was felt by some to be an asset, as it added to the fearsome appearance of those thus afflicted; there was even one epileptic who was unable to take part in several operations. It was as if they were seeking to compensate for their physical disabilities—as well as for their ugliness: one member of the Orléans group had lost half his hair, another had wine stains on his face—by an extra display of courage and ferocity. Thus, some were not only poor but physically underprivileged. A few may even have suffered from sexual insufficiencies, though most of the evidence is very much to the contrary. The 'bande d'Orgères' regularly raped farmers' wives and farm-girls. Lampião, however, would have none of this sort of thing.

The prevalence of such physical disabilities and of such visible forms of ugliness might account too for the extraordinary elegance affected by many of the leaders; the author quotes a telling inventory of Lampião's fantastic wardrobe. All concentrated much on an appearance that was designed both to strike fear into the wealthy and admiration into the poor domestic or seamstress. The Orléans gang steal clothes as much for themselves as to sell; after an attack on a farm they adjourn to an inn and, after ordering a hearty meal, they proceed to undress and put on their new finery; men who were in beggar's rags at dusk are dressed like parakeets when next seen.

There are many references to the top-hats, red waistcoats and top boots of the tall, slim red-head, 'le Rouge d'Auneau'; another member of the gang goes for three-cornered hats of fine quality (like Lampião's); they all concentrate on stealing silver shoe buckles. All of Dr. Hobsbawm's bandits seem to have favoured a profusion of silver and gold buttons, worn on any part of their clothing: many have the brilliant appearance of pearly-kings. Their concern with clothes recalls a similar obsession on the part of Glasgow razor gangs of the 1920s and 1930s. Perhaps it was all they had to show for themselves; perhaps they were thinking in terms of the ranks that they had not possessed in real armies; perhaps they were motivated by thoughts of 'le repos du guerrier'.

If any criticism can be made of this admirable book, it is that the author perhaps overstates the purely *rural* character of banditry and its anti-urban features. In eighteenth-century terms at least it is difficult to draw a clear distinction between town and country, the frontiers of which so often tend to overlap. The horse-dealer plies

between his village and the horse-market, the pedlar moves with his
tray between town and village, the carter stops off at the inn in the
faubourg frequented by his own kind, the rivermen float from place to
place. One of the leaders of the Orgères gang was 'Charles de Paris',
and he had been recruited in a Parisian inn: other members of the
group came up to the capital to organize one of their operations in
the Seine-et-Marne and to collect recruits introduced by Charles.

The 'chauffeurs du Nord' had their feet in both camps, employing village blacksmiths, urban old-clothes merchants, rural and urban
butchers, innkeepers, deserters, and so on, and they had their meeting places in a dozen towns both sides of the border. After an operation, they would head for a friendly carters' inn in a *faubourg*,
because they knew such an establishment would be open all night.
The Lyon murder gangs were city-based—and Lyon would fit into
one of Dr. Hobsbawm's categories as a frontier town; a ten-minute
walk over the pont de la Guillotière would take one into the Isère; it
was also a much better place to hide in than the countryside—and
they went out of the city at night to carry out their operations in the
neighbouring countryside, returning at dawn, to sleep in their dis-
creet, shuttered hideouts on the central peninsula or in Vaise or la
Croix-Rousse. Most of the attacks on mail-coaches under the
Directory were the work of townsmen and took place on the very
outskirts of Lyon, as the road to Paris pulled up through Vaise and
Tassin.

Perhaps Dr. Hobsbawm's emphasis on rural banditry, in con-
tradistinction to urban crime, has been suggested to him primarily
by Balkan or Brazilian examples. In France at least the two are hard
to distinguish. It is doubtful too whether 'for the genuine underworld revolutions are little more than unusually good occasions for
crime'. In French cities, there was a sharp decline in crime between
1790 and 1794; crime rates then rose dramatically in the conditions
of 1795–96. Nor did the criminally inclined appear to have gravitated
towards terrorist commitment. The case of Guénot is certainly
exceptional in this respect. The criminal and the bandit were much
more likely to find refuge, encouragement and even a sort of respectability in the service of the Counter-Revolution.

Here then are but a few indications of the many insights suggested
by Dr. Hobsbawm in his investigation of the semi-mythical world of
the Bandit Hero. He has much more of interest to say on the connexion between banditry and regionalism, as well as on the subject

of the favourable conditions offered by frontier areas, escarpments, mountain passes, rocky uplands, river estuaries and marshland. No wonder an idealized bandit was such a favourite with nineteenth-century opera and Victorian painting!

His final chapter on the anarchist Sabaté is deeply moving and compassionate, and beautifully written, with a fine visual sense ('Barcelona, that hill-compressed, hard-edged and passionate capital of proletarian insurrection.' 'Their accoutrements were the raincoat so dear to urban gunmen from Dublin to the Mediterranean'). This is human history at its very best—a worthy tribute to an utterly simple man, a plumber. He was the sort of man, the author states, who knew how to put together a motorcycle out of odd parts: he also constructed a home-made bazooka to scatter pamphlets over a football crowd.

He managed, with great doggedness, to learn to read, so as to be able to commune with Rousseau and Bakunin. He always walked *towards* the police. And he had the utmost suspicion of *any* form of organization. What one wonders, would the two *lycéennes*, his teen-age daughters—no doubt Frenchified and climbing diligently up the many-runged French educational ladder—think of their amazing father? Would they have evoked his memory with tender devotion, as did Paz Ferrer that of her almost equally single-minded father? Or would they have used the cruel slang of the *lycée* when applied to middle-age, or to the very old—'Monument historique', 'Archives nationales', and so on—to a father who had no place in the world of *Elle* and *Marie-Clair*?

The career of Sabaté may be an anachronism, his life and death historically insignificant and politically futile; but, in its utter simplicity and total optimism, it gives one some hope in the future of humanity. 'El Quico' really is dead, but is it totally impossible that some other puritan milk-bar avenger—of course from Barcelona—might not take up again his single-handed war? It seems unlikely. But the world is richer for Sabaté; and, as the author reminds us, the bandit lingers on 'and unnumbered boys from slums ... who possess nothing but the common, but nevertheless precious gift of strength and courage, can identify themselves with him ...'. 'Razor King' can safely be forgotten, unlamented, for his violence was cruel and meaningless. 'El Quico' had a message, albeit a very simple one: and, in Dr. Hobsbawm, he has got the historian he deserved. The author has reconstructed the poor plumber's amazing life with exemplary patience and tenacity, talking to his friends, visiting the scenes of his activities.

Bandits, then, is a book about people, flamboyant, cruel, simple, single-minded, ill-advised, naïve, ill-educated, under-privileged, mixed-up, touchy, unpredictable, and—above all—brave. Some were utter villains, a few, like Sabaté, were knights; all, under Dr. Hobsbawm's pen, come menacingly and marvellously alive. His book reassures us about the future of history.

17

THE COMPLETE N.E.B.

THE NEW ENGLISH BIBLE is now complete. The first proposal, in the late 1930s, was for a new Revised Version. But the outbreak of war in 1939 prevented any steps being taken to implement it. After the war the Church of Scotland put forward another proposal—for a completely fresh translation. The opinions of other churches were canvassed, and the result was the setting up in 1947 of a Joint Committee, which undertook responsibility for organizing the work and appointed three panels of translators, one for the Old Testament, one for the New Testament, and one for the Apocrypha.

The new version of the New Testament was ready first and was published in 1961. Now come the Old Testament and the Apocrypha and together with them (for good measure) a second edition of the New Testament.

In the second edition of the New Testament the changes introduced as a result of the 'numerous criticisms and suggestions which have come in from various quarters' are many; but they are all relatively minor. One of the more substantial, to which the translators themselves draw attention, is the substitution at Luke i 34 of 'How can this be! . . . I am still a virgin' for 'How can this be . . . when I have no husband?' Another is 'the Father's tribunal' at John v 45 for 'God's tribunal'. In neither instance is a different Greek text implied.

The books known as Apocrypha are by definition those books which were at one time regularly used in the Christian Church and regarded as part of the Old Testament, but which were rejected by the Protestant reformers because they lacked any extant Hebrew text and were not included in the Jewish canon. Some of them, undoubtedly, were written in Greek in the first place; others were written in either Hebrew or Aramaic, but the Hebrew or Aramaic

The New English Bible. Standard Edition: with Apocrypha. 1,824 pp. £1.75; without Apocrypha. 1,536 pp. £1.50. Library Edition: Old Testament. 1,376 pp. £2.50; Apocrypha. 378 pp. £1.25; New Testament. 474 pp. £1.25. Oxford University Press/Cambridge University Press.

originals have been lost and they are now known only from versions in Greek and other languages. Thus it comes about that the most ancient texts available of nearly all the Apocryphal books are Greek. The only noteworthy exceptions are II Esdras and Ecclesiasticus. (Of II Esdras even the Greek text has been lost, and we are dependent on the Latin and other versions; of Ecclesiasticus extensive fragments in Hebrew have come to light, though they are very far from covering the whole of the book.)

This means that the task of a translator of the Apocrypha is essentially the same as that of a translator of the New Testament. In both cases he is presented with a series of texts in Greek. But the translator working on the Apocrypha must be even more sensitive than his colleague on the New Testament in detecting Hebrew or Aramaic idioms concealed beneath the Greek, since he is dealing not only with Greek originals written by authors who often thought in Hebrew or Aramaic even when they wrote in Greek, but also with translations into Greek that on occasion have rendered their Hebrew or Aramaic originals very literally indeed. The N.E.B. translators have been conspicuously successful here.

In Ecclesiasticus they have made full use of the Hebrew fragments. Thus, at Ecclesiasticus i 3 the difficult Greek text, which the Authorised Version translated as 'in his days the cistern to receive water . . . was covered' and the Revised Version as 'in his days the cistern of waters was diminished' (with a marginal note, 'The text here seems to be corrupt'), has been abandoned in favour of the Hebrew, 'in his day they dug the reservoir'. Similarly, later in the same chapter (verse 26) 'Mount Seir' is read with the Hebrew against 'the mountain of Samaria' in the Greek.

At the opposite extreme, in Wisdom, the most obviously Greek of all the Apocryphal books, points of interest are of another kind. At iii 9 the N.E.B. follows the R.V. in omitting the final clause in the A.V. ('and he hath care for his elect'). At ii 1 the situation is reversed: the N.E.B. 'return' follows the A.V. in taking ἀναλύσας as intransitive, against the transitive 'gave release' of the R.V. At ii 23 the translators seem deliberately ambiguous: the A.V. had 'an image of his own eternity' (reading ἀϊδιότητος), the R.V. 'an image of his own proper being' (reading ἰδιότητος): the N.E.B. conflates—'the image of his own eternal self'.

In the Old Testament the problems confronting a translator are very much more complex. They arise partly from doubt about the meanings of words and partly from uncertainty about the text. To take the first point first. Whereas the New Testament and the Apocrypha added together constitute an infinitesimally small part of the whole corpus of Greek literature, much of which was written before them, the Old Testament is virtually all that survives of pre-Christian Hebrew literature and there is no Hebrew literature at all which antedates it. In the New Testament and the Apocrypha the meanings of unusual or obscure words can generally be decided by reference to the meanings and use of the same (or very similar) words somewhere else in Greek literature. But when this sort of difficulty arises in the Old Testament about the meanings of Hebrew words, often enough there is no 'somewhere else' to refer to. In the past, arbitrary meanings have been attached to many of the more obscure Old Testament words, either because the Jewish Rabbis so understood them, or because the ancient versions so translated them; and these meanings have become traditional. There has also been not a little guessing; and these guesses, too, have become traditional.

The past 150 years have seen much progress in philology everywhere, and Hebrew philology is no exception. There can be no doubt that the total number of words in the ancient Hebrew vocabulary was very much greater than the number preserved in the Old Testament. Throughout the pre-Christian period no satisfactory system was devised to indicate the vowels in a Hebrew text, which consisted almost entirely of consonants only. And there was at least one fundamental change in the script during this period. The possibility of confusion between words which look alike, but in fact are not, is immense. The philologists have sorted out many hitherto unsuspected confusions. They have, too, in many cases established meanings for words which were previously quite unintelligible, or of which the traditional meanings were highly questionable. And especially valuable in this connexion has been the application of the comparative method, whereby the meaning of an otherwise unknown word in Hebrew is determined from the known meaning of an identical or similar word in another Semitic language related to Hebrew, such as Arabic or Akkadian.

Among the many new renderings in the N.E.B. Old Testament that are directly traceable to modern philology are the following: 'perfumed herself' for 'wrapped herself' (Genesis xxxviii 14); 'his strength was not tamed' for 'his strength was not known' (Judges xvi 9); 'as birds fly upwards' for 'as the sparks fly upward' (Job v 7);

'my heart exults and my spirit rejoices' for 'my heart is glad and my glory rejoiceth' (Psalms xvi 9); 'kings and all earthly rulers' for 'kings of the earth and all people' (Psalms cxlviii 11); 'fear not, Jacob you worm and Israel poor louse' for 'fear not, thou worm Jacob, and ye men of Israel' (Isaiah xli 14); 'the train of captives goes into exile' for 'and Huzzab is uncovered' (Nahum ii 7).

As further illustration from a rather different angle and in a highly specialized field may be instanced the translators' obvious concern to identify correctly the flora and fauna of the Old Testament. Thus, the 'rose' becomes the 'asphodel', 'mulberry trees' become 'aspens', 'jackals' 'wolves', the 'porcupine' becomes the 'bustard', and the 'pelican' either the 'horned owl' or the 'desert-owl'. If a comparison be made between the A.V. the R.V. and the N.E.B. lists of the birds which 'ye shall have in abomination' (or 'you shall regard as vermin') at Leviticus xi 13–19, it will be found that out of twenty listed in all there are only six coincidences between the N.E.B. and the R.V., and only three between the N.E.B. and the A.V.

The other big problem confronting a translator of the Old Testament is uncertainty about the text. The extant Hebrew manuscripts exhibit a surprising uniformity in their text. But there can be no doubt that this uniformity is contrived. When the Rabbis, very early in the Christian era, fixed the limits of the Old Testament canon they also fixed its text; and his Masoretic Text has been carefully preserved and copied ever since. Yet when the Rabbis decided on it, it was not the only text available. This much is clear both from the remains of other types of text preserved in some of the Dead Sea fragments, and also from a number of renderings in the ancient versions. Granted that the translators of these versions often misunderstood and mistranslated their Hebrew originals, there is nevertheless abundant evidence to prove that they not infrequently had before them a different (and sometimes superior) Hebrew text to the text that has come down to us. Pre-eminent among the ancient versions is the Greek Septuagint, the whole of which is probably to be dated in the pre-Christian period, some of it being as early as the mid-third century B.C.

Consequently, the modern translator of the Old Testament must reckon not merely with the possibility but with the certainty that there is not a little corruption in the Hebrew text in front of him. He will be prepared to improve it where he can in the light of the versional and Dead Sea evidence; and he is also likely to resort from time to time to at least a modicum of purely conjectural emendation.

A very simple example of this approach in operation in the N.E.B. is the substitution of 'Edom' for 'Syria' at II Samuel viii 12. 'Edom' is in fact read by a few of the Hebrew manuscripts. It was certainly read by the translators of the Septuagint and the Syriac versions. It appears in the parallel passage in Chronicles (I Chronicles xviii 11). It makes much better sense in the context. And the difference in Hebrew is of one letter only (אדם for ארם), so that the corruption is easily explained.

A similar corruption is assumed in the N.E.B. at Deuteronomy xxi 3, where the A.V. and the R.V.'s 'an heifer which hath not been wrought with' is replaced by 'a heifer that has never been mated' (עבר for עבד): here there is no external support for the change, only conjecture. Much more conjectural is 'Saul was fifty years old when he became king, and he reigned over Israel for twenty-two years' (I Samuel xiii 1): the Hebrew has 'Saul was a year old when he became king, and he reigned over Israel for two years': what the translators have done is to try and make a semblance of sense out of nonsense; but their 'fifty' and 'twenty-two' are pure guesswork. At Isaiah xiv 4 a conjecture of long standing has been confirmed by one of the Dead Sea manuscripts: hence 'See how the oppressor has met his end and his frenzy ceased' for '. . . the golden city ceased'. At Amos vi 12, 'Can the sea be ploughed with oxen?' instead of 'Will one plough there with oxen?' is obtained by dividing the same consonants into different words and reading them with different vowels.

As an example of a more fundamental change in the N.E.B. may be cited the beginning of the Prayer of Solomon at the Dedication of the Temple (I Kings viii 12):

And Solomon said:
O Lord who hast set the sun in heaven,
    but hast chosen to dwell in thick darkness,
here have I built thee a lofty house,
    a habitation for thee to occupy for ever.

Here the first line of the quatrain is an addition to the Hebrew text— restored on the basis of the Septuagint. There are a number of such additions and restorations. On the other hand, some verses and parts of verses are omitted as glosses (e.g. Ezekiel i 14). And there are many transpositions: thus, Job xli 1–6 follows on xxxix, and Isaiah xli 6–7 is sandwiched between xl 20 and 21.

The reader's attention is drawn to the more outstanding of these changes in the footnotes, which also supply much miscellaneous information about the text, the versions, and such other matters as the meanings of Hebrew names—for instance, we are informed at Joshua v 9 that Gilgal means 'Rolling Stones'. The Revisers of 1885 set the pattern for this kind of note. The translators of the N.E.B. have improved upon it, and their notes are a most valuable feature of their work.

To sum up. In estimating the significance of the N.E.B. it is important to remember that the translators were instructed to produce 'a completely new translation'. In this they differed from the Revisers who were commissioned merely to 'revise' the A.V. of 1611. When using the R.V. one is always conscious that its authors felt keenly the limitation of their commission and that they would often have preferred to incorporate into their text readings which the terms of their commission allowed them only to draw attention to in the margin. The translators of the N.E.B. suffered from no such limitation. They were left completely free to decide on their text and then to turn it into English as best they could in the light of the most up-to-date knowledge and techniques. The N.E.B., therefore, offers the reader the very best that modern scholarship can give.

Not everyone, of course, least of all among the scholars, will approve of everything. Some will note the absence of certain readings and renderings which they will think should have been accepted: others will deplore the presence of others which they will think should have been rejected. And they will argue. Meanwhile, more discoveries will be made (especially in the Old Testament area) and fresh proposals put forward for solving difficulties. And so we may look forward to several 'editions' in the years that lie ahead—perhaps even to a 'revision'.

So far as the non-specialist is concerned, reactions will likewise vary, not only between one individual and another, but also in the same individual according to his familiarity with the traditional rendering in particular passages. For example, if Jeremiah xiii is being read in church from the N.E.B. few members of a congregation are likely to be seriously upset by verse 21 appearing as:

> What will you say when you suffer
>   because your leaders cannot be found,
> though it was you who trained them
>   to be your head?

rather than as:

What wilt thou say, when he shall set thy friends over thee as head, seeing thou thyself hast instructed them against thee?

The probability is that no one will notice anything. But the situation is likely to be different when the reader goes on to inquire two verses later: 'Can the Nubian change his skin . . ?' Though it is only fair to the translators to point out here that they continue with the traditional '. . . or the leopard its spots?' Despite their fondness for mutations in the animal kingdom, they have not looked kindly on the suggestion, first advanced by that prince among the earlier Hebrew philologists, Wilhelm Gesenius (1786–1842), that we should continue instead '. . . or the tiger his stripes?'

18

DUCKS AND DRAKES

UNTIL VERY RECENTLY, the movement of people and goods has been restricted to the interface between two media, and of the four possible interfaces on this planet only two have been exploited. Travel takes place in ships at the interface between water and air, and in a variety of vehicles at the interface between solid earth and air. Devices to travel on the bed of the sea (the earth/water interface) would seem to have limited utility, gliders skimming on the outer edges of the atmosphere (the air/space interface) have been suggested, but not yet used, as one means of aiding spacecraft re-entry. The present century has also seen the growth of travel within three of the available four media: airships and aircraft in the air; submarines in the sea; spacecraft in space. Movement in solid media has been left to the earthworms.

Travel at an interface is inherently attractive, particularly where large loads are to be carried. The lower medium (earth or water) can be relied upon to support the vehicle, and all of the available power can be used for providing motion. In an aircraft, on the other hand, power must be used both for support and motion: this is particularly obvious in the case of the helicopter. The principal defect with travel at an interface is the resistance to motion which occurs due to friction and other causes between the vehicle and the supporting medium. The history of transport engineering has been mainly concerned with reducing this drag, or increasing the propulsive power available to overcome it.

On land, reduction of drag was achieved in two ways—improving the vehicle and improving the surface on which it ran. The first led from the sledge to the wheel and the roller bearing: the second produced the tarmacadam road and the steel rail track. Propulsion changed from man to draught animal to steam to internal combustion engine or electric motor. On water, it is not possible to

---

ROY MCLEAVY (Editor): *Jane's Surface Skimmer Systems.* 312 pp. Sampson, Low, Marston. £4.20.

improve the supporting surface, and attempts at drag reduction must concentrate on the vehicle itself. Resistance to a ship's motion occurs due to two principal causes—wave making, and skin friction due to the movement of the wetted surface through the water. Much research has gone into producing hull forms to minimize the total drag due to both wave making and skin friction. The progression of prime movers on water has been much the same as on land, with the significant addition of the wind; the means of movement have been the paddle, the oar, the sail, the paddle wheel and the screw propeller.

In all conventional modes of travel at an interface, the vehicle is in contact with the supporting medium, either over a fairly limited area as in the case of a motor car, or over a large area as in the case of a ship, where support comes by displacement of a mass of water equal to that of the vessel. Clearly most of the resistance to motion is associated with this contact and for more than a century engineers have been considering schemes whereby the vehicle could be supported by the surface without touching it.

Two basic ideas have evolved. In one, applicable to land or water, a cushion of air is interposed between the vehicle and the supporting medium. In the other, applicable only to water, the hull behaves like a conventional ship when at rest, but as it gathers speed it rises out of the water on legs supported by small aircraft-type wings (foils) which travel just below the surface. In this second scheme, contact with the lower medium is not lost entirely, but there is negligible wave making and the wetted area, and thence the skin friction, is very small.

Air-cushion vehicles have been built for over fifty years, but their study received a major impetus from the experiments of Christopher Cockerell in the 1950s. Cockerell's coffee tins have something of the quality of Watt's kettle in their appeal from domestic to technological affairs. In his first experiment, Cockerell blew air from a hair dryer through an inverted coffee tin on to a pair of scales, and measured the thrust. In his second experiment he placed one tin inside a slightly larger one and blew air through the space between them: the thrust was markedly increased. This principle of a circular curtain of downward flowing air, containing the cushion air within it, was used in the first hovercraft, the Saunders Roe N1. The SR-N1 successfully completed its first Channel crossing in July, 1959, finishing the trip on Dover beach and thus demonstrating the

P

amphibious capability of this new type of vehicle. It soon became clear, however, that the hover height attainable with this type of craft (6–12in.) was insufficient, since the vehicle could only travel over smooth ground or fairly calm water. To increase the hover height it was necessary to contain the cushion air by a material barrier, rather than the air curtain of Cockerell's patent. Two possibilities existed: a rigid side wall or a flexible skirt. The rigid side wall cannot be used on land; at sea it must be sufficiently immersed to provide an adequate seal for the expected wave heights, and the wetted area produces significant drag. A flexible skirt, which will glide over the obstacles encountered, while maintaining cushion pressure with minimum leakage, can be used on land or water and produces less drag than the immersed sidewall.

Most of the effort in hovercraft development has been put into the study of compliant skirts. The original SR-N1 was subsequently fitted with 4ft skirts, enabling it to clear solid obstacles 3½ft. high, and the current SR-N4 Mountbatten class, used by British Rail and Hoverlloyd for cross-Channel services, has 8ft. skirts and can maintain a service speed of 40–50 knots in 10ft waves. It has been said that the development of a satisfactory skirt is 'as significant to the hovercraft as the pneumatic tyre is to the motor car'. Certainly the economic feasibility of hovercraft operation is closely related to skirt life.

As well as amphibious hovercraft, there is much interest at present in tracked air cushion vehicles, the most advanced project being the Orléans to Paris Aérotrain designed for speeds of 155–185 m.p.h. Tracked Hovercraft Ltd. have suggested to the Roskill Commission a 250 m.p.h. link between the third London airport and the city at a passenger cost no higher than current first-class rail fares. One advantage of conventional hovercraft on land is that they can move over unprepared surfaces: for example, they are proposed in Israel for collecting the banana harvest—banana groves are littered with dead fronds and branches and irrigation pipes so that wheeled vehicles cannot enter. Another advantage is that the air cushion prevents damage to the surface or to the supported object. The former point is of importance in protecting crops—the Central Electricity Generating Board have an air cushion vehicle to carry parts for transmission towers over farmland, and air cushion crop sprayers are being made in many countries. The latter point has found application in the hoverbed, used to support patients with extensive skin burns.

Boats which, at speed, rise out of the water on small submerged wings (hydrofoils) were first built successfully by the Italian airship designer Forlanini in 1905. His work attracted the interest of Alexander Graham Bell, the inventor of the telephone, and Bell eventually bought Forlanini's patent and began to construct his own hydrofoils on the Bras d'Or Lakes near Halifax, Nova Scotia. One of these boats achieved a water speed record of 71 m.p.h. in 1918. These early hydrofoils used ladder foils—the small wings being arranged like the rungs of a ladder and the number of rungs immersed diminishing as the boat increased speed. Most modern seagoing hydrofoils achieve the same effect by having foils in the shape of a shallow V, only a small part near the apex being immersed at high speed. For reasons of stability, vee foil boats cannot have very long legs, and so they are unsuitable for use in large waves, but numerous boats of this type operate successfully in coastal waters in waves up to about 5ft. The largest sea-going vee foil boat, carrying 150 passengers and eight cars, runs between Gothenberg and Fredrikshavn at 36 knots in $7\frac{1}{2}$ft. waves. At the other end of the size spectrum a vee foil sailing dinghy has achieved 30 knots in 18in. waves.

In order to cope with open ocean conditions, long legs and fully submerged foils must be used. Fixed fully submerged foils are inherently unstable and so the boat is provided with pivoted foils controlled by an autopilot. The autopilot maintains the boat in a smooth flight almost irrespective of the wave conditions. A typical example is the Grumman Dolphin carrying 116 passengers at 48 knots in 10ft. waves. The largest hydrofoil of this type is the U.S. Navy's 320-ton Plainview, intended to travel at more than 70 knots.

Development of vee foil boats has taken place mainly in Italy, although the most advanced vessel of this type is almost certainly H.M.C.S. Bras d'Or. The United States has been principally responsible for submerged foil construction. Most hydrofoils in operation are, however, of neither of these types. The U.S.S.R. has a major network of rivers and canals, where the water is smooth but sometimes shallow. In 1945 Dr. Rostislav Alexeyev began work on the design of a hydrofoil suitable for these conditions. The Alexeyev system makes use of the fact that the lift on a foil running just below the surface decreases as the surface is approached. The main foils run a few inches below the surface and in addition there are sub-foils which just touch the surface under normal running conditions: these sub-foils assist take-off and prevent the main foils sinking. If the

P*

main foils rise they lose lift and thus return to their correct
position.

The first passenger-carrying hydrofoil using the Alexeyev system,
the Raketa, was launched in 1957. Several hundred Raketas are now
in use in the Soviet Union, and a number have been exported. The
Raketa carries 50 passengers at 32 knots in calm water. Alexeyev's
Meteor, which entered service between Gorki and Moscow in 1960,
carries 150 passengers at 35 knots, and the Sputnik (1961) 300
passengers at 41 knots. The first Soviet gas turbine hydrofoil, the
Burevestnik, carries 130 passengers between Gorki and Kuibyshev at
53 knots. The larger Alexeyev hydrofoils can travel in moderately
rough water. The cost of transport by hydrofoils in the U.S.S.R. is
stated to be lower than by ship or bus, and it is expected that they
will eventually replace all conventional passenger ferries on inland
waterways.

We have, then, two means of travelling at an interface with little
or no contact with the supporting medium. The hydrofoil, developed
to commercial success in Italy and Russia, and the hovercraft, very
largely a British invention, and as yet commercially unproven. For
travel solely over an unobstructed waterway of adequate depth the
hydrofoil seems likely to lead for some years to come. There are,
however, waterways where because of shoals or rapids or floating
obstacles such as log rafts or ice the hovercraft alone could function.
For amphibious operation the hovercraft offers an almost unique
capacity, and it will clearly be used for such purposes as inshore
rescue and military landing craft. The agricultural benefit of having a
load carrier which will not damage crops will also be exploited (the
Polish horse-drawn hover platform affords a pleasing combination of
tradition and innovation). Both the seagoing and tracked hovercraft
and the hydrofoil have the advantage that over medium distances
they are faster than alternative means of transport, and for passenger
travel this may secure them a place in the vehicle spectrum. Whether
they can compete with aircraft for passengers or ships for goods over
longer distances is uncertain. The United States Government has
recently commissioned a research programme to determine the feasibility of building and operating 4,000 to 5,000-ton air cushion ships
having speeds of 80 to 100 knots. Certainly their proponents have
always believed that the commercial attractiveness of hovercraft
would increase with size, although one of the most flourishing markets at present seems to be for small sporting vehicles.

Jane's Surface Skimmer Systems, now in its third year of issue, is in the main a catalogue of aircushion vehicles and hydrofoils, listed by countries and manufacturers. Small separate sections deal with power plant and operators. The book is compiled largely from information supplied by the manufacturers, but this is reduced to a fairly standard format, which aids comparison between vehicles. The arrangement of the book is generally satisfactory, although there is some duplication of information and the quality of a number of the photographs is very poor. As well as the lists of vehicles and brief editorials there are an extensive glossary of terms—very necessary in a growing field, where the general reader may not be entirely familiar with yaw port (see puff port) or finger skirt (see skirts)—and four contributed papers.

The first paper, by Commander J. M. Lefeaux, gives a very clear explanation of British Rail's choice and construction of terminals for the first cross-Channel hovercraft service, and of some of the teething troubles with the first SR-N4. J. M. Berthelot writes on the economics of *aérotrain* systems. He suggests that the cost per passenger mile will be comparable with present second-class rail fares, in spite of the much higher speeds. The reason is that maintenance costs are low, that of the track (a major item with conventional railways) being negligible and that of the carriage being less than for a wheeled vehicle subjected to concentrated loads and vibration. M. Berthelot does not envisage fixed timetables, but small units departing either when full or at maximum intervals of (say) 12 minutes. Radar guidance would be used for traffic control in preference to a crew. Commander N. T. Bennett discusses the work of the Interservice Hovercraft Unit. A naval party has used an SR-N6 (Winchester) in the Falkland Islands. The hovercraft has been used inland, over stone runs, bogs and streams, and at sea between the 200 islands. Weather in the Roaring Forties produces strong gusty winds and short, steep seas, and the navy found the extensive kelp beds around the islands of great assistance in permitting fast running. An army hovercraft squadron at Singapore has used Winchesters for moving men and stores ashore and afloat and for rescue operations over deep mud.

The longest of the contributed papers is by E. K. Liberatore on 'The Giant S.E.S. and Global Mass Travel'. Mr. Liberatore's paper is divided into two main parts. The first starts with the thesis that an American's home is not his castle but a 'self-packaging, self-propelled, people container' (motor car), and that he is frustrated by the existence of the oceans. Mr. Liberatore's solution is the provision of sixty 15,000-ton S.E.S.s (surface effect ships), travelling at 150 m.p.h. and bringing Europe the inestimable benefits of 20 million American self-propelled people containers per year. The car would be the family's cabin (below decks) for the 24-hour journey time, but as a concession to a deficiency in present day automobile design, each car would be allocated a minute 'comfort station'. The return fare for a people container and its contents would be $200. As well as people, other expected loads are self-propelled spiritual facilities and de-salination plants.

The second part of Mr. Liberatore's paper is headed 'Is it worth it?' Via synergistic education, mobile birth control instruction centres and computers with a conscience he assures us that it is.

Jane's Surface Skimmer Systems follows *Jane's Fighting Ships* (1897), *Jane's Aircraft* (1909) and *Jane's World Railways* (1951). Each provides an annual record of the state of the art, and each will be of great value to future historians of technology. What is more intriguing is who reads, and who purchases, the current issues. Small boys and model makers will find a wealth of the minutiae that they adore ('. . . foilborne propulsion is supplied by two G.E. LM1500 marine gas turbines of 14,000 b.h.p. continuous rating, connected by Z-drives through the main struts to two stainless-steel, super-cavitating fixed propellors of 4ft. 4in. diameter at the end of the propulsion pods on the main foils . . .'), but at four guineas they are more likely to go to the library than to purchase the yearbook. And if they are the principal devotees, why did *World Railways* appear so late on the scene? Do manufacturers study their rivals' products in *Jane's* or operators prospective purchases? It does not seem very likely—they can get more detailed information more directly. Even the most enthusiastic of hoverers or skimmers can hardly want it as a bedside book—it's much too heavy to hold. Perhaps we might offer to some budding sociologist in search of an M.Sc. subject, 'Who reads *Janes*?' And do those who do not read it know what they are missing? Because if you want information, give or take a few criticisms, it is a very well produced book.

INDEX

This index, in addition to referring to articles and reviews in the present volume, also shows other major reviews of the year which have appeared in the *T.L.S.*
Date references and page numbers *in italic* are to articles and reviews in the *T.L.S.* not reprinted in this volume. Page numbers in parentheses are given only where the reference is not immediately obvious from the article.